I09011O8

IMAGES
of America

STOW AND MUNROE FALLS

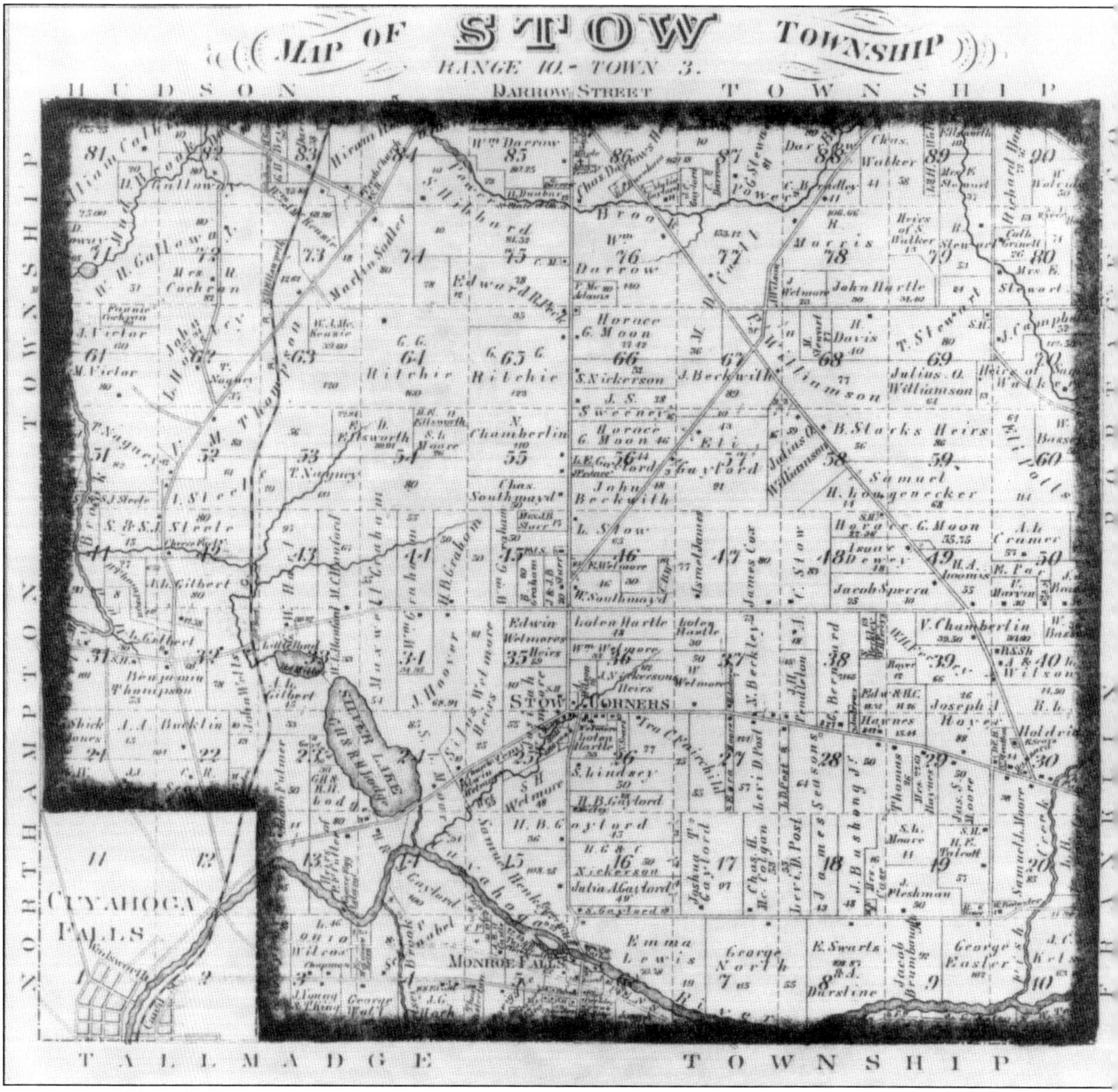

Although the settlement of Stow, Ohio, was founded in 1804, Stow Township was not organized politically until Portage County was formed in 1808. At that time, Stow Township consisted of portions of Stow, Cuyahoga Falls, Munroe Falls, and Silver Lake. The township became part of Summit County when it was formed in 1840. Cuyahoga Falls remained part of Stow Township until 1851, Munroe Falls remained until 1921, and Silver Lake remained until 1926. (Stow-Munroe Falls Public Library.)

On the Cover: A private company provided fire protection service for Stow before the Stow Volunteer Fire Department was organized on January 16, 1933. The first fire truck, pictured here, was a converted Model-T Ford truck, which was eventually turned over to the Stow Fire Department by the private company. Names on the back of the photograph include, from left to right, Marie Caspari, Lillian Boekley, Mary Gauthier, Avelave Sell, Betty Green, Shelly Musson, Esther Murdock, and Dal Barden. (Fred Long.)

IMAGES
of America

STOW AND MUNROE FALLS

Beth E. Daugherty on behalf of
Stow-Munroe Falls Public Library

ARCADIA
PUBLISHING

ISBN 978-0-7385-8388-4

Published by Arcadia Publishing
Charleston, South Carolina

Printed in the United States of America

Library of Congress Control Number: 2010927466

For all general information contact Arcadia Publishing at:
Telephone 843-853-2070
Fax 843-853-0044
E-mail sales@arcadiapublishing.com
For customer service and orders:
Toll-Free 1-888-313-2665

Visit us on the Internet at www.arcadiapublishing.com

To members of the Stow and Munroe Falls Historical Societies for their dedication to the preservation of the community's history for future generations

Contents

Acknowledgments		6
Introduction		7
1.	Early Days in Stow and Munroe Falls	9
2.	Unique People and Special Places	23
3.	School Days	45
4.	Neighborhood Clubs and Organizations	71
5.	Worshipping, Shopping, and Doing Business	85
6.	Two Communities Looking toward the Future	103
Bibliography		127

Acknowledgments

Stow and Munroe Falls have a rich and related history, as evidenced by the variety of photographs featured in Images of America: *Stow and Munroe Falls.* These images have been selected from several collections, including those of the Stow-Munroe Falls Public Library (SMFPL), the Stow Historical Society (SHS), the Munroe Falls Historical Society (MFHS), and local historian Fred Long (FL). Several generous individuals, including Lyn Bisesi, Charles and Jean Call, Howard and LaVerne Corathers, Cheryl Crowe, and Leona Farris, have contributed images as well. Each image in the book is designated to its source.

This book would not have been possible without the generosity of those who have donated their photographs, oral histories, and personal documents to the Stow-Munroe Falls Public Library Local History Collection. My deep gratitude goes to the Stow and Munroe Falls Historical Societies for sharing their historic photographs and also to Charles and Jean Call for contributing images that depict rural life as it once was. I would also like to recognize the late Ruth Hanson, local reporter, and photographer of many of the Fourth of July parade images in this book.

I am most grateful to Fred Long, who donated the use of his vast photograph collection and also spent many hours proofreading, correcting, and assisting with the content of this book. Author of *Recollections of Living and Working in Stow, Ohio 1936 to . . .* and *Stories from a Stow Native*, Fred's knowledge of local people, places, and events is invaluable.

Material for the book's content was derived from a variety of sources, most notably *Biographical and Historical Data of Stow* by Frank A. Green, *Stow, Ohio—Shadows of Its Past* by Peggie Seitz James, and *History of the Village of Munroe Falls* by Katheryn Myers. To read more in-depth narratives about Stow and Munroe Falls please refer to the bibliography for a complete list of print resources.

Sincere appreciation goes to the Friends of the Stow-Munroe Falls Public Library for their support of this project and to my coworkers for their understanding and assistance in making this book a reality. Lastly I would like to thank Arcadia editor Melissa Basilone for her expertise and guidance in creating this photographic history of Stow and Munroe Falls.

Introduction

Images of America: *Stow and Munroe Falls* focuses on the people, places, and events in the shared history of Stow and Munroe Falls, Ohio. Through images, it traces the communities from their founding as settlements in the Connecticut Western Reserve to their status as cities entering the 21st century. The early pioneers, including those who accompanied William Wetmore, Joshua Stow's land agent, in 1804 and William Stow in 1809, had a difficult life. They had to contend with privation, isolation, harsh winters, and wildlife, including bears, wolves, panthers, and rattlesnakes. They worked hard to turn their wilderness settlements into villages with schools, churches, businesses, and social activities for the community. Among the images selected from the collections of Stow-Munroe Falls Public Library, Munroe Falls Historical Society, Stow Historical Society, and local historian Fred Long are those of founding families, commercial businesses, early churches, school classes, social club members, and special places.

The history of the Stow and Munroe Falls communities began with the settling of the Connecticut Western Reserve, land reserved for Revolutionary War veterans. In 1796, Joshua Stow, of Middletown, Connecticut, accompanied the Connecticut Land Company, a party of surveyors headed by Gen. Moses Cleaveland, to the Western Reserve in Ohio. Stow was the commissary of the group. At that time, the reserve was surveyed and divided into townships, laid out in five mile square grids. Township No. 3, range 10 was purchased in 1804 by Joshua Stow. Stow's agent, William Wetmore, employed Joseph Darrow to survey the new township into 160-acre lots. In 1804, Wetmore arrived with a party of settlers, including his wife and six children; Gregory Powers, his wife and eight children; Thomas Rice, his wife and two children; and single men Josiah Starr, John Campbell, and Titus Wetmore—William's half-brother. William Wetmore built the second house in Stow Township, the first being built by William Walker, who believed he was building in Hudson Township, north of Stow. Once the land was surveyed, Walker purchased lot 89, which included his cabin and the land he had cleared. Joshua Stow himself never lived in Stow but traveled here at least 13 times.

In 1809, a large party of settlers led by William Stow, cousin of Joshua, came to southern Stow Township. The settlers called this village Kelsey Mills but changed it to Florence in 1817. Both communities were part of Stow Township, which was organized politically in 1808 as part of Portage County. William Wetmore was the first justice of the peace and his half-brother Titus was the first postmaster.

Stow and Munroe Falls pioneers valued education and religion. Fifteen students attended the first school held in 1806 in the former Walker home. The first schoolhouse was built near Stow Corners in 1810, and the first schoolhouse in Munroe Falls was built about 1816. By the late 1800s, the area had eight school districts with 10 one-room schoolhouses. The new Stow Township Centralized School was built in 1907. Church services began in 1806, when a small group of Presbyterians first met in the home of deacon Stephen Butler. Early churches included the United Presbyterian in the northwest section of Stow Township known as Little Ireland,

Stow Disciples of Christ located in Stow Cemetery, and the Methodist Episcopal Church in Munroe Falls.

Stow Corners, now the intersection of Kent and Darrow Roads, became the center of community life in the 1800s. Ezra Wyatt built the first house at the Corners in 1806. The first post office was in the home of Titus Wetmore on the northwest corner. Other establishments included a tavern, a stagecoach stop, a school, and a nearby sawmill. A whiskey distillery was built on the east side of Stow Pond (Silver Lake) by Judge William Wetmore, who employed John Graham as distiller.

Along with a growing population came the need for cemeteries. Maple Lawn Cemetery, first known as Darrowville or Darrow Street Cemetery, was situated in Darrowville on the border of Stow and Hudson. Darrowville was settled by Joseph Darrow, hired by William Wetmore to survey Stow Township, and his brother George, who built cabins along the trail later named Darrow Street near the border of Hudson Township. Joseph and his wife, Sally Prior, gave the community a 1-acre site to be used as a cemetery. The first burial was in 1807 when Sally Powers, wife of Capt. Gregory Powers, died shortly after giving birth. The site of the Stow Cemetery was part of Josiah Wetmore's farm along what is now U.S. Route 59. The first burial in Stow Cemetery was Elizabeth Gaylord in 1809. Wife of Johnathon Gaylord Sr., she died shortly after making the trip from Middletown, Connecticut. The first burial in the O'Brien Cemetery, located just north of the Stow border in Hudson Township, was in 1806.

As settlers moved into southern Stow Township, the village of Florence, renamed Munroe Falls in 1837, grew. Arriving with the William Stow party in 1809 were Johnathon Gaylord and his family, his brother Samuel Gaylord, Frederick Wolcotts' family, Francis Kelsey, Isaac Wilcox, and William McClelland. Settling near the banks of the Cuyahoga River, these pioneers soon established industries and small businesses. A sawmill and gristmill were built in 1817. In 1836, Edmund and William Munroe of Boston, Massachusetts, purchased the mills, as well as several hundred acres of property from local farmers. Their plans for a prosperous town based on the production of silk did not materialize due to the death of the silkworms and the financial panic of 1837. The Munroe Falls Manufacturing Company, owned by the Munroe brothers and their associates, started a bank to extend credit via its own printed currency. Eventually the company went bankrupt and the currency became worthless. Munroe Falls, however, continued to do well. The Pennsylvania and Ohio Canal, and later the Baltimore and Ohio Railroad, carried goods and passengers to Munroe Falls. A small hotel was built on the canal about 1842. By the end of the 19th century, Munroe Falls had a post office, school, general store, dress shop, and the Munroe Falls Paper Mill.

Although remaining mostly rural in character, Stow and Munroe Falls entered the 20th century with improved roads, increasing school enrollment, growing industries and businesses, and active social and religious organizations. Early clubs and organizations included the Portage and Summit County Pioneer Association, the Stow Culture Club, and the Darrow Street Grange. The communities continued to grow, with farms and horses giving way to housing developments, cars, and parks. Volunteer fire departments were organized in Stow in 1933 and in Munroe Falls in 1948.

In 1921, Munroe Falls was incorporated as a village and was no longer a part of Stow Township. It became a city in 1991. Stow was incorporated as a village in 1957 and became a city in 1960. Through the hard work and determination of their citizens, both communities successfully made the transition from rural township to city status while maintaining their shared school district, shared library, and shared history. Stow and Munroe Falls remain good places to live, work, and raise a family.

One

Early Days in Stow and Munroe Falls

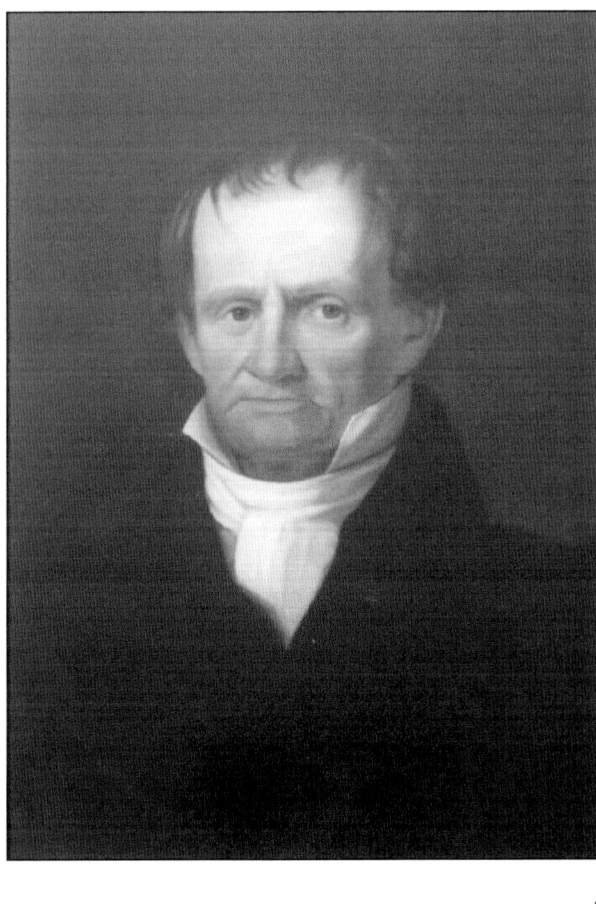

Joshua Stow was born on April 22, 1762, in Middlefield, Connecticut. He was part of the Moses Cleaveland team that surveyed the Western Reserve in 1796–1797. When Stow first saw the area of the future Stow Township, he described it as "one of the prettiest and most romantic spots in the Western Reserve." He purchased Township No. 3, Range 10 in 1804 as an investment for $14,154. This portrait of Stow hangs in the Stow Historical Society Heritage House Museum, compliments of one of his descendants, Faith Stow Hamilton, of Middletown, Connecticut. (SHS.)

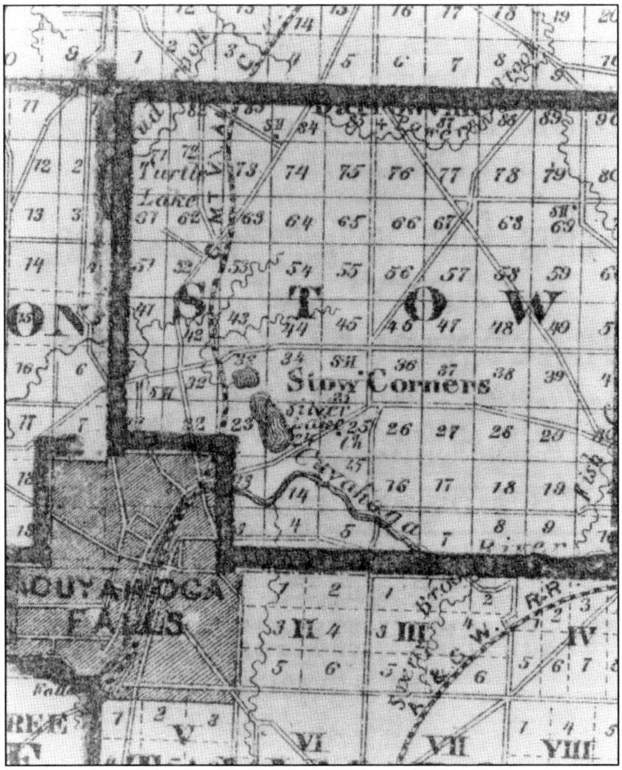

This map shows a close-up view of the area known as Stow Corners, the center of community life for many years. Located at the intersection of what are now Darrow and Kent Roads, Stow Corners held a post office in the Titus Wetmore home, a stagecoach stop, tavern, a school, and several residences in the early 19th century. The first house in Stow Corners was built by Ezra Wyatt in 1806. (MFHS.)

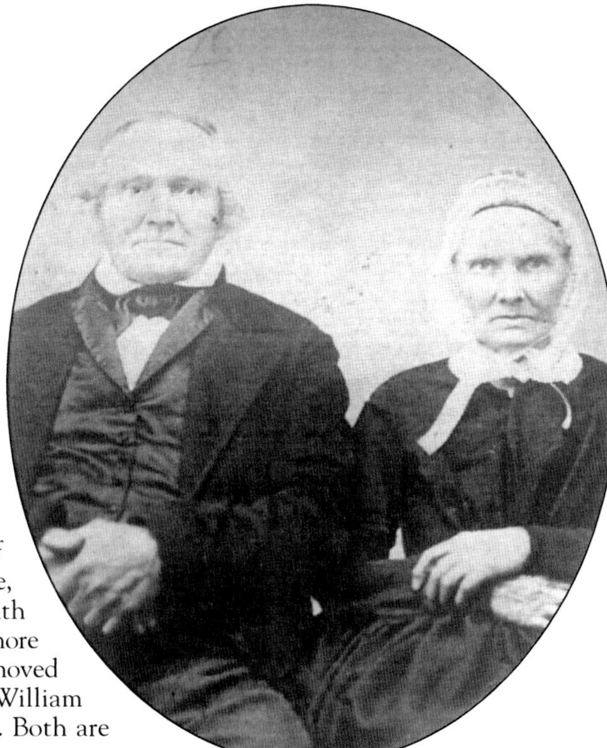

William Stow was born in 1776 in Middletown, Connecticut. In 1809, he bought 300 acres from his cousin Joshua and settled on the south bank of the river at Munroe Falls. He and his wife, Margaret (Peggy) Gaylord, brought with them their six children and had four more children after arriving. In 1839, they moved to a farm on Darrow Road in Stow. William died in 1853, and Peggy died in 1864. Both are buried in Stow Cemetery. (FL.)

Silas Wetmore and Mary Birge were married in 1846. Silas Wetmore was the son of Edwin Wetmore and his first wife, Polly Wetmore (a distant cousin). Edwin was the son of William Wetmore V and Anna Ogden Wetmore. William came to Stow in 1804, bringing his family (Edwin was six years old at the time) and a group of other settlers. The trip from Middletown, Connecticut, took 42 days by covered wagon. Silas was born on Fourth of July, 1821. He and Mary (born in 1827) had two sons, Charles Birge and Edwin Simeon. Silas held various township offices, and he and his wife were workers in the Disciples of Christ Church. He worked as a farmer with his father and died in 1871, one year before his father. Mary outlived her husband by 32 years. She was a "fine looking, educated woman" and kept a hospitable home, according to historian Frank Green. (Both FL.)

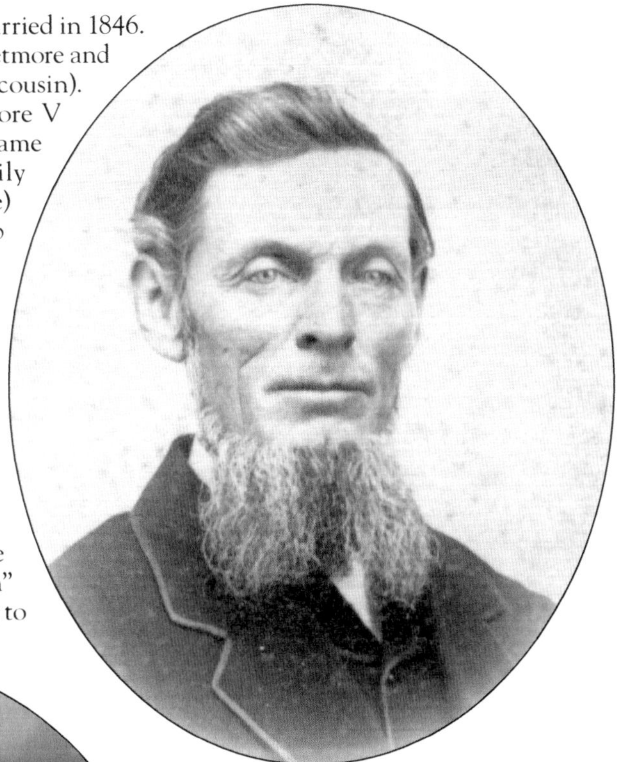

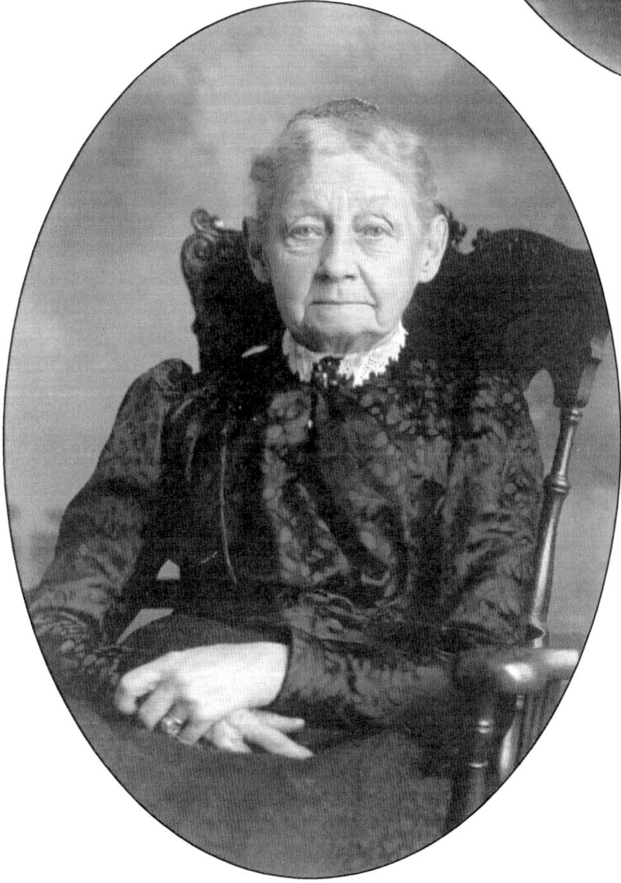

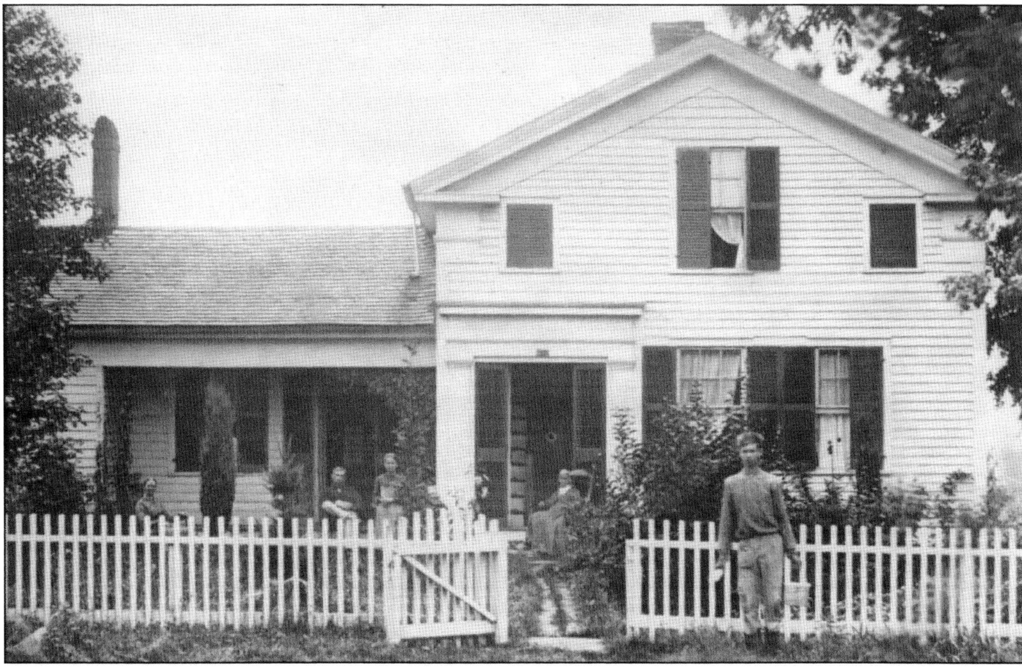

Joseph Butler built this house for Erastus Southmayd in 1832 on 46 acres of land purchased from Thomas Rice for $96. Southmayd was married, first to Anna Wetmore, daughter of Caleb Wetmore, and later to Clarissa Rice, daughter of Thomas Rice. William Southmayd, son of Erastus by Clarissa, sold the home to Edwin Simeon Wetmore in 1881. Wetmore and his wife, Lurie Green, raised their four children in the home. The house was moved to Hale Farm in 1966. (FL.)

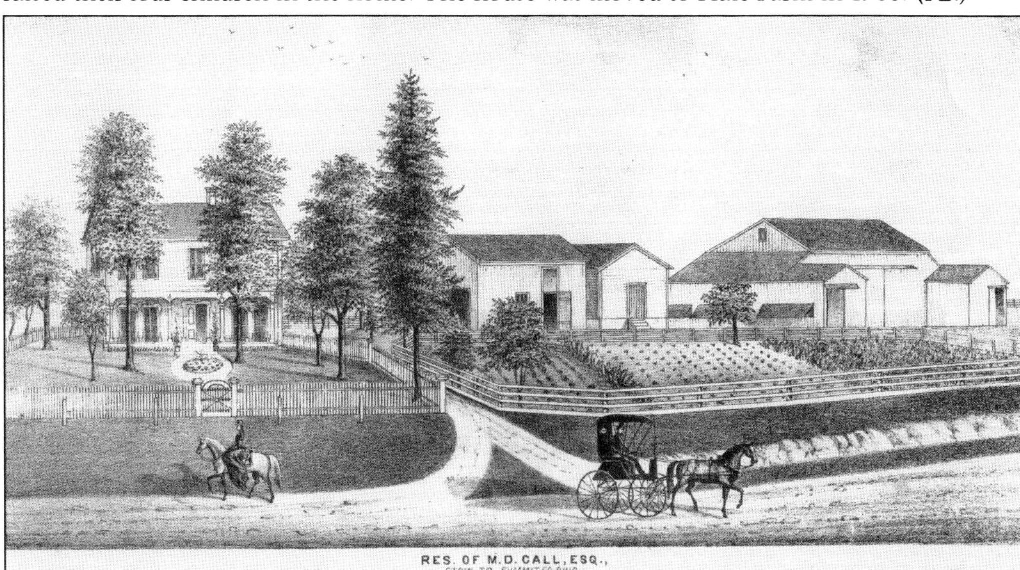

This drawing of the Moses Call farm is taken from the 1874 Combination Atlas Map of Summit County. The Call farm was originally built by Josiah Starr, who arrived in 1804 with the William Wetmore party. At that time, Starr was not yet 18 years old. He purchased lot 77 in Stow Township to farm, and in 1808 he married Mary Cannon of Aurora. Their daughter Harriet Maria married Moses D. Call in 1842. (SMFPL.)

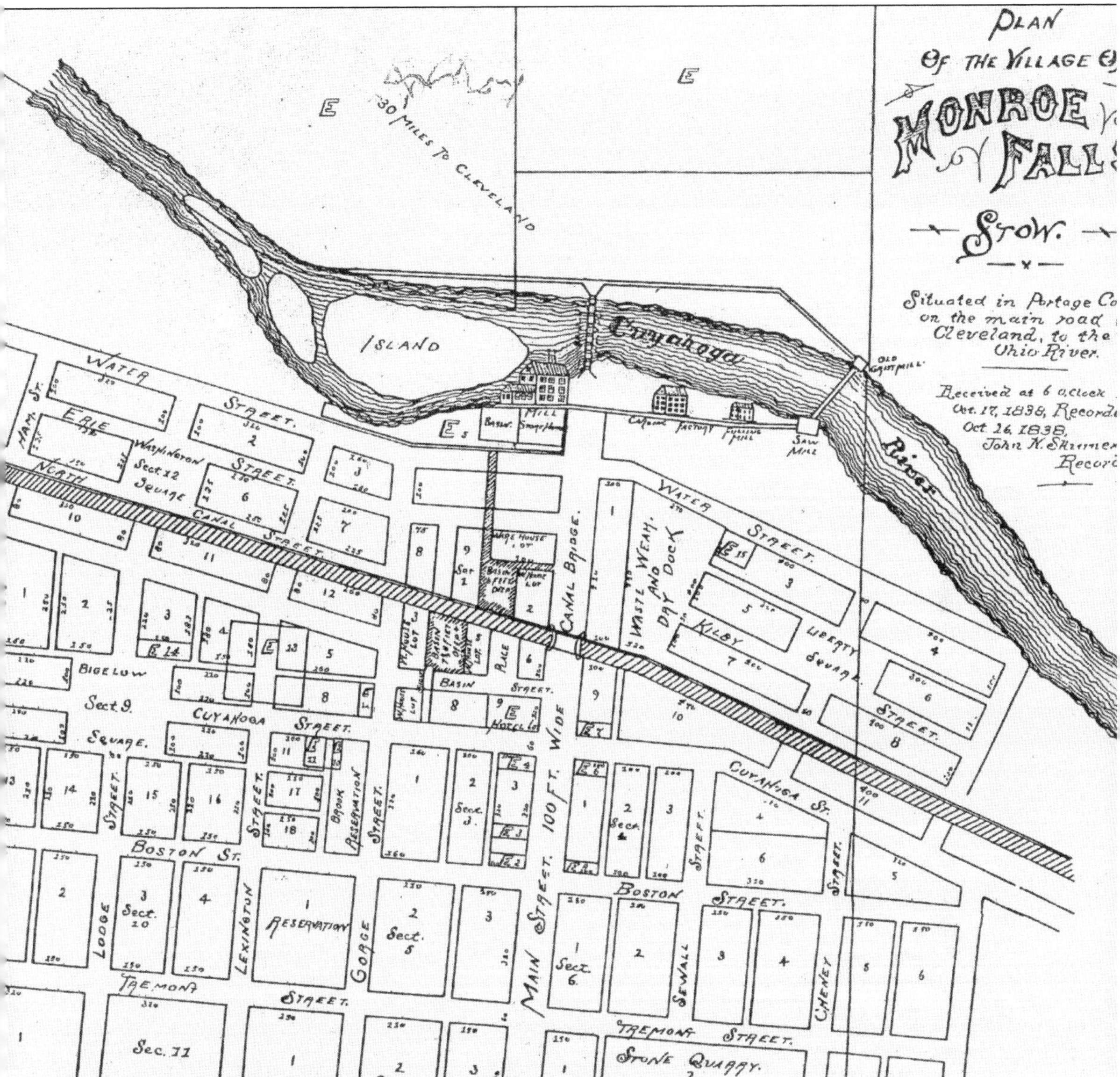

The first group of settlers who came to the area now known as Munroe Falls in 1809 included the William Stow, Gaylord, Wolcott, Kelsey, Wilcox, and McClelland families. They purchased land from Joshua Stow and built their cabins near the Cuyahoga River. The settlement was first called Kelsey's Mills before becoming Florence. A sawmill, gristmill, carding factory, a distillery, and other small businesses were established. In 1836, Edmund Munroe of Boston, Massachusetts, purchased several hundred acres of land, including waterpower, mills, and other improvements. He intended to make the area a "metropolis of importance." Two hundred and eleven acres were mapped showing the proposed village of Munroe Falls, which was incorporated in 1838 in Portage County. In 1837, a charter known as the "Munroe Falls Manufacturing Company" was granted by the legislature of Ohio to Edmund Munroe, his brother William Munroe, and their associates. The Munroes intended to make their fortune by manufacturing silk. Mulberry trees were imported and silkworms were shipped in. Unfortunately the silkworms did not survive, and the financial panic of 1837 destroyed their plans. (MFHS.)

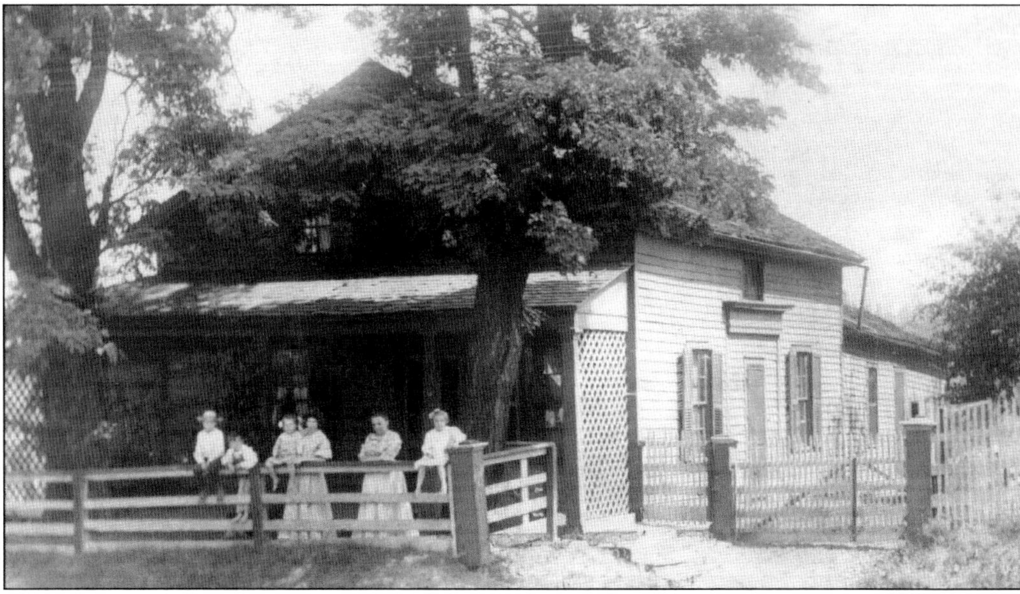

This Munroe Falls house, located on the north side of the Pennsylvania and Ohio Canal, was originally built as a tavern or small hotel in approximately 1842. Folks standing behind the fence in front of the house are identified as Leon Happoldt, Edward Happoldt, Beatrice Happoldt, Mrs. Gustav Happoldt, Mrs. Conrad E. Happoldt (Almeda Ebel), and Laura Happoldt Wolf. The first canal boats arrived in Munroe Falls on August 6, 1840, having left New Castle, Pennsylvania, on August 4. (MFHS.)

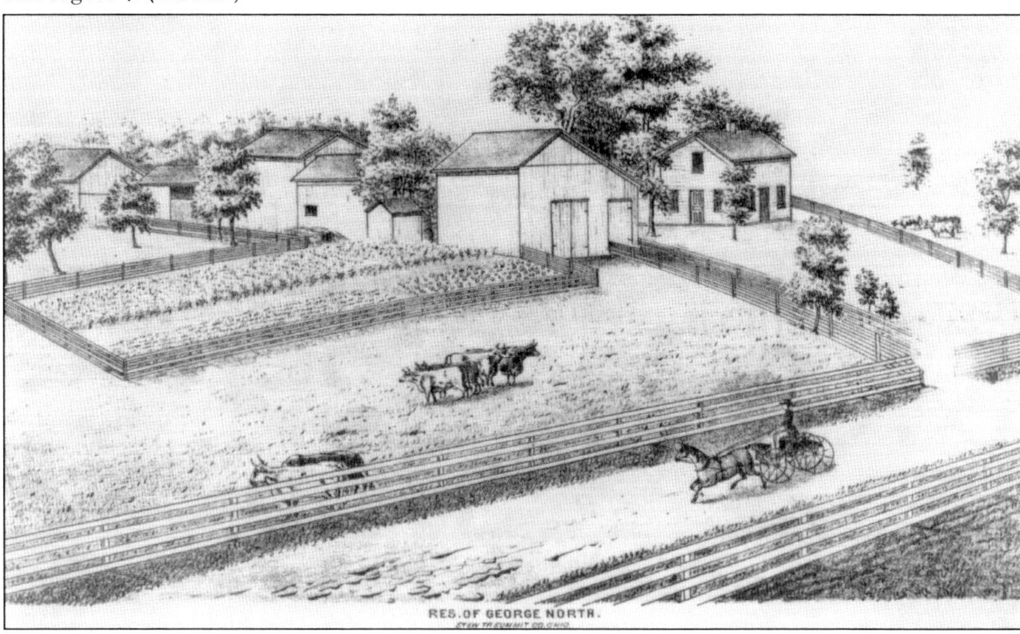

This drawing in the 1874 Combination Atlas Map of Summit County depicts the farm of George North in Munroe Falls. The farmhouse belonging to one of the area's pioneer families was built about 1836 and remained in the family's possession well into the 20th century. Lester North, grandson of George North, was the first employee of J. J. Lawson, founder of the Lawson's Milk Company. North descendants still reside in Stow and Munroe Falls. (MFHS.)

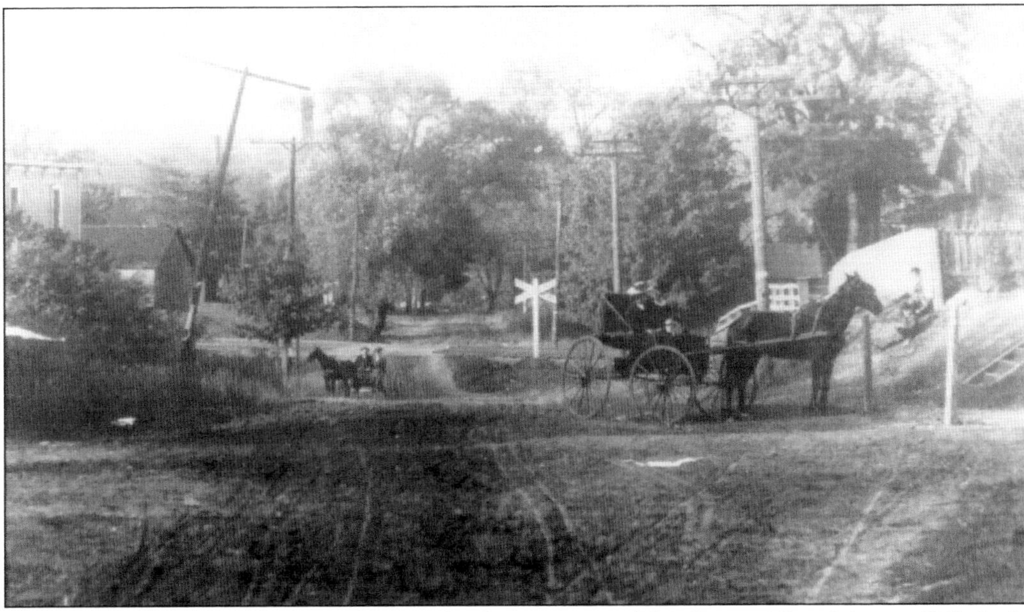

This turn-of-the-20th-century photograph of Main Street (U.S. Route 91) in Munroe Falls looks north toward Stow. The steps to the right lead to the Dixon-McCracken General Store. After the Pennsylvania and Ohio Canal was discontinued in 1868, the Pittsburgh, Youngstown, and Chicago Railroad purchased the property and laid tracks following the canal bed. In 1890, the property was purchased by the Baltimore and Ohio Railroad. (MFHS.)

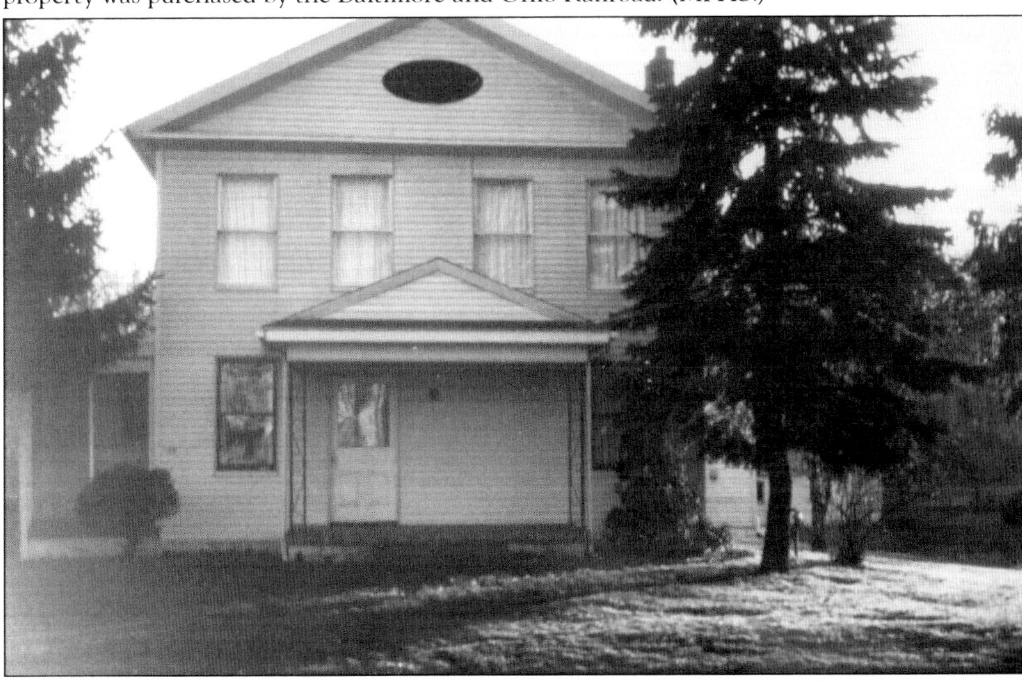

This building at 83 Munroe Falls Avenue currently houses the Munroe Falls Historical Society Museum. The two-story structure is an example of the Greek revival architectural style. The house first appeared on the 1851 Summit County Tax Duplicate as "frame house" under the name of Owen Brown, father of abolitionist John Brown. (MFHS.)

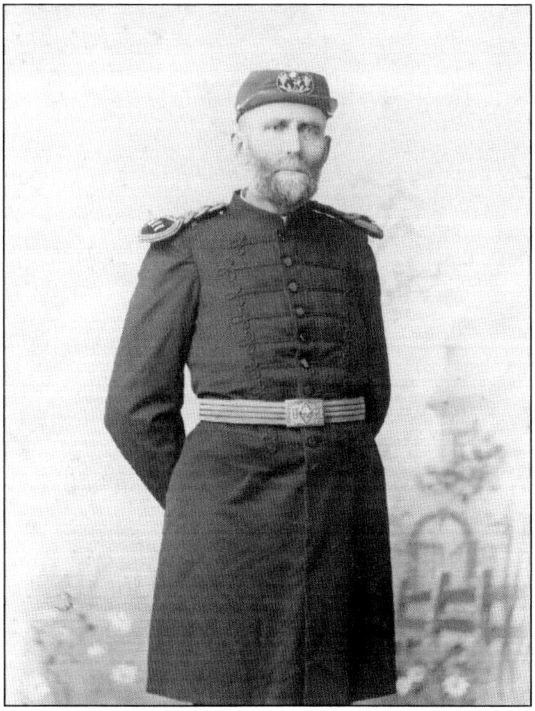

Francis Marion Green, pictured here in his Civil War uniform and at the pulpit of the Stow Disciples of Christ Church, was the son of Philander Green and Tarissa Root. Philander was the son of Samuel Green and Lucy Bailey, who came to Ohio from Connecticut in 1810. Philander was a preacher at the Disciples of Christ Church. Francis, born September 28, 1836, taught school for several years. He was ordained a minister in the Disciples of Christ in 1863. He attended Hiram College, known then as the Western Reserve Eclectic Institute. Green led a distinguished life, and according to his son, Frank Green, preached in "about every town and hamlet on the Western Reserve and in 27 or 28 states in our Union." He was known for his writings, including a biography on Pres. James A. Garfield. He served one term in the Ohio Legislature after being elected in 1885. (Both FL.)

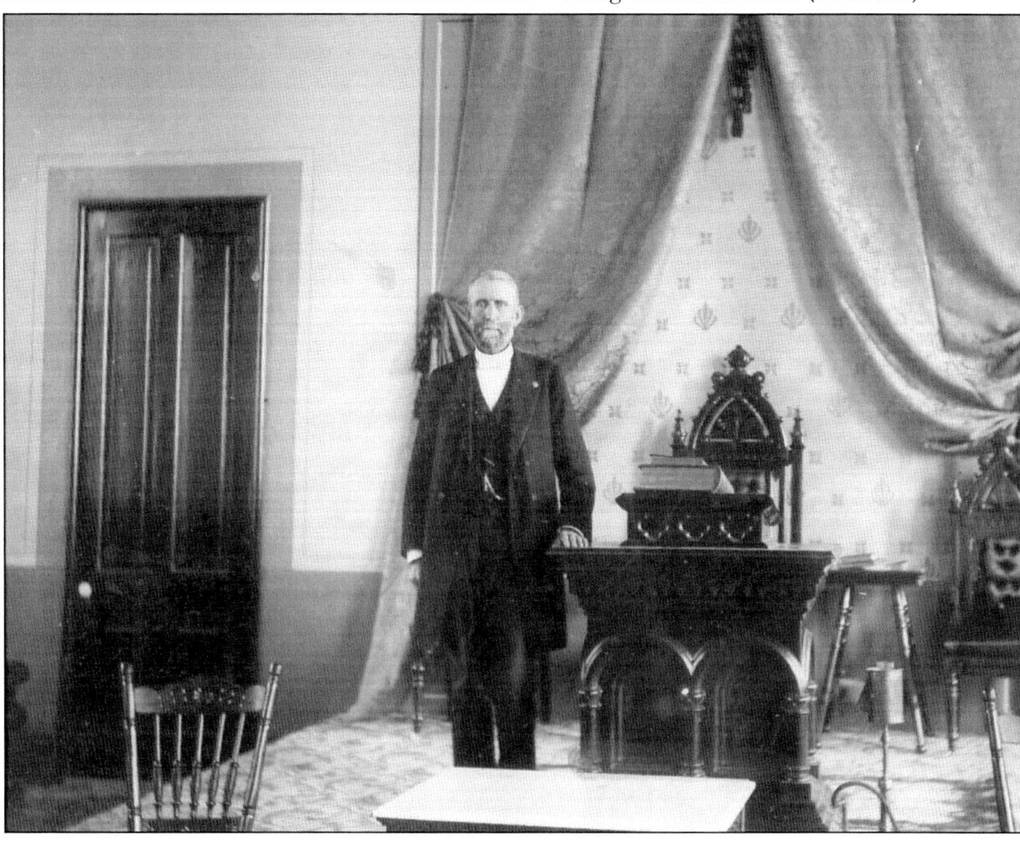

James A. Garfield met Francis M. Green at Hiram College when Garfield was a teacher there. Both men were members of the Disciples of Christ, both served in the Union army during the Civil War, and both were staunch Republicans. Garfield was a guest minister at the Stow Disciples of Christ at the invitation of Green. Green wrote a biography of President Garfield, *A Royal Life: Or, the Eventful History of James A. Garfield.* (FL.)

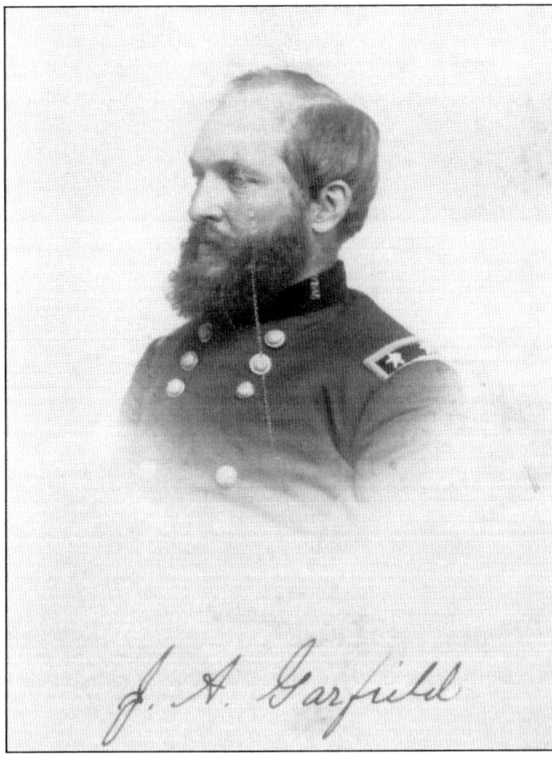

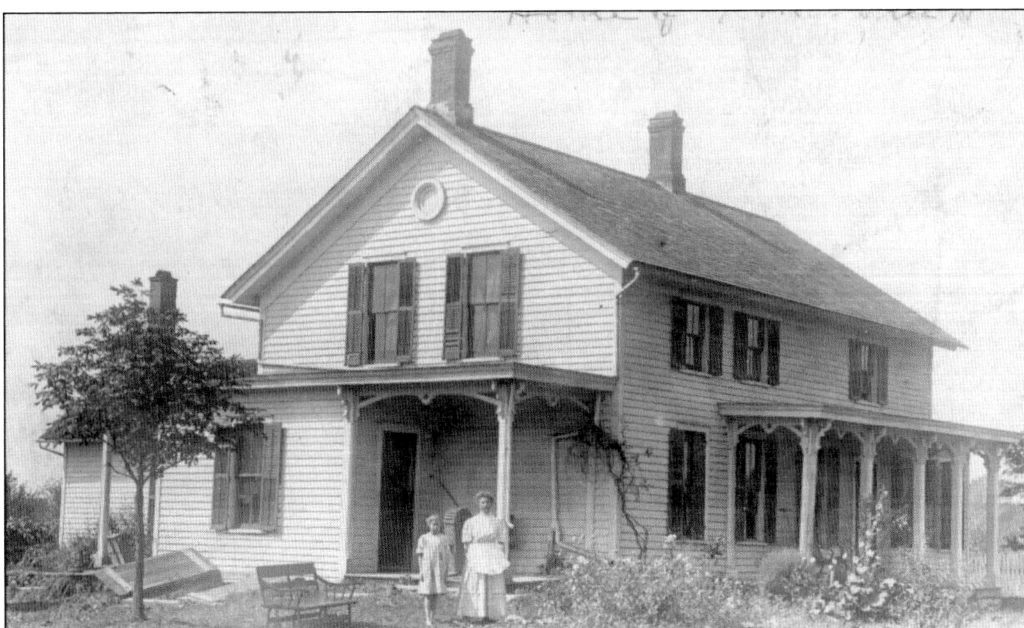

Francis Marion Green married Ellen Stow in 1862. They raised their five children in their home located on the south side of Graham Road diagonally across from the Albert Cheney Stow home. The back of this postcard, written by their son Frank A. Green, states that the main part of this house was built in 1876. The two large rooms on the back of the house are a bedroom and his father's (Francis's) study and library. (FL.)

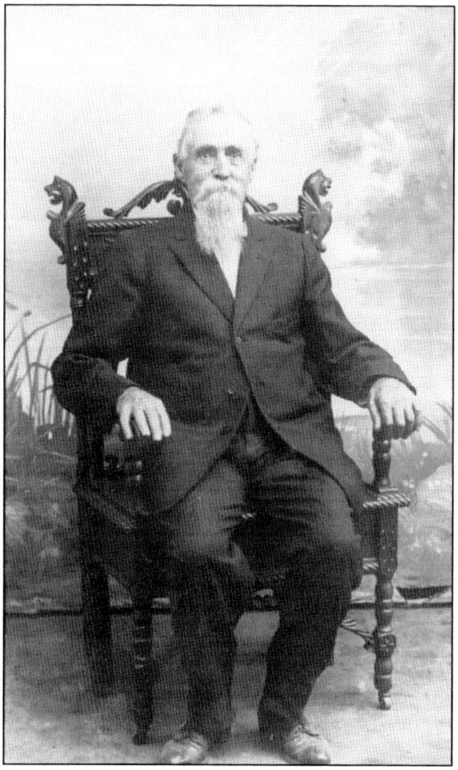

Orison Moore II (at left), born in 1848, was the youngest son of Samuel and Sally Moore, settlers on the east bank of Silver Lake. Moore married Clara (Clarissa) Wetmore, daughter of Edwin Wetmore and his second wife, Polly Bell. Edwin was the son of Stow pioneers William and Anna Wetmore. The Moores had seven children, three of whom (Grace, Arthur, and Henry) lived to adulthood. Daughter Grace, seen here posing with her hat in her lap, was the oldest of the seven children. Grace never married. She died in 1934 and is buried in Stow Cemetery. (Both FL.)

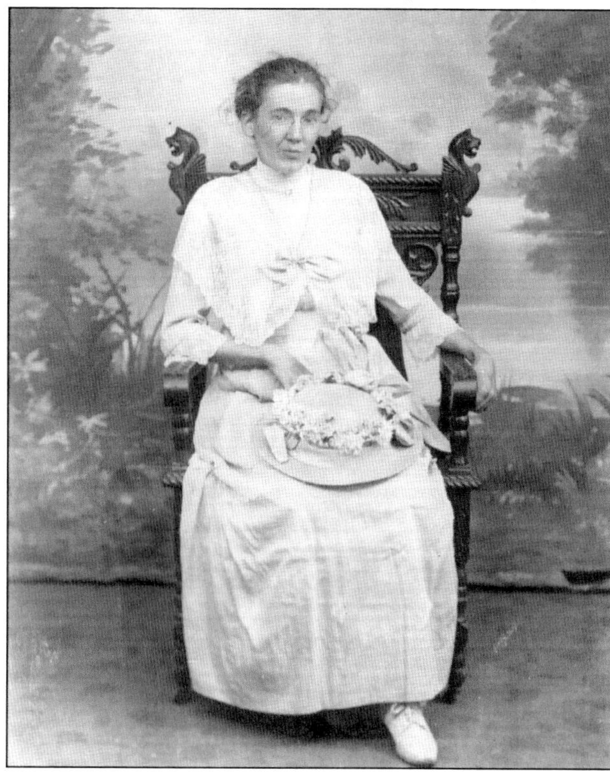

Mr. and Mrs. Newman Chamberlain lived in Stow Township during the 1800s. Their son Frederick (known as Dr. Fred) became a dentist. He and his wife, Demarus, had a daughter, Blanche, who grew up to marry Arthur Wetmore, son of Charles B. Wetmore. Charles was the son of Silas and Mary Wetmore. Arthur was a successful businessman who owned a general store in Stow and was widely known for his expertise on flowers. (FL.)

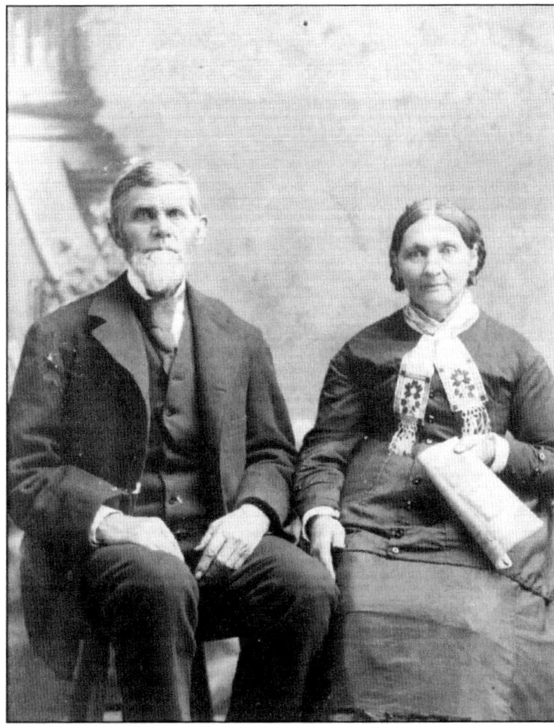

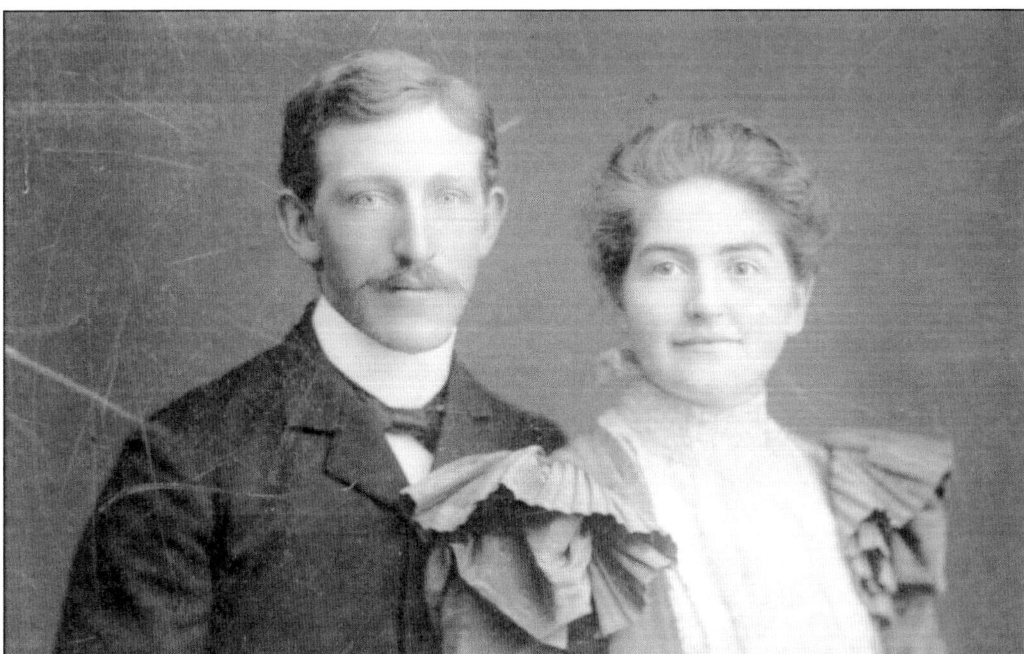

John S. Hibbard (born in 1872) married Nancy Barbara Housley (born in 1876) in 1897. Hibbard was the son of Simpson and Sarah Hibbard. Simpson's father, William, came from Ireland to Stow in 1833 and married Catharine Sadler shortly after. Their farm became one of the finest in Stow Township. Nancy Barbara was the daughter of John and Nancy Housley, who arrived in Stow in 1871. John and Nancy Hibbard had four children—Sarah, James, Loftin, and Lorin. (SMFPL.)

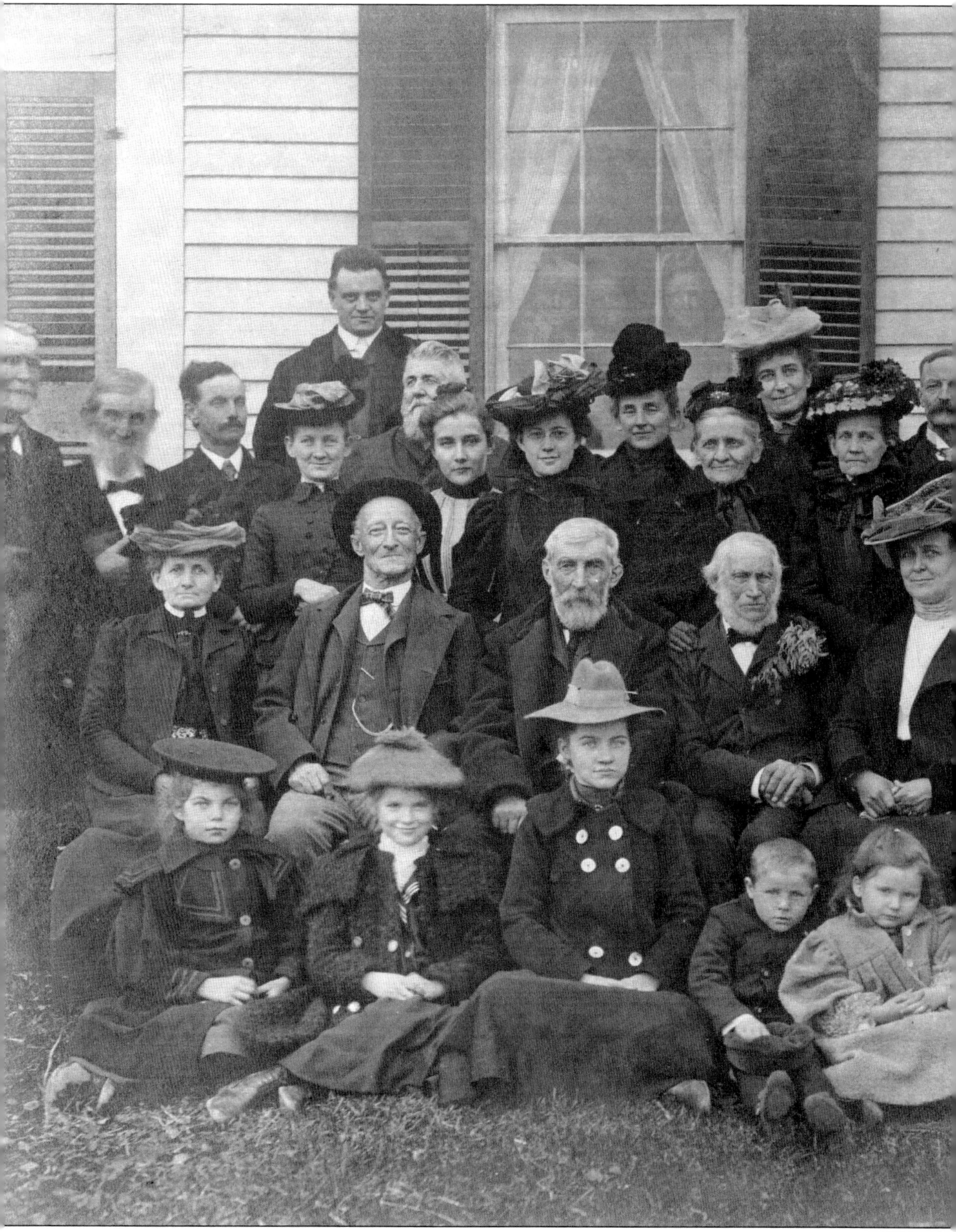

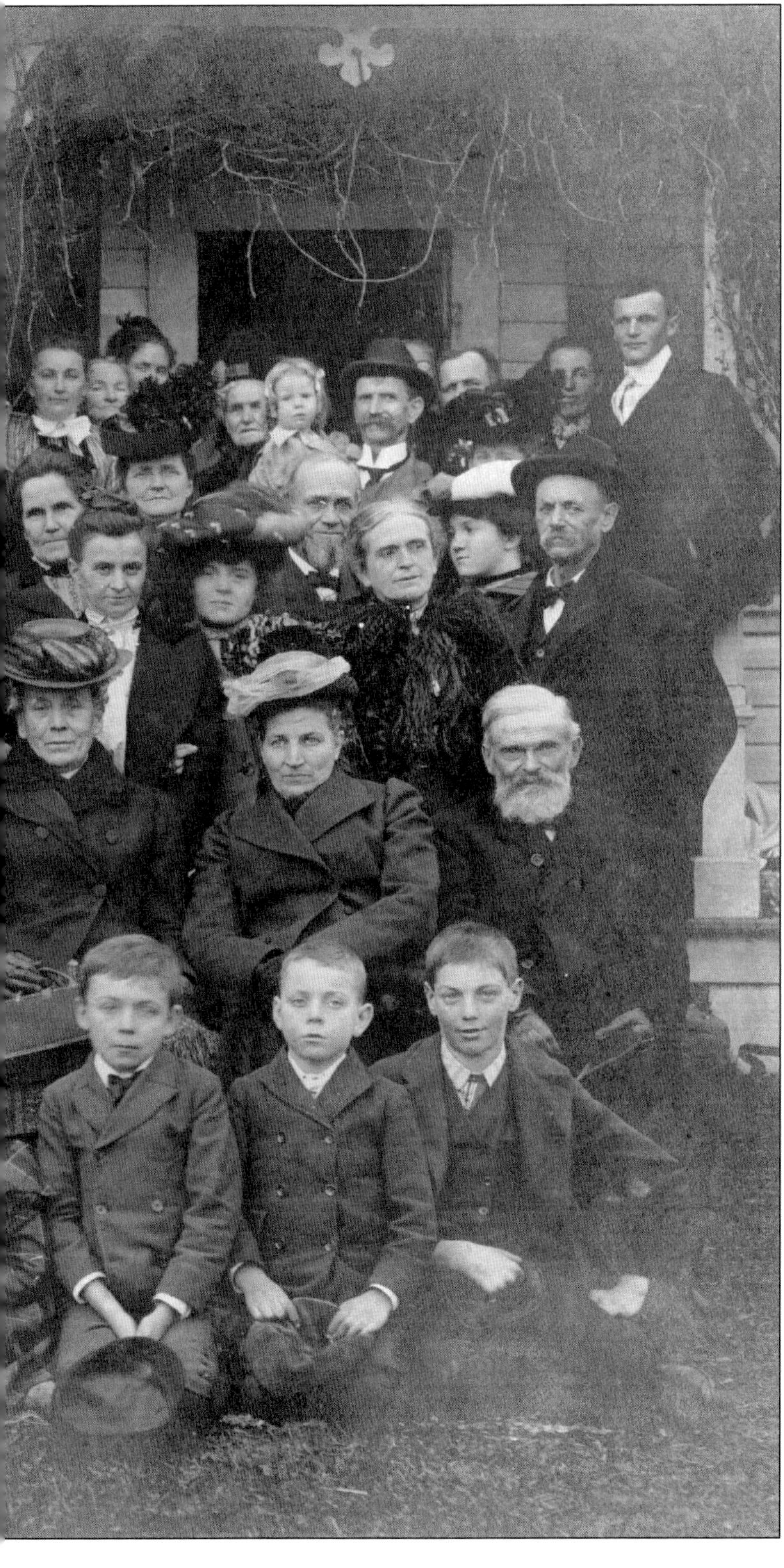

Friends and family gathered to celebrate the 66th wedding anniversary of Albert Cheney and Almira Stow on November 22, 1901. Attendees included, from left to right, (first row) Mary Wetmore, Jeanie Hillyard, Elno Grubb, Ford Grubb, Ellen Hillyard, unidentified, Carroll Cox, Albert Cox, and Lawrence Wetmore; (second row) Martha (Matt) Beckley, Laverett Beckley, Noel Beckley, Albert Cheney Stow (wearing boutonniere), Ida Nickerson, Mrs. Josiah Wetmore, unidentified (above), Mrs. Homer (Lottie Durbin) Campbell, J. O. Williamson, Mrs. Williamson, Hazel Johnson, Len Gaylord, Mrs. Ralph Lodge, and Ralph Lodge (below); (top rows) Francis Marion Green, Seth Wetmore, Edwin Wetmore, Daisy Hill, William Hill (above Daisy), Milton Danforth, Hattie Olin, unidentified, Mary Graham, Maxwell Graham, Hannah Prior, Styles Prior, William Wetmore, Julia Wetmore (below), three unidentified, Mrs. Leonard Gaylord, Mrs. John Beckwith, unidentified child, Nell Fields, two unidentified, and George Miller. (SMFPL.)

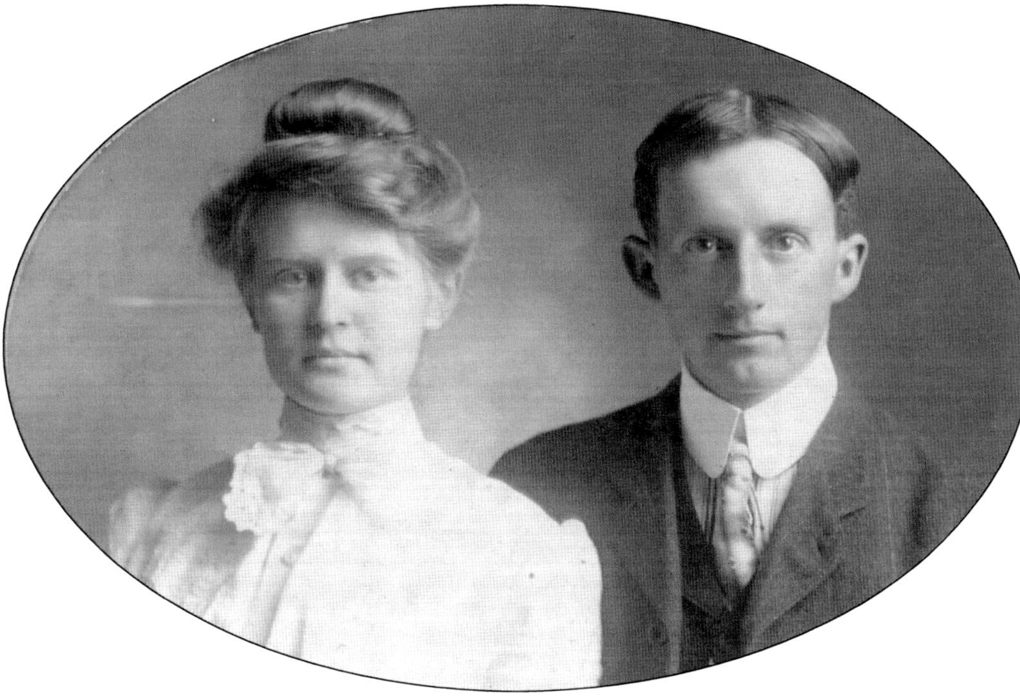

This is the wedding photograph of Howard and Florence Gaylord, who were married on May 2, 1902, in Holloway, Michigan. Gaylord was the great-grandson of Munroe Falls pioneer Johnathon Gaylord Jr. Howard and Florence lived in Munroe Falls after their marriage and raised their seven children there. Gaylord was the Munroe Falls constable and marshal for 36 years. He is remembered as also being in charge of security for Adell Durbin Park. (SHS.)

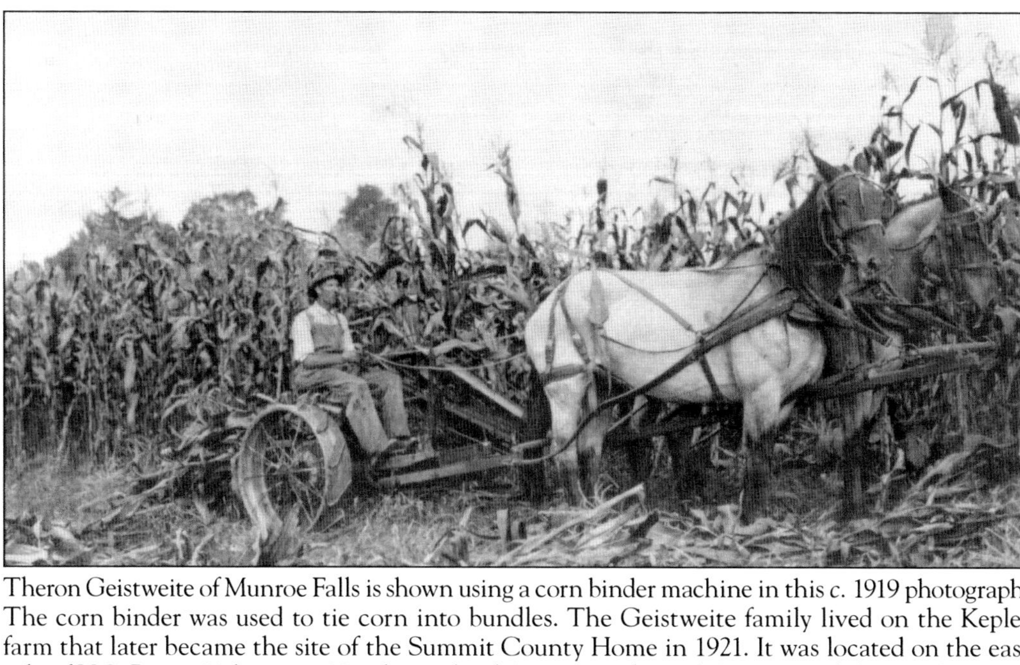

Theron Geistweite of Munroe Falls is shown using a corn binder machine in this c. 1919 photograph. The corn binder was used to tie corn into bundles. The Geistweite family lived on the Kepler farm that later became the site of the Summit County Home in 1921. It was located on the east side of U.S. Route 91 between Northmoreland Avenue and South River Road. (MFHS.)

Two

UNIQUE PEOPLE AND SPECIAL PLACES

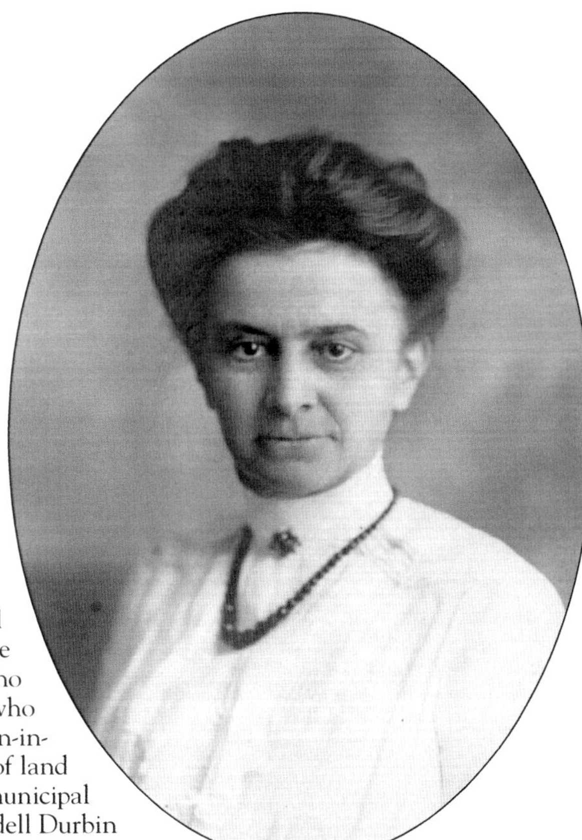

Adell Edmunds Durbin, born on the Fourth of July, 1862, was raised by her uncle Seth and aunt Lucy Wetmore until she married Robert Durbin in 1880. She and Robert had two daughters, Jessie, who married Don Williamson, and Lottie, who married Homer Campbell. In 1939, her son-in-law Homer Campbell donated 29 acres of land on U.S. Route 91 in Stow to be used as a municipal park. The park opened in 1948 as the Adell Durbin Park and Arboretum. (SMFPL.)

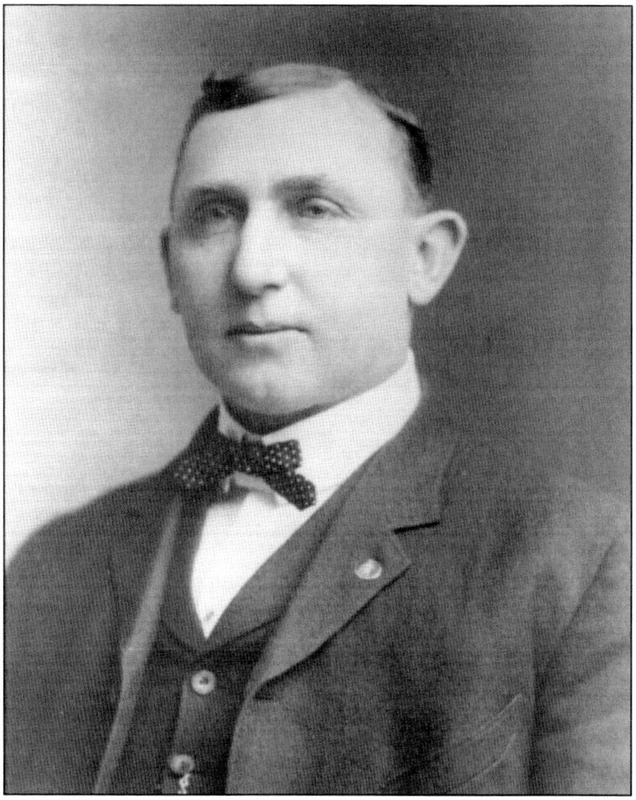

Charles Senn came to Munroe Falls in 1889 to take charge of the Cleveland Paper Company plant. The Cleveland Paper Company was incorporated as the Munroe Falls Paper Company in 1899 with president John Silk of Massillon, vice president Charles Silk, secretary and treasurer F. B. Silk, and superintendent Senn. Senn, his wife, Mary Dixon, and their four children were active in the Munroe Falls community and were members of the Methodist Episcopal Church. (MFHS.)

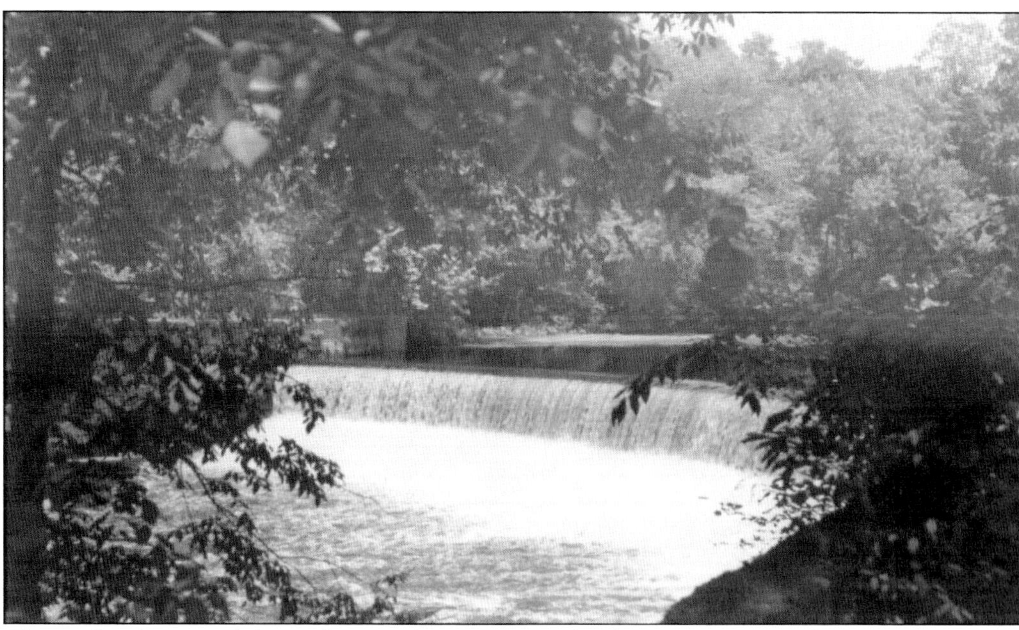

This undated postcard shows the Cuyahoga River at the dam in Munroe Falls. In 1817, a log dam was built to provide power for a sawmill and gristmill, which were constructed the following year on either side of the dam. The dam was rebuilt several times but continued to be used as a power source and as a site for recreation until 2005. (FL.)

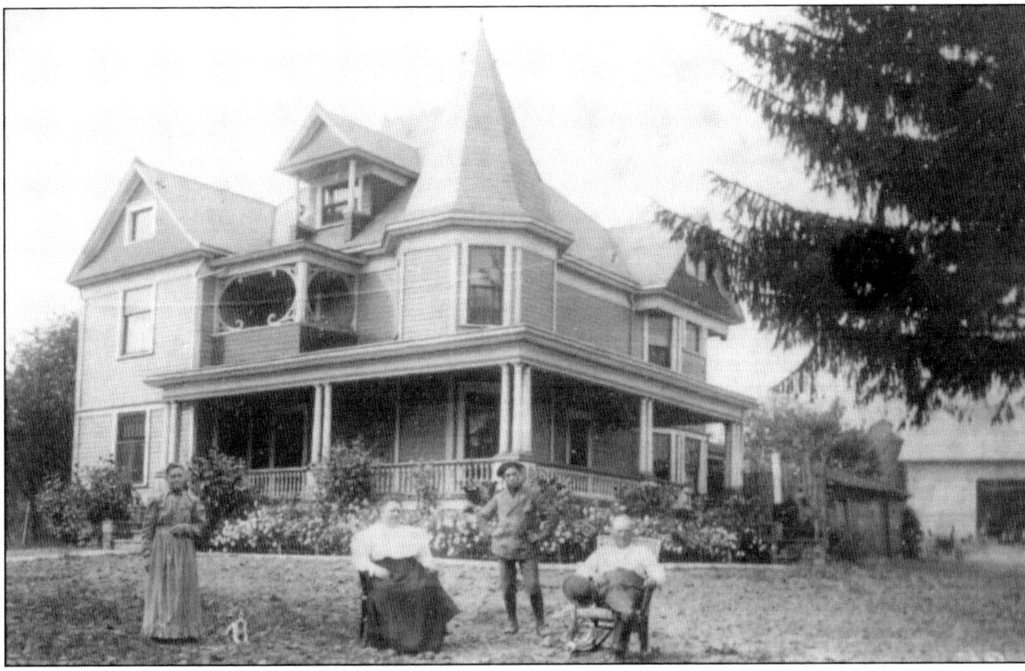

Otis Thompson built this house located on Hudson Drive in Stow Township in 1906. It was described in *Centennial History of Summit County, Ohio* as "probably the finest rural residence in this county." Thompson purchased the site of his 171-acre farm in 1888 and named it the Crystal Creek Stock Farm for the breeding of trotting and draft horses from registered stock. Pictured from left to right are the family's housekeeper, Mrs. Thompson, her son Roy Otis Thompson, and Otis Thompson. (FL.)

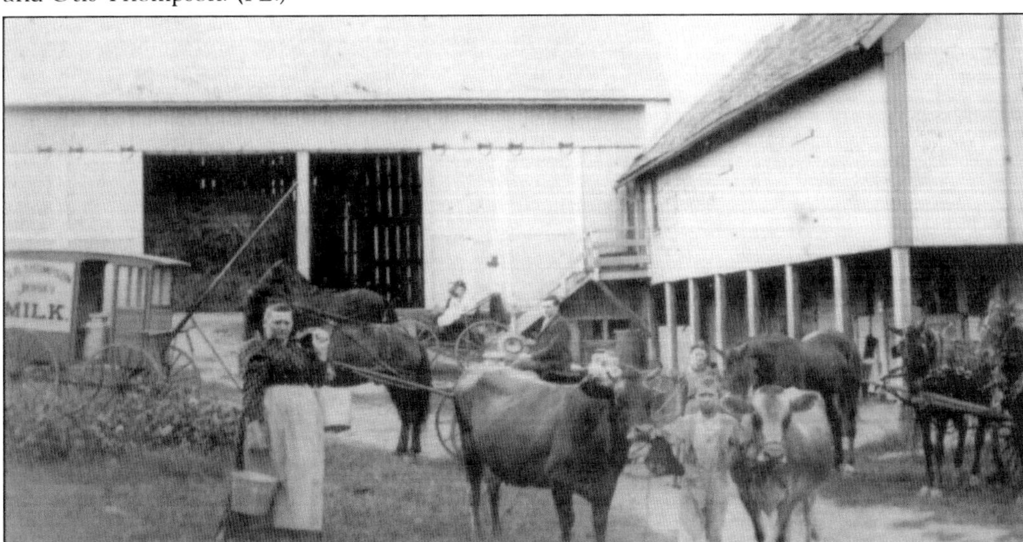

About the time Otis Thompson retired from horse breeding, he started raising celery on 25 acres. He became known as the "Celery King" because of his success at being the largest grower in this part of Ohio. He also grew corn, wheat, and oats. Thompson was director of the Summit County Agricultural Society for 14 years. Pictured from left to right are Mrs. Thompson, Otis Thompson, and Roy Otis Thompson. (FL.)

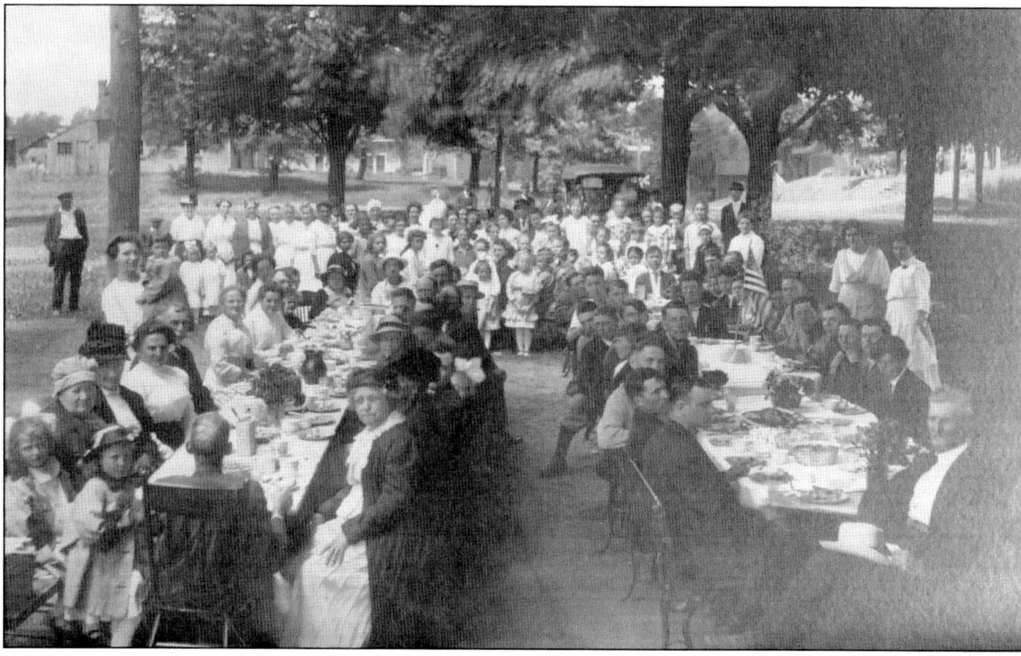

The Munroe Falls community picnic was held at the Munroe Falls Town Hall about 1913. In the early 1900s, George Dixon ran a general store in Munroe Falls that carried items such as groceries, dry goods, feeds, and coal oil for lamps. He was an agent for the B&O (Baltimore and Ohio Railroad) station and also served as Munroe Falls postmaster. (MFHS.)

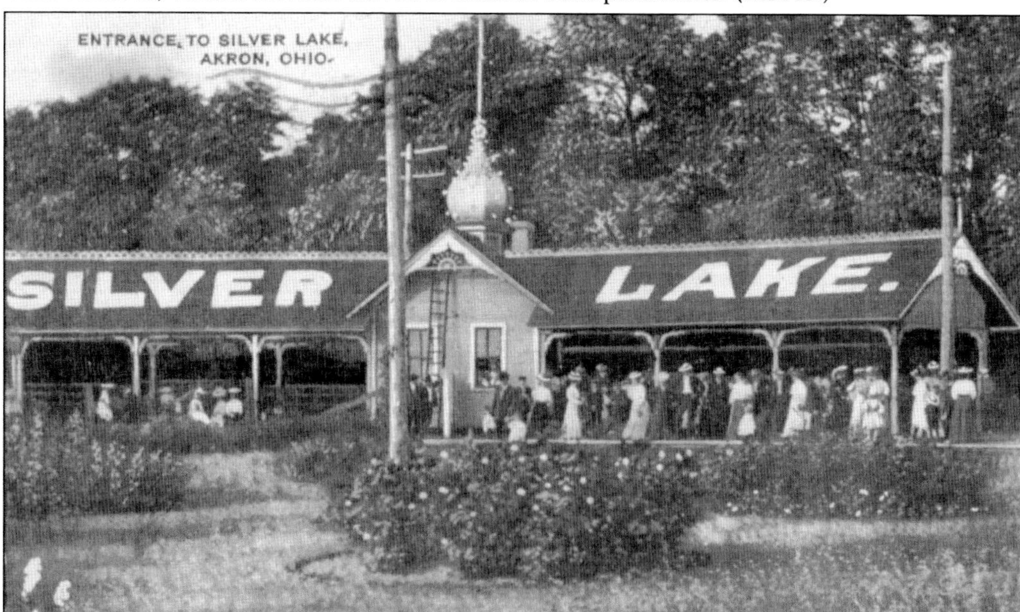

This postcard of the train station entrance to Silver Lake was mailed in 1908, a time when Silver Lake Amusement Park was in its heyday. One of the traditions every summer was for the Summit County Farmers Institute to have their annual picnic at Silver Lake. For 30 years, the last Saturday in August was "Farmer's Picnic Day." Ralph Lodge wrote that 10,176 people attended this picnic in 1908. (FL.)

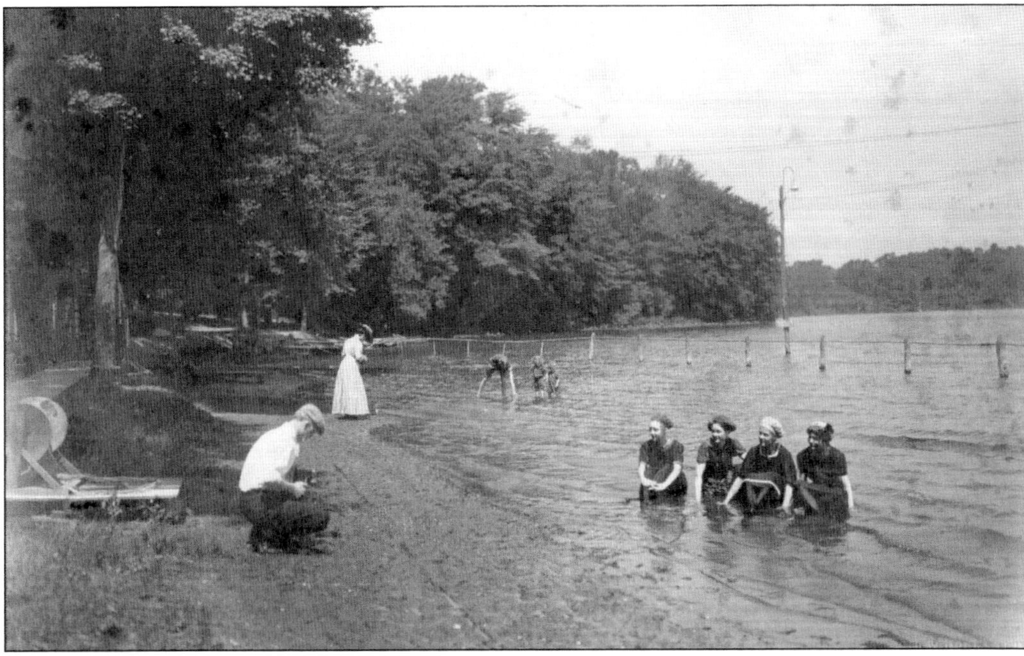

Silver Lake, formerly known as Stow Lake or Wetmore's Pond, was purchased by Ralph H. Lodge in 1876. He later purchased land bordering the lake and opened the area to picnickers and those seeking amusement and recreation. According to Lodge's son William R. Lodge, "When people heard that father paid $1,300 for just the lake, they thought he was crazy." (SMFPL.)

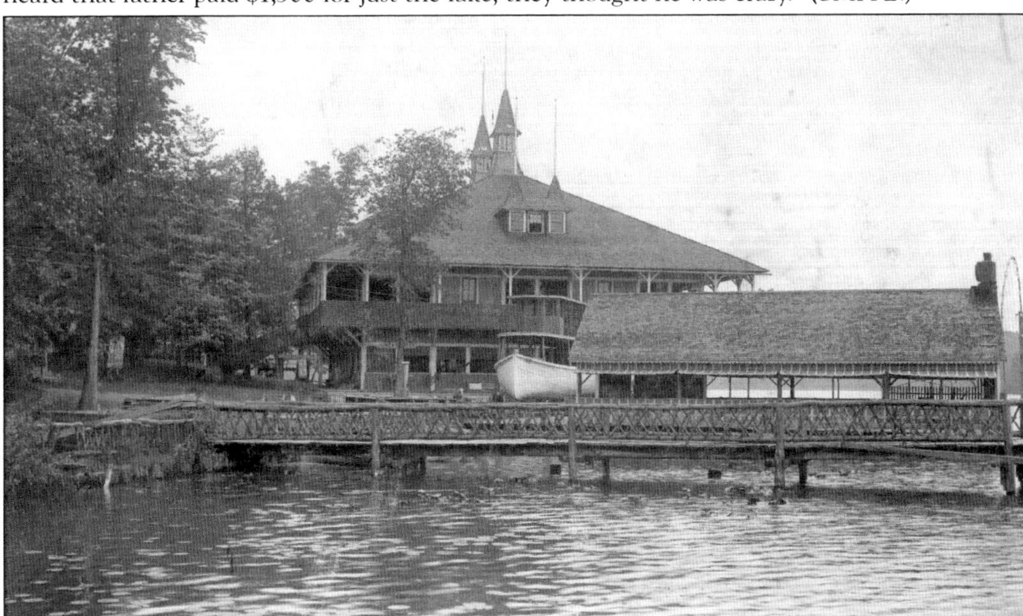

Silver Lake Amusement Park became one of the biggest attractions in Ohio. It included a dance hall, a stable, boating, fishing, swimming, roller coasters, a baseball diamond, bear pits, elk and deer grounds, menagerie, and a hotel. The peak years were between 1906 and 1911. This photograph is of the dance hall overlooking Silver Lake in the early 20th century. William Lodge wrote that "200 to 300 couples made just a nice crowd." (SMFPL.)

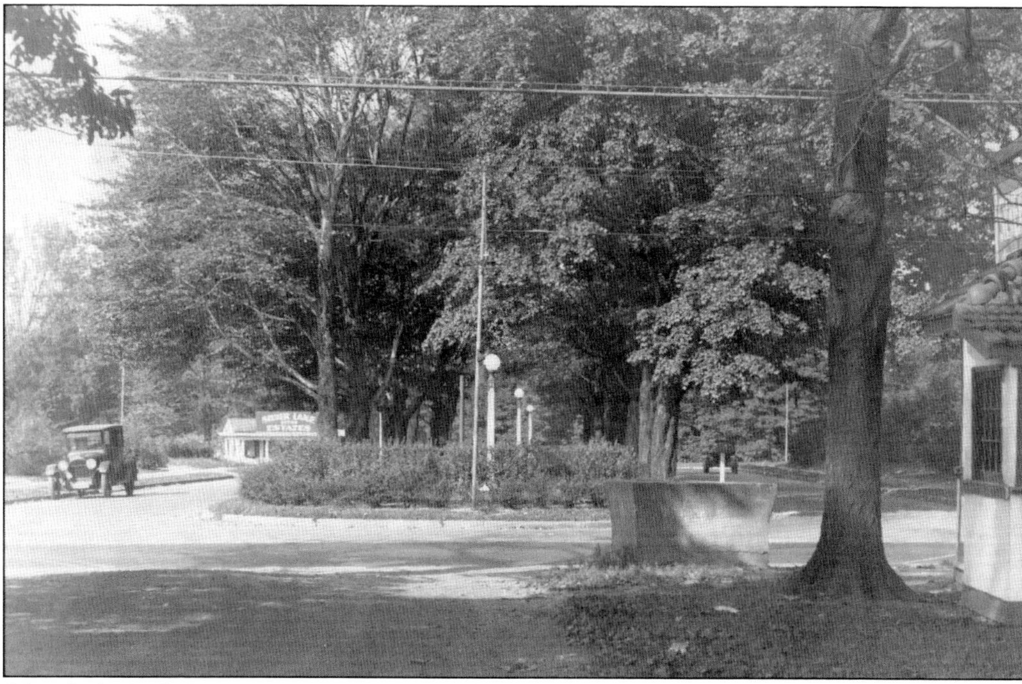

Silver Lake Park Company was incorporated in 1902 by members of the Lodge family. Because of incorporation, the company was able to finance new features for the park and successfully manage the business during the next 16 years. By 1918, attendance at the park had slowed because of World War I and lack of transportation. The majority of shareholders voted to sell the property. The Silver Lake Improvement Company then developed the 542 acres, selling residential lots in Silver Lake Estates. (SMFPL.)

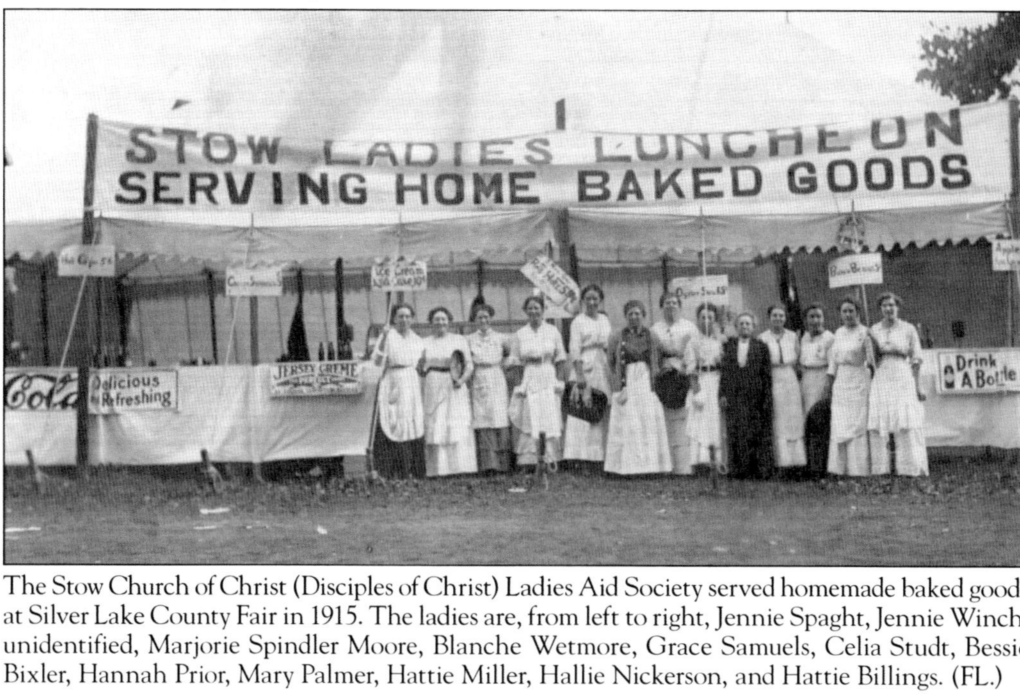

The Stow Church of Christ (Disciples of Christ) Ladies Aid Society served homemade baked goods at Silver Lake County Fair in 1915. The ladies are, from left to right, Jennie Spaght, Jennie Winch, unidentified, Marjorie Spindler Moore, Blanche Wetmore, Grace Samuels, Celia Studt, Bessie Bixler, Hannah Prior, Mary Palmer, Hattie Miller, Hallie Nickerson, and Hattie Billings. (FL.)

World War I soldier Roger Moore was born in Munroe Falls to Henry and Martha Moore. Henry and Martha had the largest family in Munroe Falls, with 21 children. Roger was a casualty of World War I and was buried at age 23 in Stow Cemetery in 1918. (MFHS.)

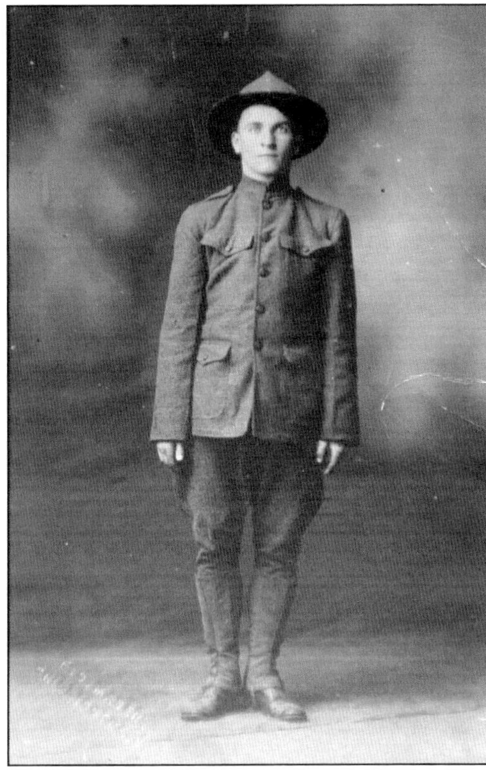

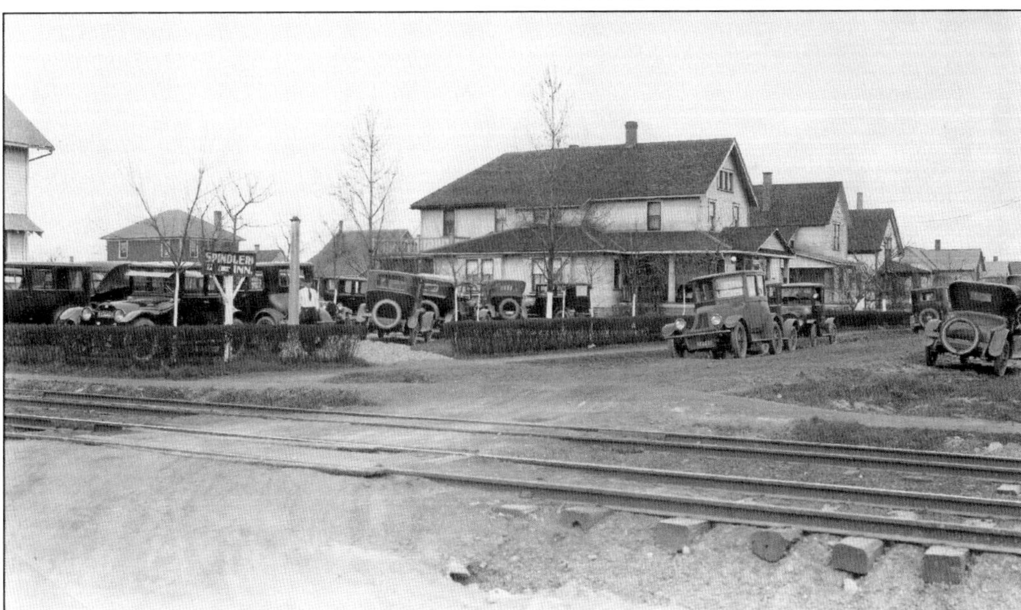

This photograph shows the Spindler Inn in Cuyahoga Falls in 1921. Mrs. Spindler had managed the Gaylord Inn, opened by the Lodge family at Silver Lake Amusement Park, for many years. The first year the Gaylord Inn was open, Mrs. Spindler served over 10,000 $1-per-plate chicken dinners. The Spindlers also served family-style chicken dinners in their own establishment, which was in business until 1943. (FL.)

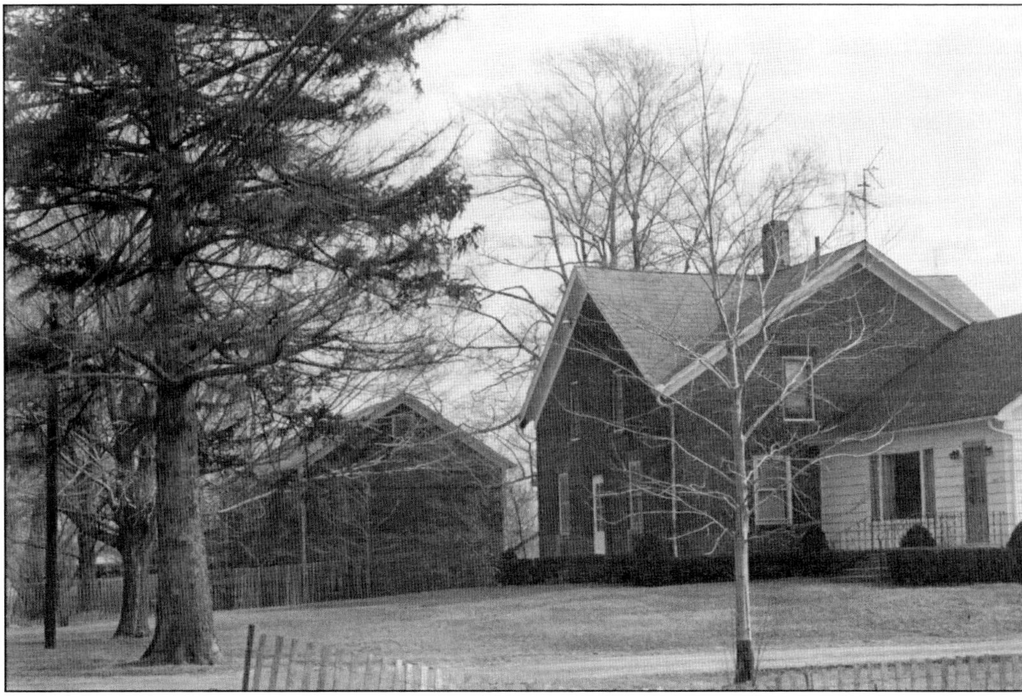

The Stewart-Hanson farmhouse is located on Call Road in Stow. Thomas Stewart settled on this land in 1832 and built a two-story log cabin with his brother Robert. He later bought out his brother's share and built the redbrick house in 1855. Orrie Stewart, the youngest daughter of Robert and his wife Catherine, married Charles Edward Hanson. They acquired the farm in 1897, and it remained in the Hanson family for three more generations. (FL.)

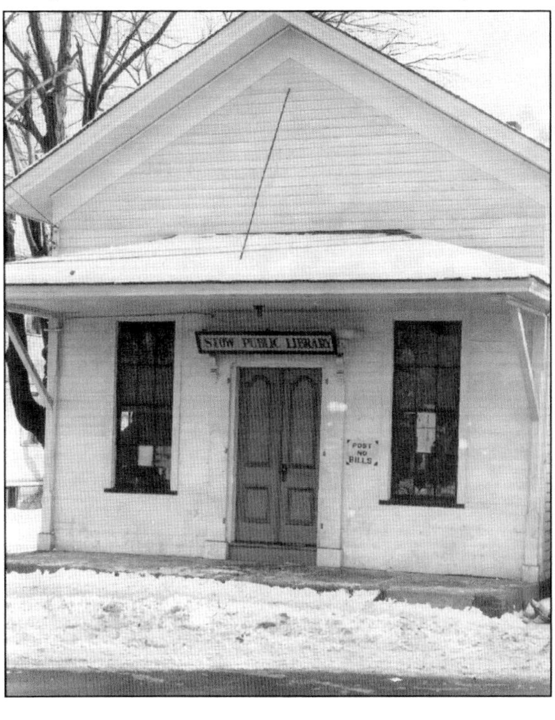

From 1924 to 1930, Stow Public Library resided in the Stow Township Hall. The library board of trustees met for the first time in the library in May 1924. Opening night of the library was officially held on January 21, 1925. Mrs. Donald (Jessie) Williamson, daughter of Adell Durbin, was hired as the first librarian. The library's first budget of $4,800 provided service to the public library, high school library, and grade school library. (SMFPL.)

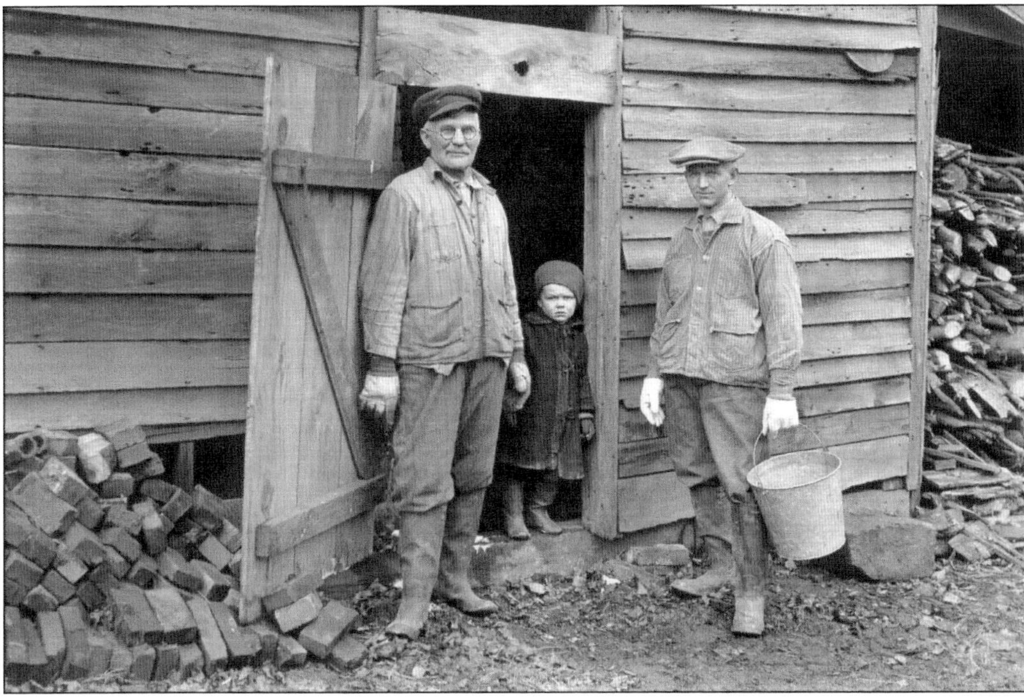

Charles A. Call (left) stands with grandson Charles E. Call and son Howard M. Call in front of their sugarhouse about 1925. Charles A. was the third generation to farm the property of early settler Josiah Starr. In 1884, an additional grove of 144 maples trees was planted to supplement the maples already on the property. This maple grove was considered just as valuable as any other part of the farm because it supplied maple syrup as well as wood. (CJC.)

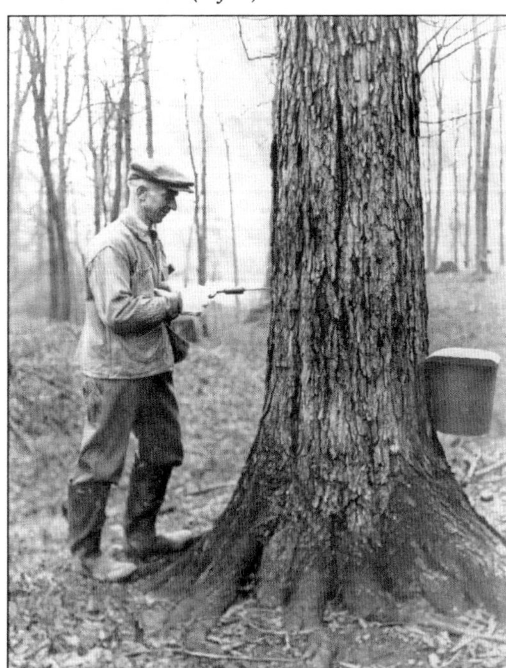

Howard M. Call is seen here tapping a maple tree in the wood lot at the Call farm. Production of maple syrup was an important part of the farm operations. Maple trees are tapped in early spring when daytime temperatures are above freezing while nighttime temperatures fall below freezing. (CJC.)

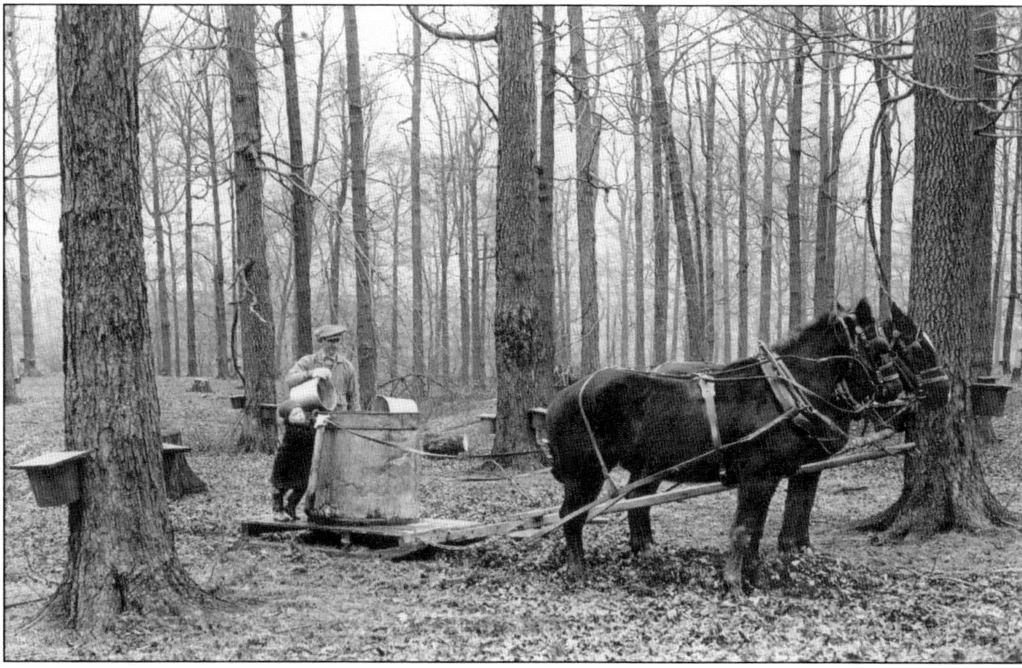

Howard M. Call and son Charles pour maple sap into a gathering barrel in this c. 1925 photograph. Once full, the barrel was carried by sled to the sugarhouse, where it was evaporated and filtered to produce maple syrup. Approximately 40 gallons of sap are needed to produce one gallon of syrup. In 1927, this wood lot was fenced off to allow nature to take its natural course of reestablishing timber. (CJC.)

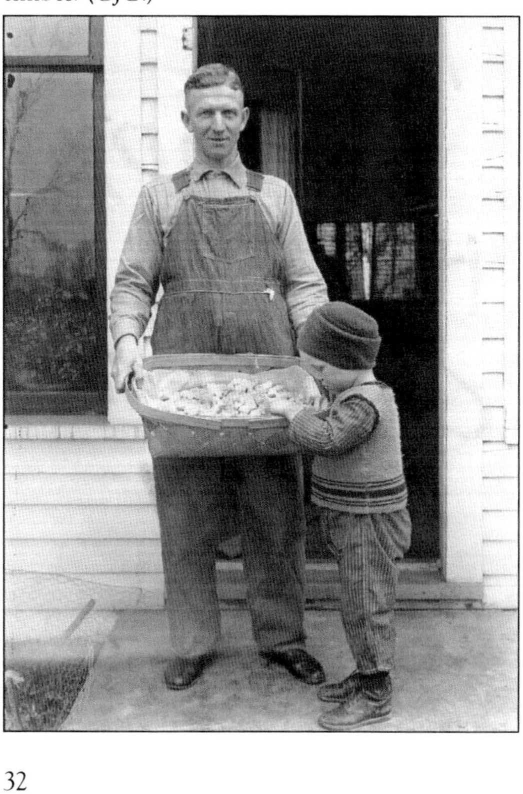

Howard Call (pictured here with son Charles) took over operations of the Call farm from his father in 1927. He received a degree in agriculture from Ohio State University about 1908. Having learned that lime applied to the soil would correct the problem of declining yields, Call worked at rebuilding the land and became one of the most successful and progressive farmers in Ohio. (CJC.)

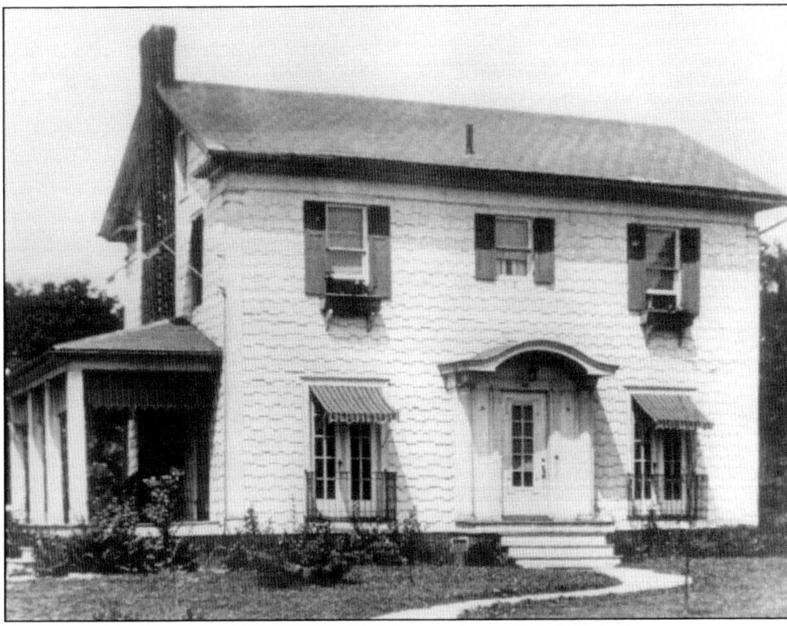

This house was originally a tavern, which stood at the northeast corner of the Darrow and Kent Roads intersection. In 1874, the building was converted to use as a parsonage for the Disciples of Christ Church. It was moved to its present location at 3614 Elm Road in Stow around 1920. (SHS.)

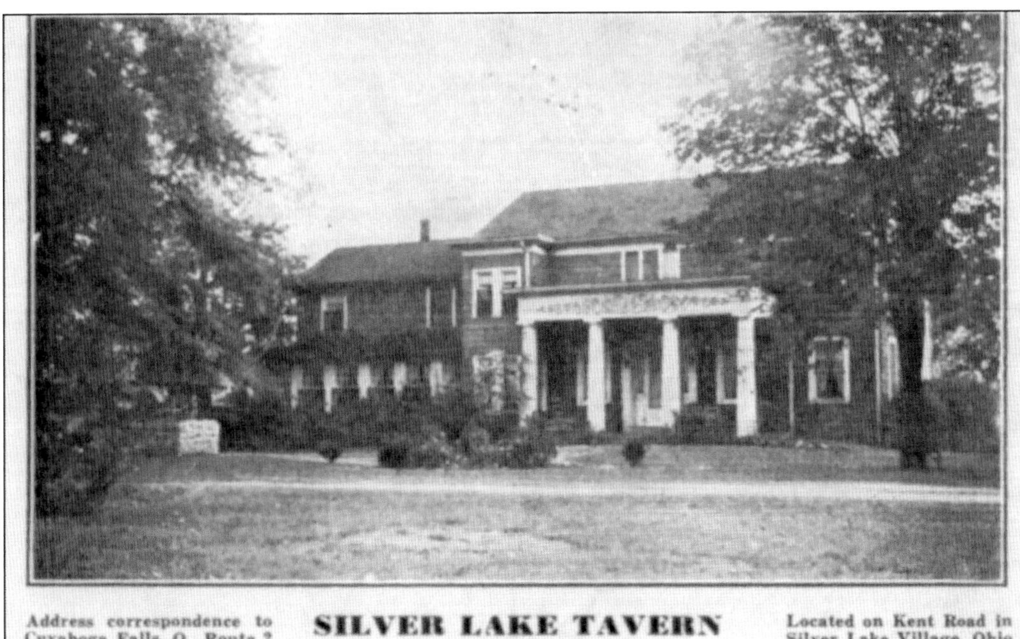

This postcard of Silver Lake Tavern was mailed from Kent, Ohio, in 1932. Located on Kent Road in Silver Lake Village, the tavern was a popular dining spot. The back of the postcard reads, "An inviting home in which to dine and entertain. Call Walbridge 1031 for reservations. Mr. and Mrs. E. D. Eckroad." The tavern, which is now used as a residence, was moved to allow the building of the Church in Silver Lake. (FL.)

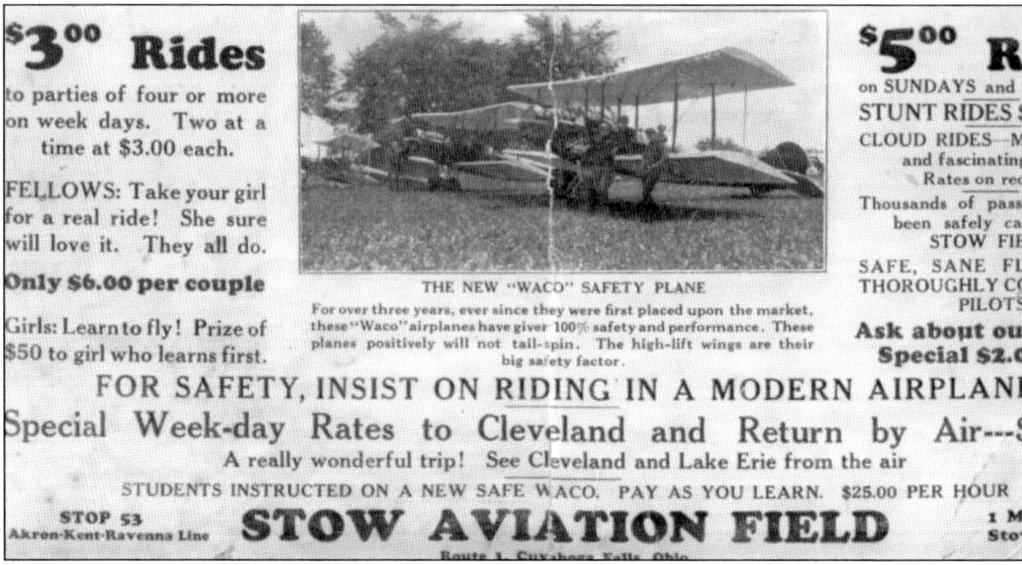

This poster promoting Stow Aviation Field advertises plane rides for $3 and flying lessons for $25 an hour. In 1927, Frankie Renner learned to fly at the Stow Airfield and became the Akron area's first licensed female pilot. She later became manager and owner of the field and salesman of Waco planes. Her flying career ended after a fire destroyed a hangar and eight uninsured planes. The airplane in the photograph is an example of the type of aircraft that might have used Stow Airfield. People in the photograph are unidentified. Stow Airfield is now the Kent State University Airport. (Both FL.)

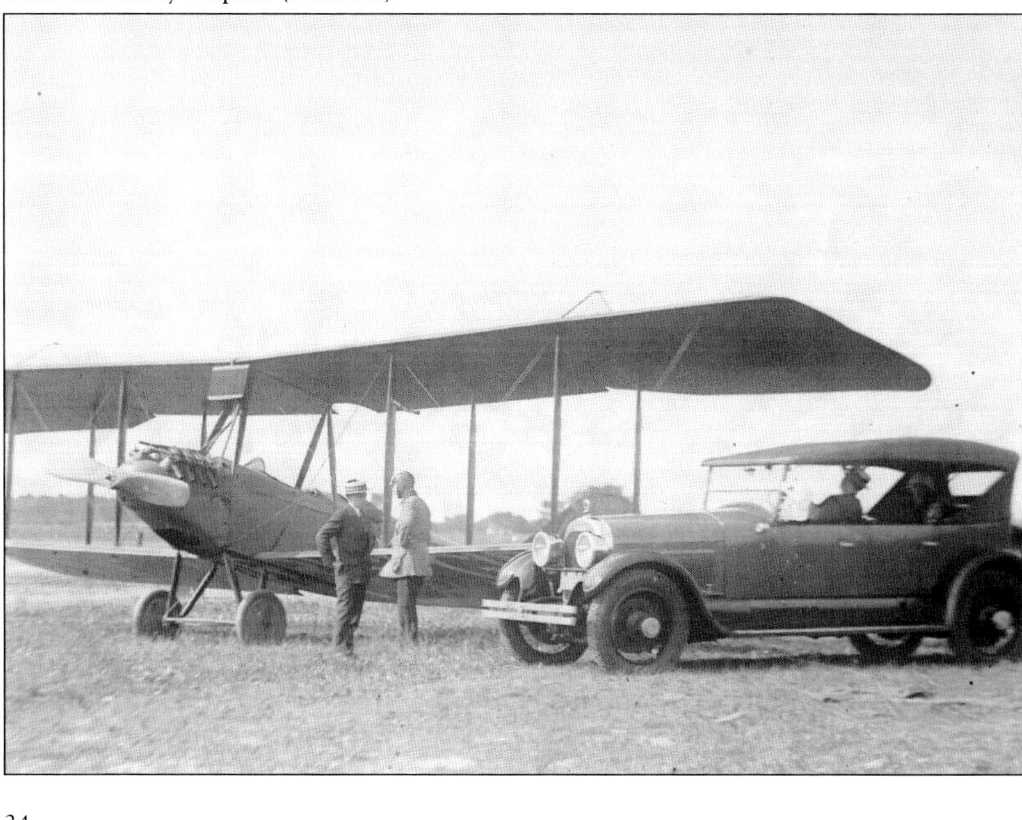

Frank Green, daughter Elizabeth Stow Green Cowles, and granddaughter Kathryn stand at the grave site of William Stow in Stow Cemetery about 1940. Green was the son of Francis Marion Green and Ellen Stow, the daughter of Albert Cheney and Almira Stow. Albert was the first child born to William and Margaret Stow after they arrived in the area of Munroe Falls in 1809. (FL.)

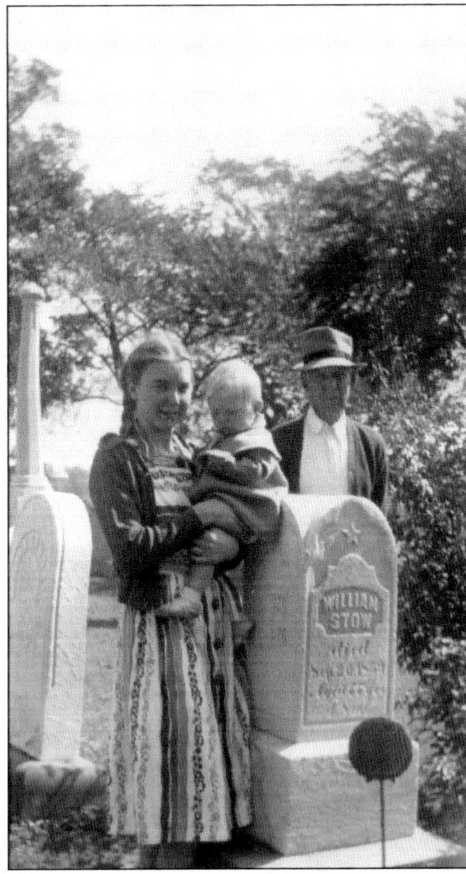

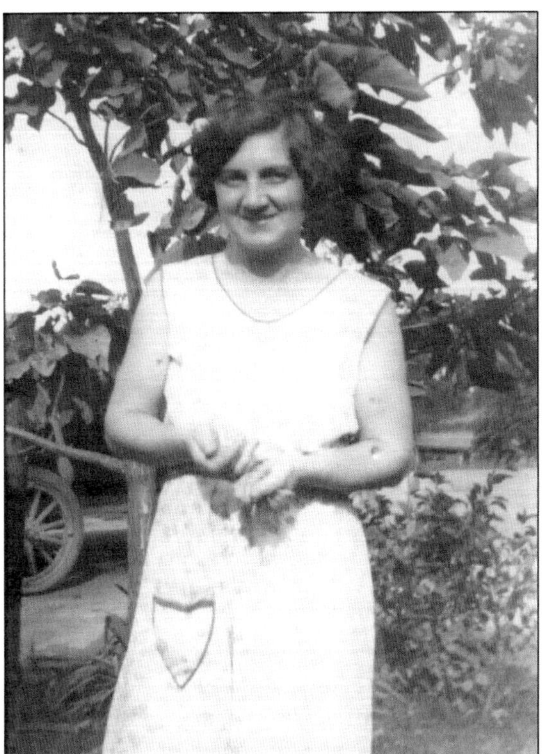

Sarah Hibbard Amlung, pictured in 1940, was born in Stow to John and Nancy Hibbard. Married to Arthur Amlung in 1921, she was a charter member of the Stow Historical Society and helped establish the historical society's park museum. A registered nurse, she was also a member of the Metz Missionary Society and Stow United Presbyterian Church. Sarah, her husband, and brothers donated Meadowbrook Lake to the City of Stow in 1966. (SMFPL.)

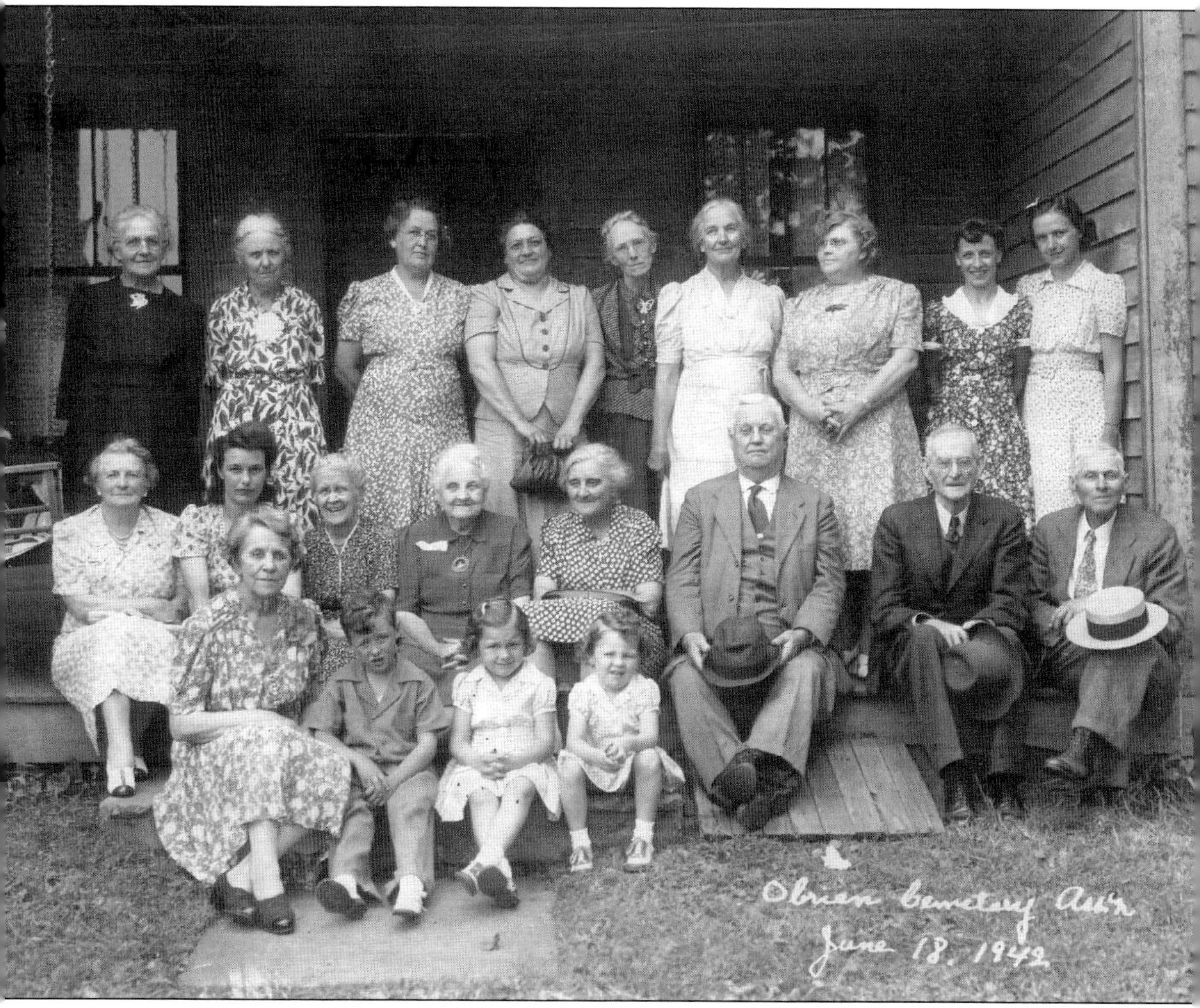

Members of the O'Brien Cemetery Association in this 1942 picture include, from left to right, (first row), Mrs. Howard (Neva) Roose, three unidentified children; (second row) Mrs. McDonald, MaryBelle Christ Poole, Mrs. W. C. Ritchie, Mrs. Jennie Raleigh, Minnie Sadler, Henry Ritchie, William Ritchie, and Howard Roose; (third row) Mrs. John (Nancy) Hibbard, Mrs. Fannie Harrington, Mrs. Lillian Tavis, Mrs. Angie Reed Weaver, unidentified, Maggie Ritchie Christ, Beatrice Raleigh Paul, Harriet Weaver Smith, and Edith Weaver Smith. The association was formed to care for the O'Brien Cemetery, which is located in Hudson Township, just north of the Stow border. Most of the burials in the cemetery actually took place before it was platted in 1880. The first known burial was of Mary Deacon on August 15, 1806. Although it was in Stow Township, the area near O'Brien Cemetery was called "Little Ireland" because so many Irish settled there. Many Irish immigrants came to the Western Reserve to work on the canals, but the Irish Protestants who settled in Little Ireland were farmers. The name "Little Ireland" was changed to Metz in 1886. (FL.)

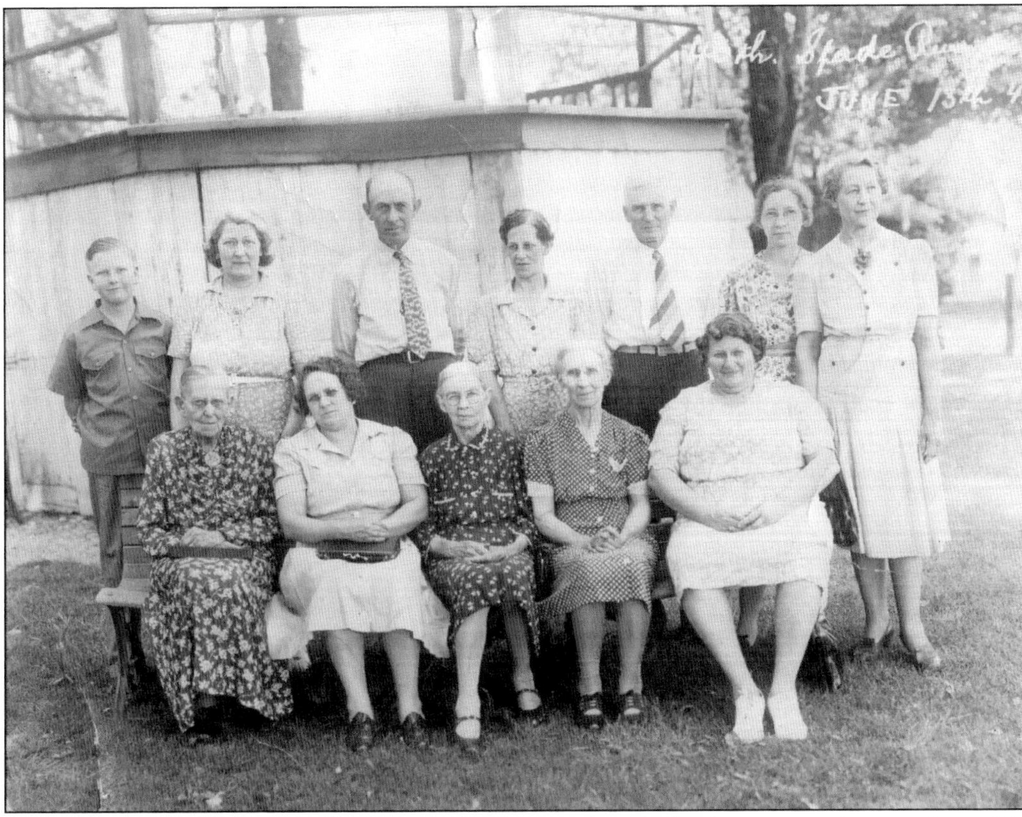

Descendants of Frank and Sarah Ellen Spade gathered for this family reunion photograph in 1942. Frank (1845–1927) and Sarah (1853–1938) lived for many years on the county line road between Summit and Portage Counties. Lulu Swinehart, second from left in the first row, is a great-aunt of Stow's Fred Long. (FL.)

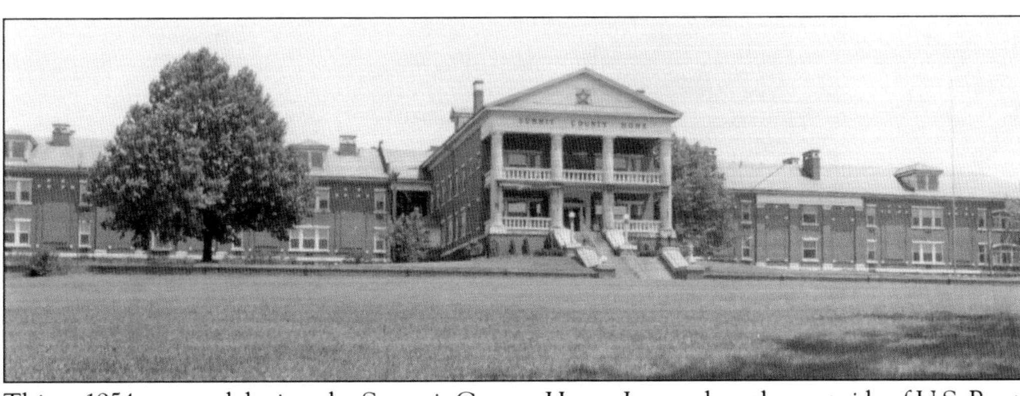

This c. 1954 postcard depicts the Summit County Home. Located on the east side of U.S. Route 91 in Tallmadge, Ohio, just south of Munroe Falls, the Summit County Home, or Infirmary, opened in 1921 to house the poor and indigent. The property was farmed to provide food for the residents. The home was closed in 1970 and demolished in 1980. (FL.)

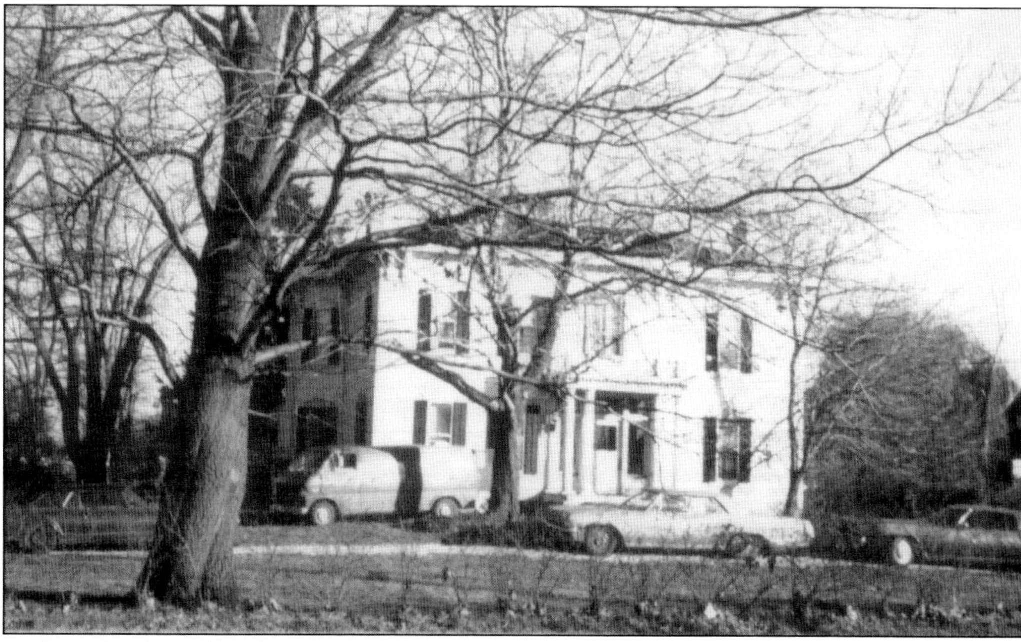

William Rattle and his family maintained a summer residence in this home at 364 North Main Street in Munroe Falls. Acquiring the property in 1848, the Rattle family owned more than 100 acres of land bordering both sides of North Main Street. Later owners of the home were William Perrine, the Fageol family, Harry Schrank, and Russell Werts. In 1961, new owners Ken and Ruth Alexander turned the home into a restaurant known as Alexander Manor. (MFHS.)

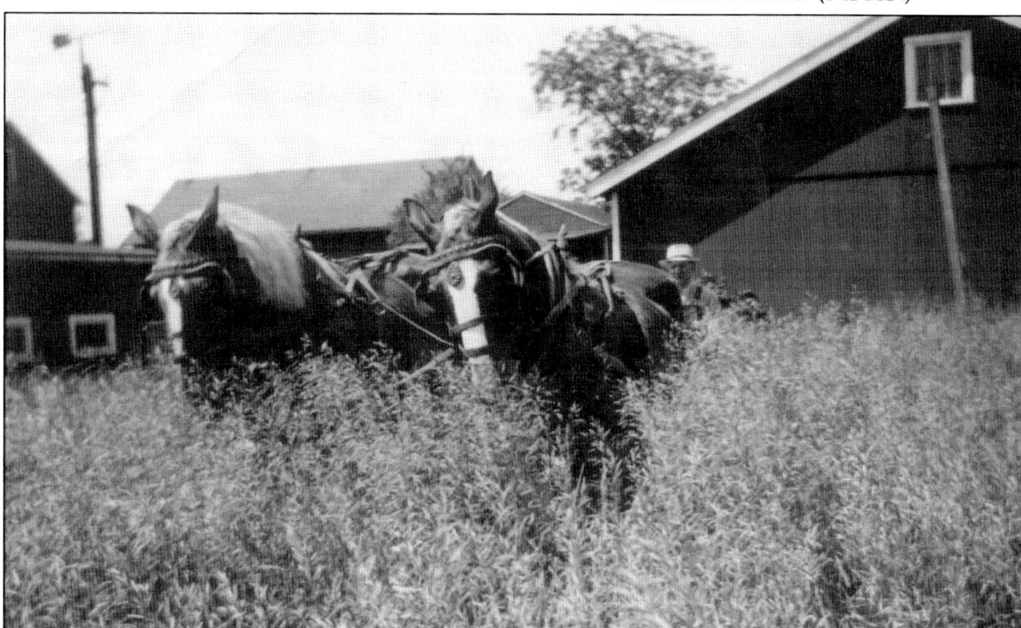

Five generations of Calls have farmed the property acquired by their ancestor Josiah Starr, when he came to this area from Middletown, Connecticut, in 1804. Starr came to take possession of the 180 acres of land he had purchased in 1803 from the Connecticut Land Company for $1.50 an acre. Howard M. Call is pictured here cutting hay in the 1940s. (CJC.)

This photograph from the 1950s shows Charles E. Call using a buck rake and hauling hay in from the field to the barn on his Call Road farm in Stow. Call and his wife, Jean, continued the farming tradition of his ancestors while modernizing and mechanizing the operations. Besides dairy farming, the Calls were involved in the production of eggs, certified seeds, and maple syrup. (CJC.)

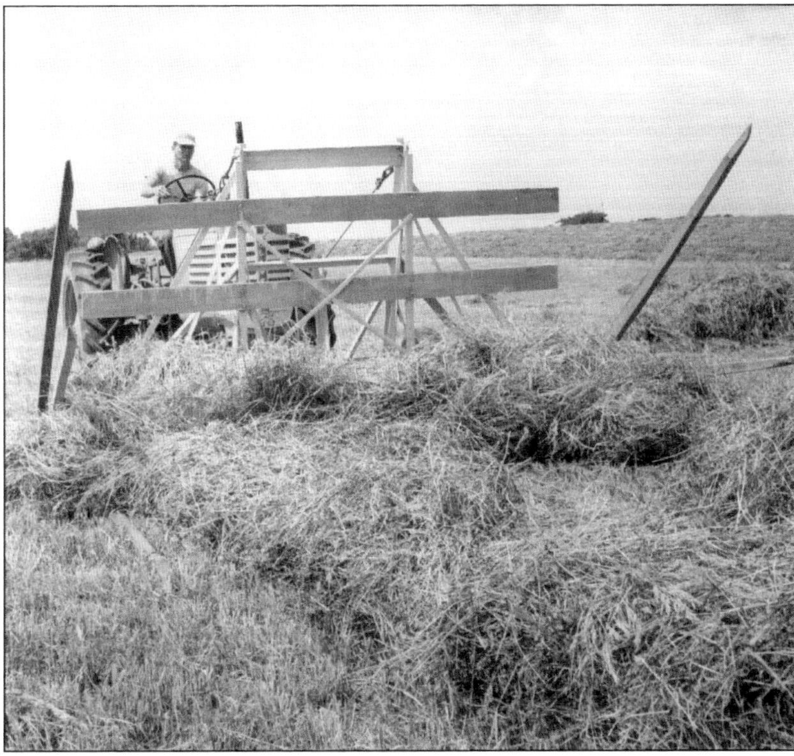

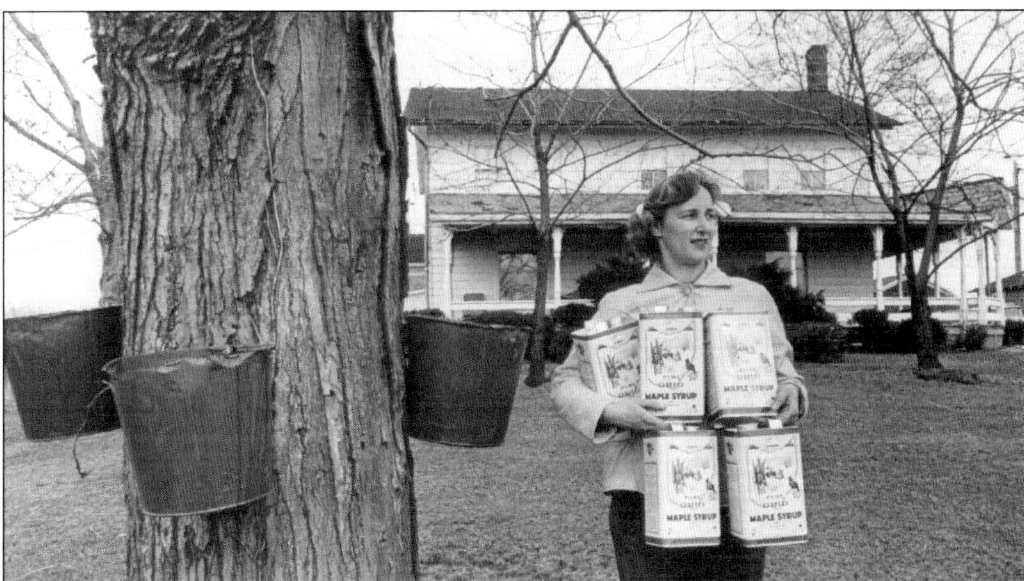

Jean (Point) Call stands in front of the Call farmhouse holding cans of maple syrup produced on the farm in the mid-1960s. She has lived on the farm since her marriage to Charles E. Call in 1944. Jean has been active in farm and community life, with involvement in the Summit County 4-H Club, the Stow Historical Society, and state and local farm bureaus. She was the first female member and president of the Summit Soil and Water Conservation District. (CJC.)

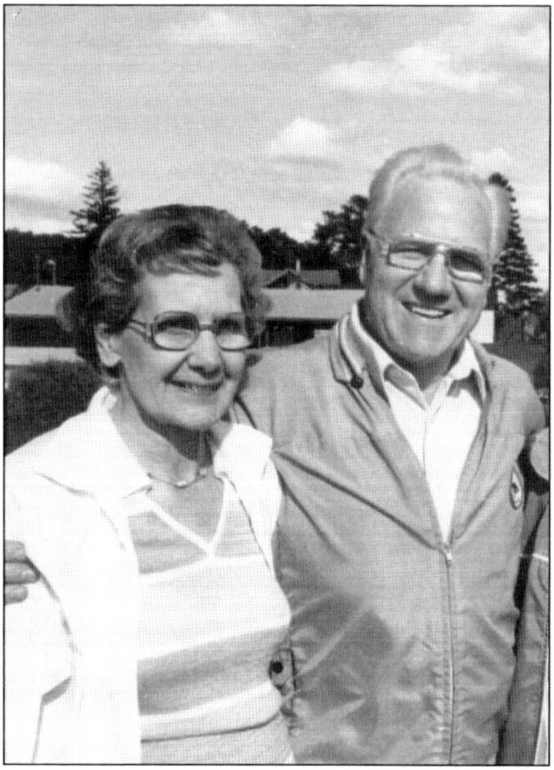

Frank and Dorothy Schmiedel became residents of Young Road in 1944. Both were longtime members of the Stow Historical Society and active in the local community. A contractor by trade, Frank Schmiedel was a past president of the Stow Fraternal Order of Police Association, a member of the Stow Chamber of Commerce, and writer of the Stow Men's Garden Club monthly newsletter. Dorothy Schmiedel, a talented homemaker, worked closely in the family's Fox Den Fairways business. (LB.)

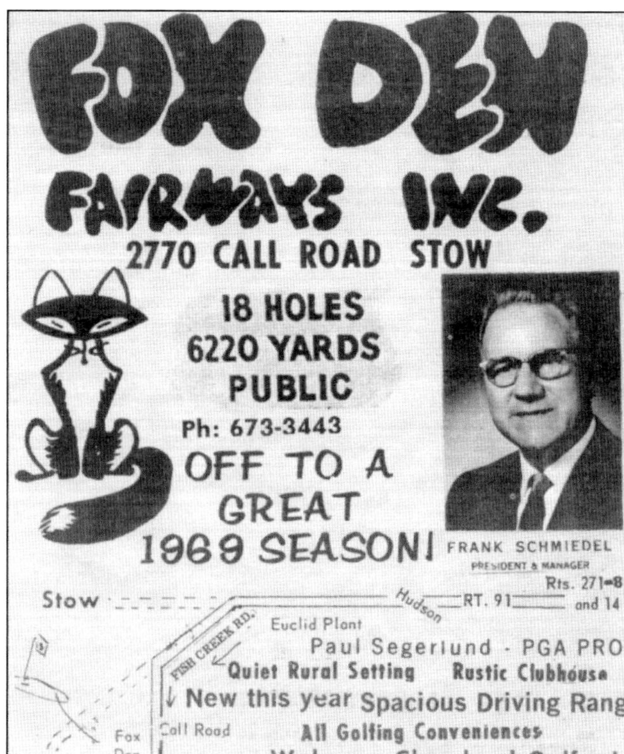

Frank and Dorothy Schmiedel developed Fox Den Fairways across from their home on 150 acres of the former Hanson farm. The golf course on Call Road opened in the spring of 1967 with parking for 200 cars. The course turned into a family affair, with each of the Schmiedel children working at the course over the years. (LB.)

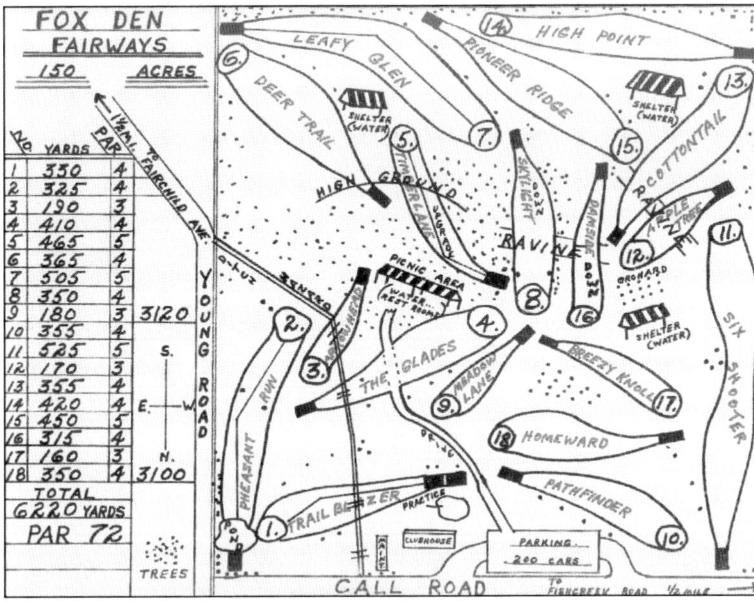

Frank Schmiedel designed the scorecard for Fox Den Fairways, and Clayton Woike, Dorothy Schmieldel's nephew, designed the original Fox logo. The Schmeidels named each one of the holes, such as Pheasant Run, Leafy Glen, and Deer Trail, according to early farm memories. Fox Den was privately owned until it was bought by the City of Stow on February 1, 2006. (LB.)

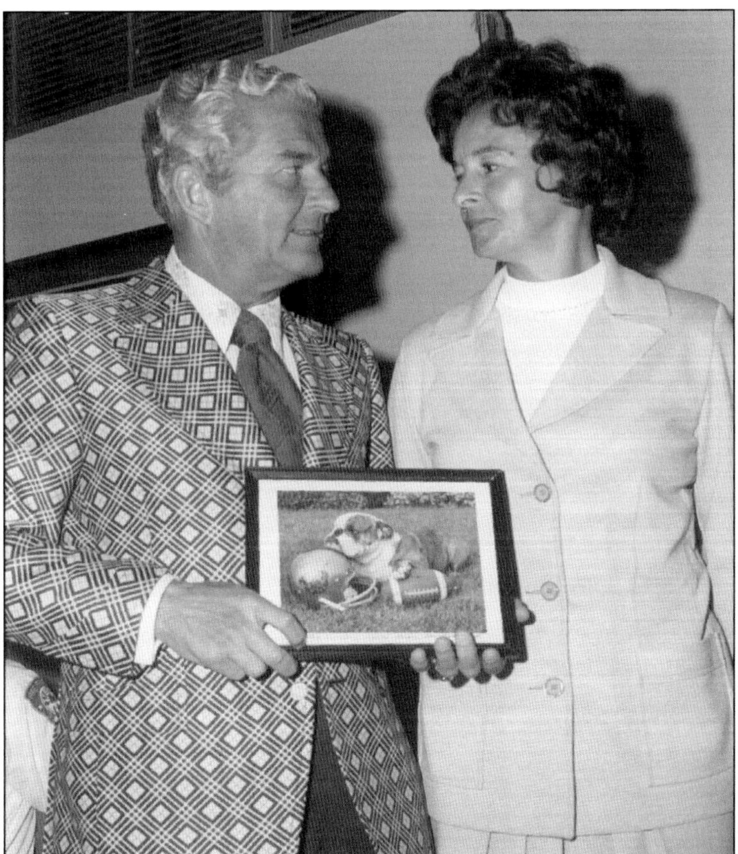

Jim Graner, pictured holding a photograph of the Stow bulldog mascot, was a well-known sports announcer for Cleveland station WKYC (channel 3) and for the Cleveland Browns Radio Network. Graner worked with Gib Shanley, announcing games first on station WERE-AM (1300), then on station WHK-AM (1420) from 1963 to 1974. Graner was a 1937 graduate of Stow High School. The woman with Graner is unidentified. (FL.)

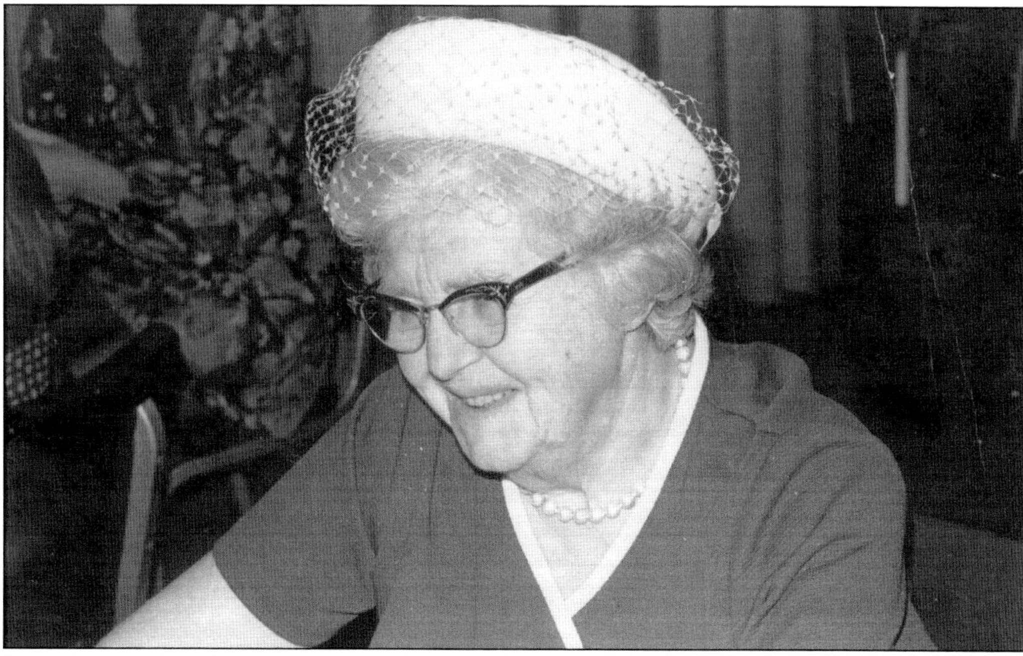

Lena Osman, founder and owner of Osman's Pies, is seen here at an employee Christmas party in the 1970s. Mrs. Osman began selling pies in Stow in 1949 after having been the head chef at the Stow Smorgasbord. She handed down the business to her son and daughter-in-law, Richard and Ethel Osman, who then handed it down to their daughter Cheryl Crowe, who operated the business with her daughter Wendy. (CC.)

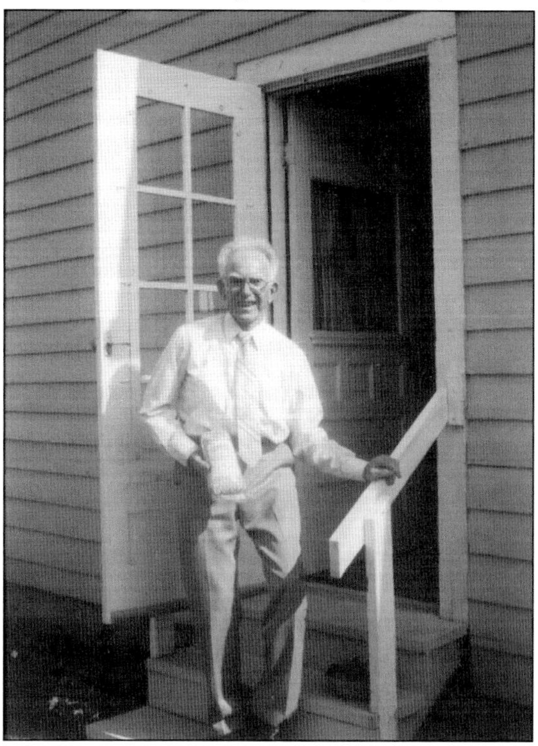

Floyd M. Darrow, known as the "Popcorn King," was one of Stow's most well-known residents. He was a descendant of Stow Township surveyor Joseph Darrow. In 1806, Joseph purchased property on the Hudson-Stow border, and it remained in the family for 172 years. The Darrows went into the popcorn business in 1933, at one time selling as much as 80 tons of popcorn a year to businesses and individuals. (SHS.)

Educator and Stow Historical Society member Paul Coleman (left) points to the sign indicating that the White House Tavern (built in the 1830s) will be restored at Silver Springs Park. The tavern was originally located at the corner of Graham and Fishcreek Roads. It offered food and drink to those traveling by stage. The house was donated to the city by developer Stan Boltz to make way for the Graham Road Plaza. (SHS.)

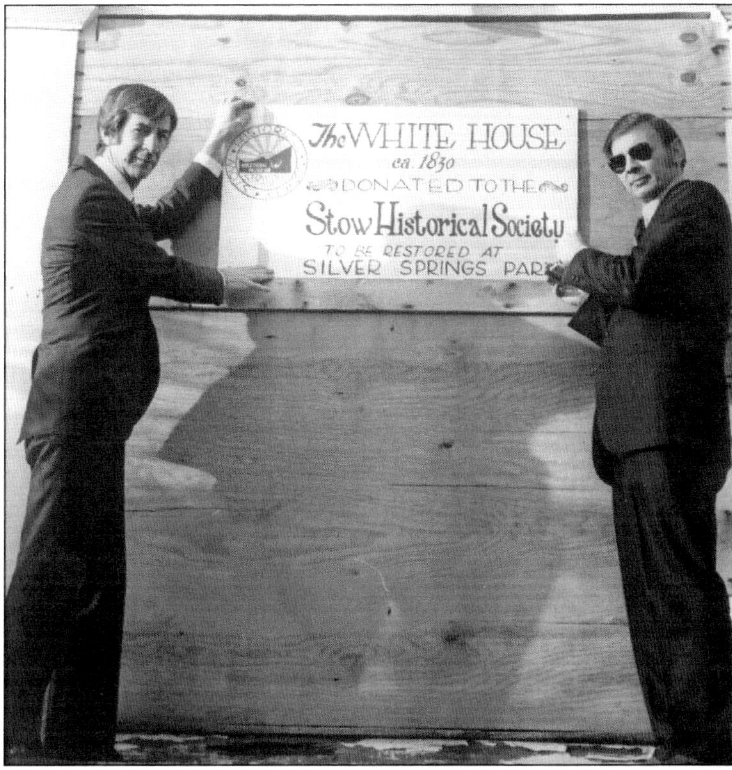

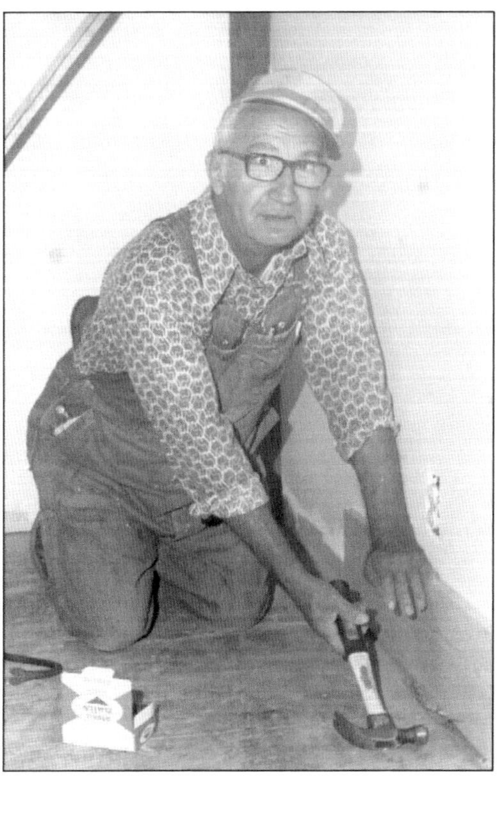

Tom Troyer of Stow is pictured working on the Heritage House belonging to the Stow Historical Society. Troyer helped restore the old house after it was moved from its original location at the corner of Graham and Fishcreek Roads to Silver Springs Park. He and his wife, Dorothea, received the Stow Citizens of the Year award from Mayor C. Paul Hutchison in 1979. (SHS.)

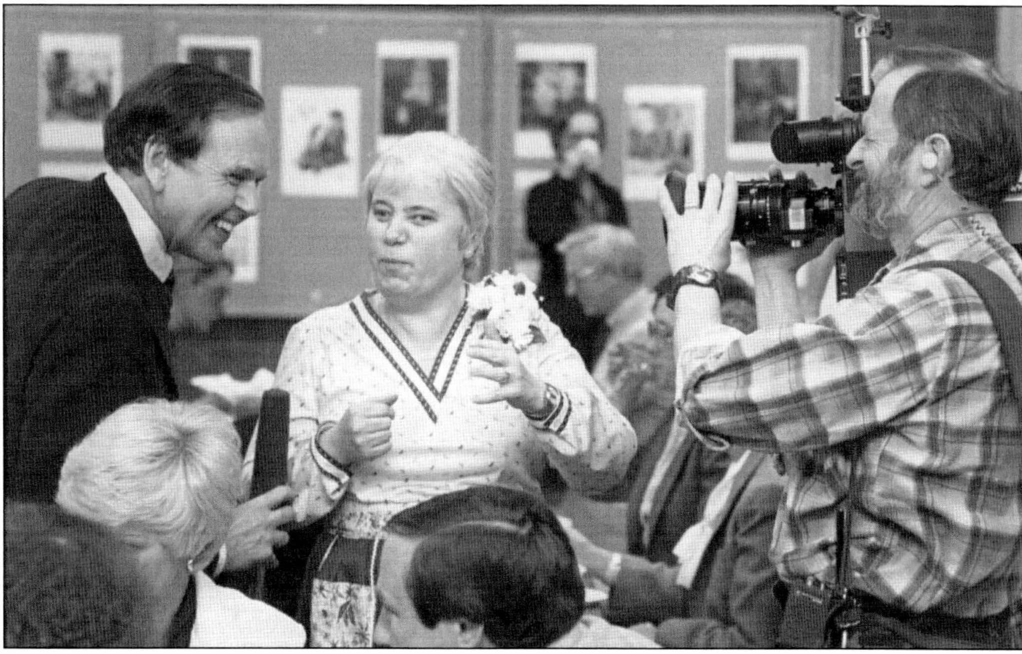

Doris Jyurovat, known for her love of books and motorcycles, began working at the Stow Public Library part-time when she lived next door. She became a full-time employee in 1960 and director of the library in 1964. Mrs. "J," as she was known by the community, retired in December 1985. This picture, taken in 1982, shows her being interviewed by Del Donahoo for a "Del's Folks" segment on WKYC-TV. (SMFPL.)

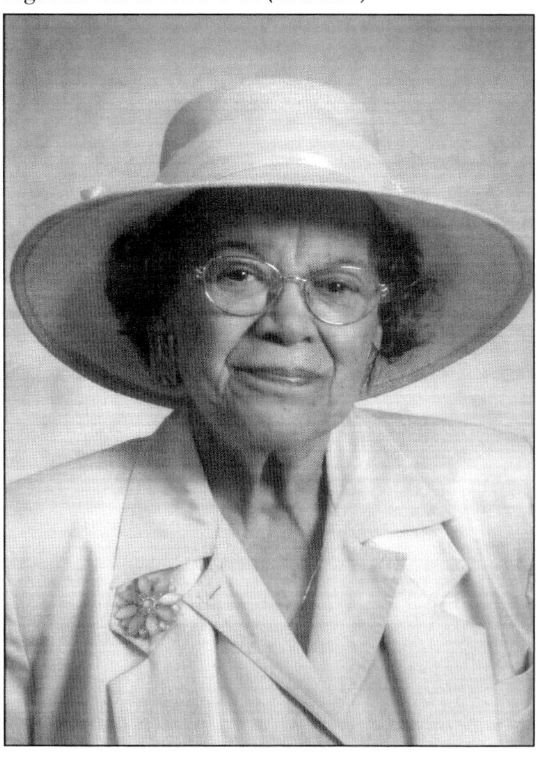

Leona Farris and her husband, Dr. Melvin Farris, moved to Stow in 1954 with three of their four children. Dr. Farris was a general practitioner who made house calls, having received his doctorate in medicine from Ohio State University in 1943. Mrs. Farris was involved in many school and community activities. In 1969, she was the first African American woman hired as an assistant professor at the University of Akron. (LF.)

Three

SCHOOL DAYS

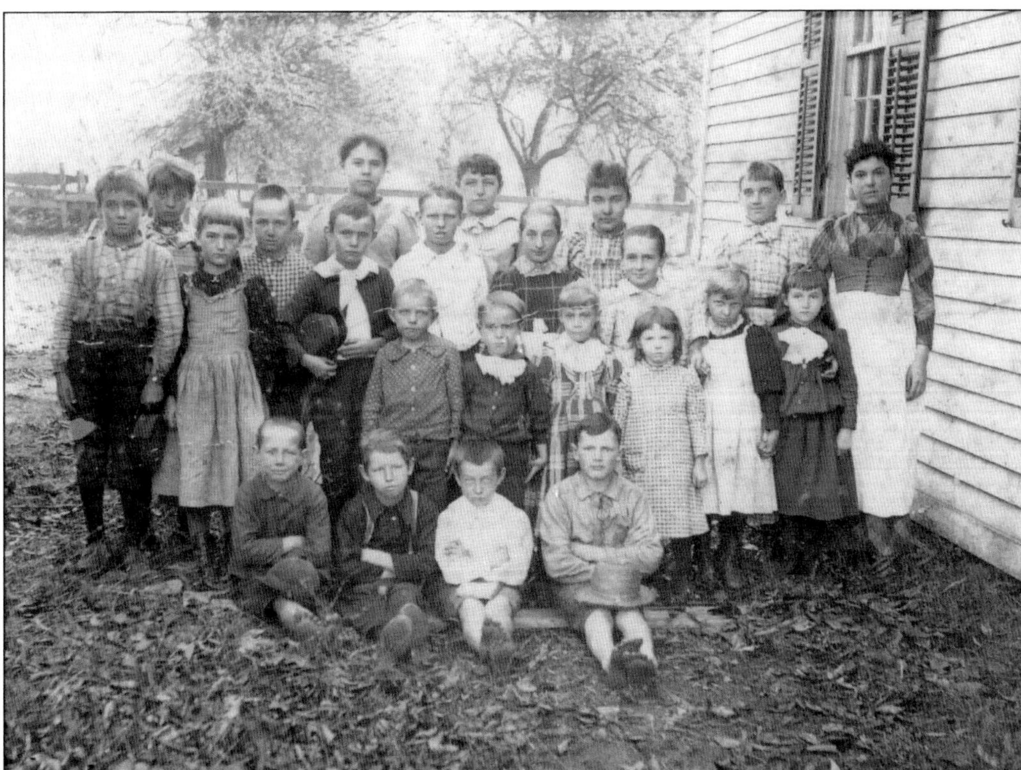

A teacher and her students pose for this 1893 photograph outside one of Stow's one-room schoolhouses. In 1835, Stow established the first of eight school districts, each district containing a one-room schoolhouse for grades one through eight. If a student wished to pursue higher education, he or she traveled to Kent or Akron for high school. (FL.)

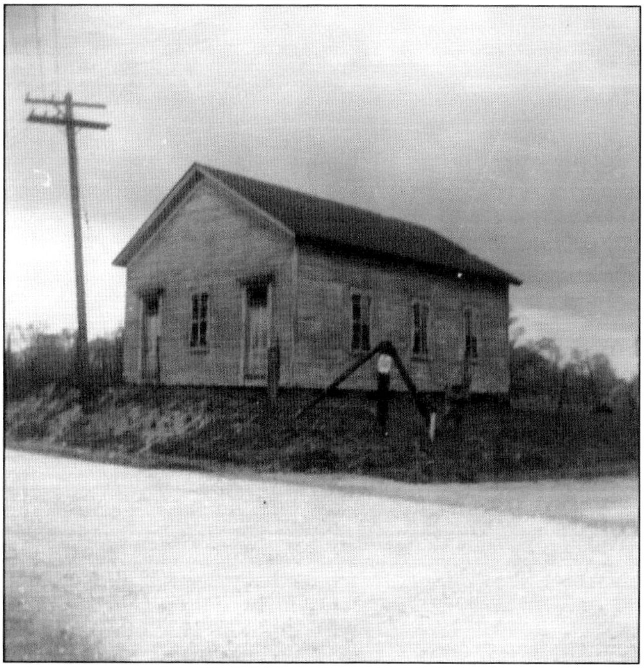

The one-room schoolhouse at Stewart's Corner (the southwest corner of Call and Young Roads) was just 1 of the 10 schoolhouses used by Stow students during the 1800s. In 1853, the Stow School District had a population of 334 students, and Moses Call was acting director of the schools. The schoolhouse has since been moved 500 feet north of its original location and has been used as the Green Valley United Baptist Church. (FL.)

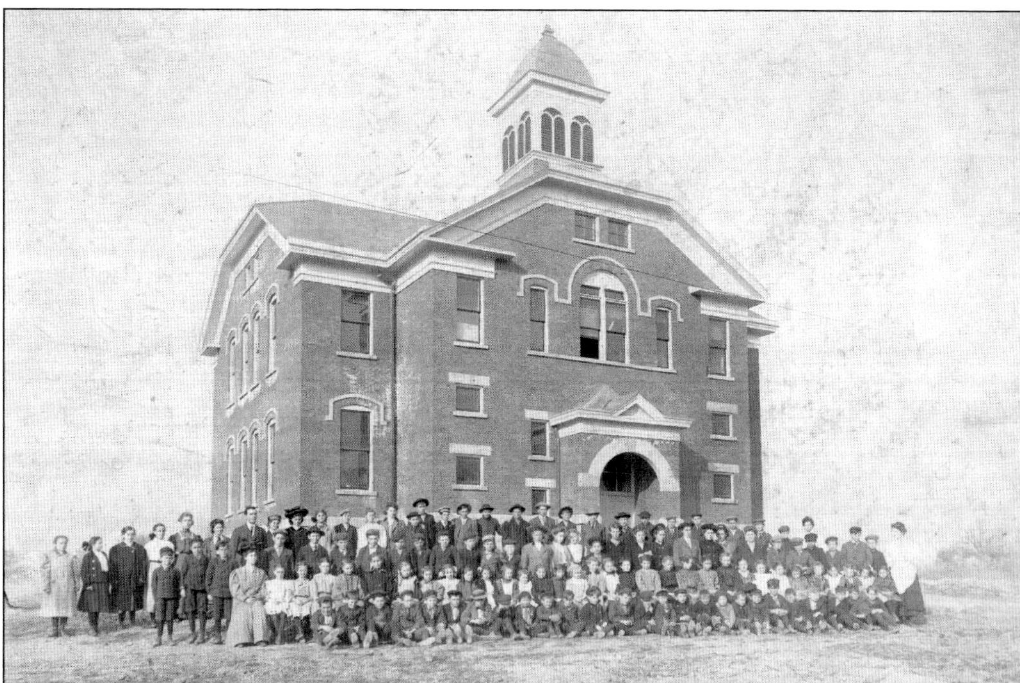

The Stow Township Centralized School was opened in 1907, allowing all Stow students to attend the same building. Curriculum improvements took place immediately, expanding the range of courses offered at both the elementary and high school levels. High school courses included American literature, bookkeeping, Latin, algebra, geometry, English literature, physics, botany, physical geography, economics, and zoology. About 200 students attended school in Stow at this time. (MFHS.)

This Munroe Falls one-room schoolhouse, shown here in the early 1900s, was built in 1885. The first schoolhouse in Munroe Falls was built in 1816. At that time, teachers earned a very small wage and were "boarded around" among the families in the district. (MFHS.)

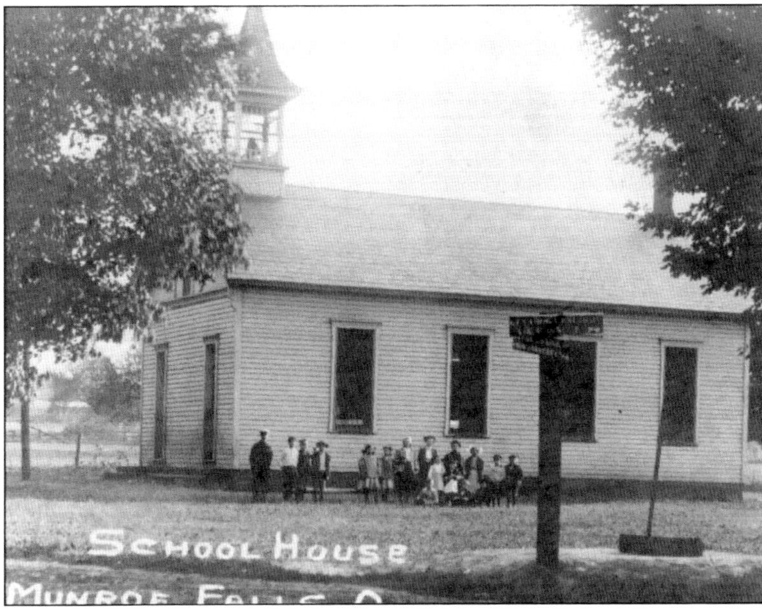

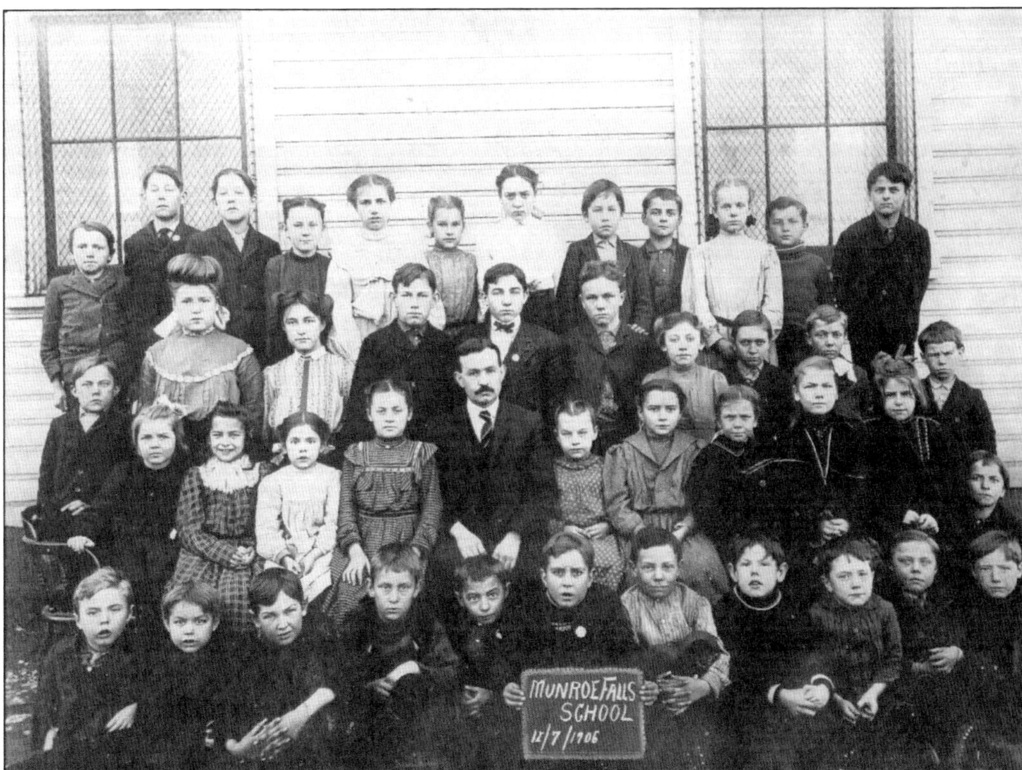

On November 7, 1906, the students of Munroe Falls School gathered with their teacher to have their photograph taken. According to former student Alice (Dixon) Wilson, students learned to spell by participating in the "spell downs" held at the school. The Munroe Falls School District was dissolved by the Summit County Board of Education and joined the Stow Township Centralized School District in 1916. (MFHS.)

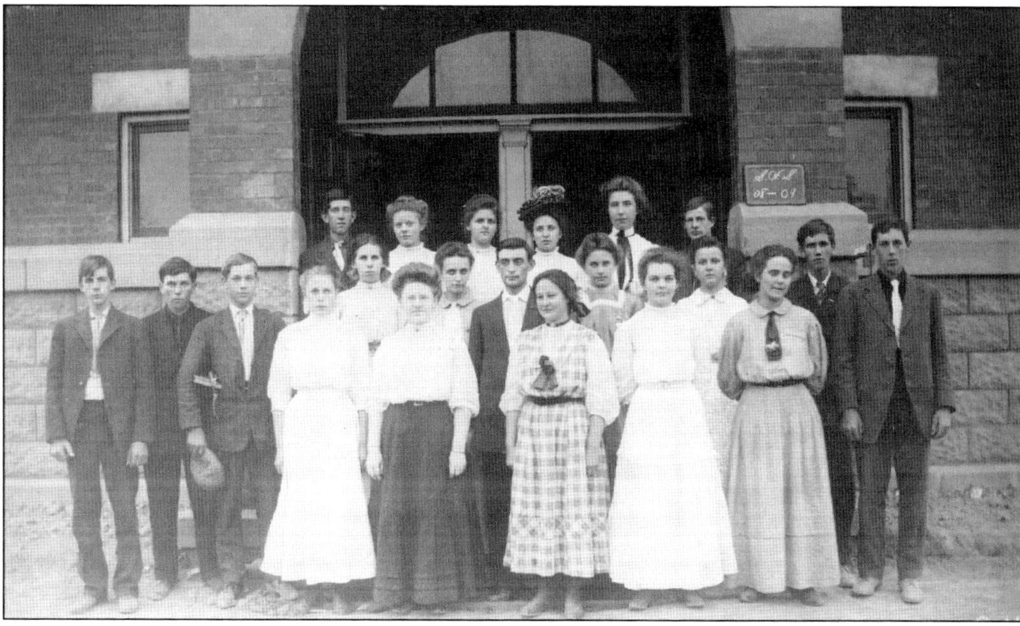

Stow High School students and their teachers stand in front of the brand new Stow Township Centralized School in 1908. The high school and grade school students attended the same school, and the high school consisted of only three grade levels at that time. The class of 1909 was the first to graduate from the centralized school. Graduates were Dorra Darrow, Blanche Dickenson, Emma Hansen, Lottie Hansen, Hallie Nickerson, Delila Staats, and Mary Wetmore. (SMFPL.)

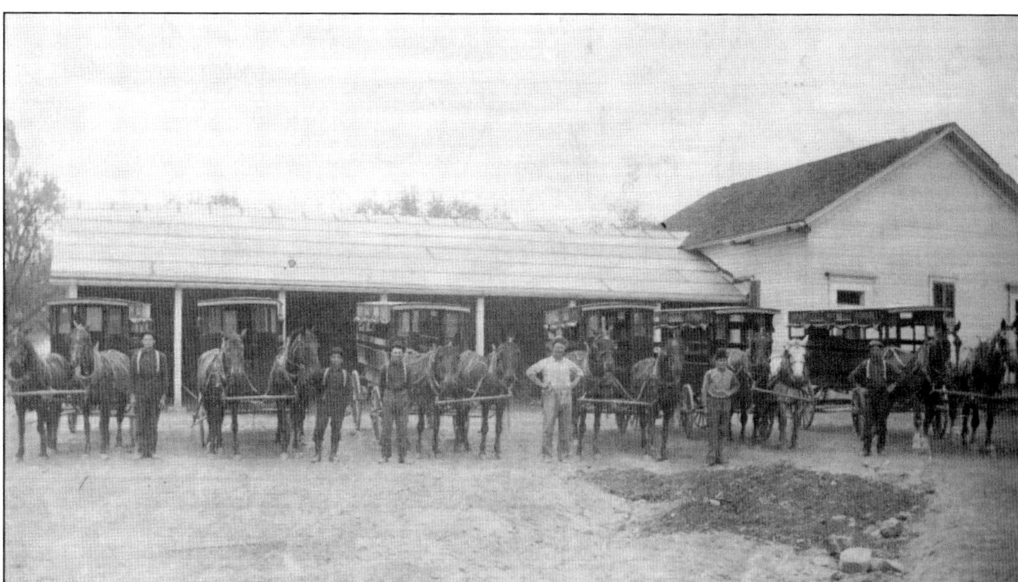

After the Stow Township Centralized School was built in 1907, the Stow Board of Education hired teams of horse wagons and drivers to transport students back and forth to the school. The "bus" stable was on the west side of the property of Stow Centralized School. Two of the drivers in this photograph are Mr. Felmey (second from left) and William Allen (fourth from left). By 1911, there were five bus routes. (FL.)

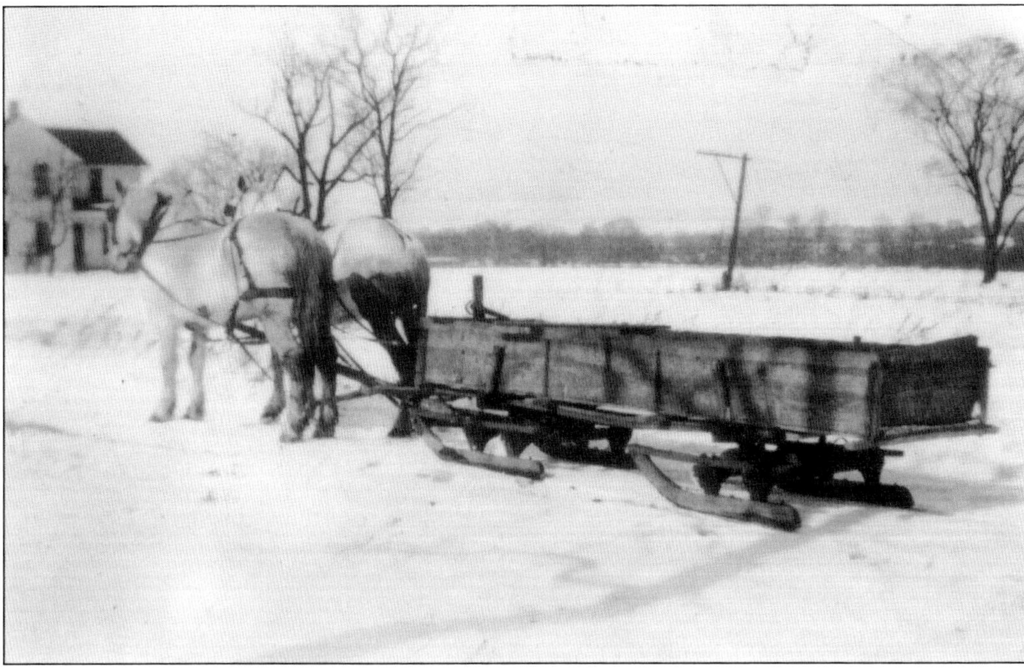

Before buses, there were horses. Teams of horses and drivers were paid $2.50 a day to transport Stow students to the new centralized school after the closing of the one-room schoolhouses in the early part of the 20th century. When the snow was too deep for wagons, students were transported by sled. The horses pictured here are Kate and Nellie. (FL.)

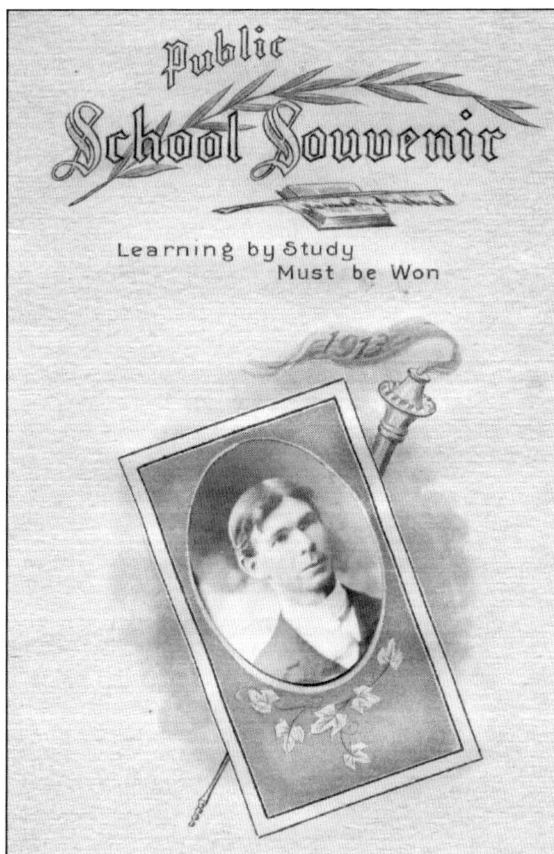

This souvenir booklet was presented at the end of the 1913 school year to the 57 students in the class of Munroe Falls teacher N. S. Marsh. "Learning by study must be won" was the adage on the front of the booklet. (MFHS.)

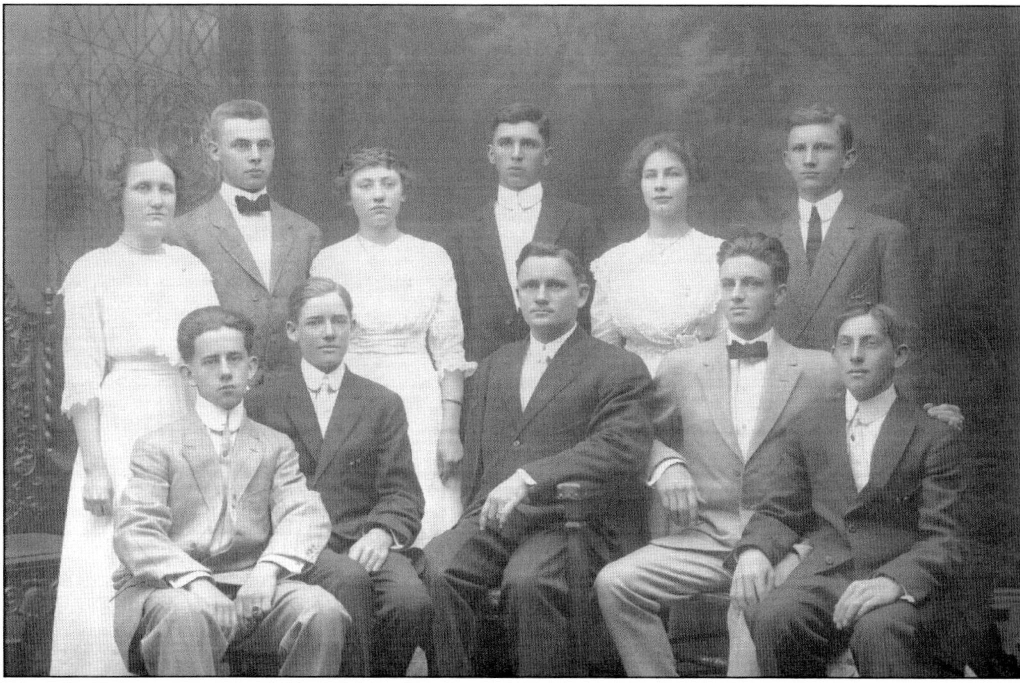

The class of 1913 was the fifth graduating class of Stow's Centralized School. By 1913, two additions had been added to the school because of overcrowding. The school would not have a twelfth grade until 1916. From left to right are (first row) Simpson Hibbard, Edgar Nickerson, principal C. A. Flickinger, Martin Billings, and Clifton Mellin; (second row) Gertrude Ritchie, Roy DeHaven, Stella Gaylord, Coy Palmer, Helen Welker, and Paul Hagelbarger. (SMFPL.)

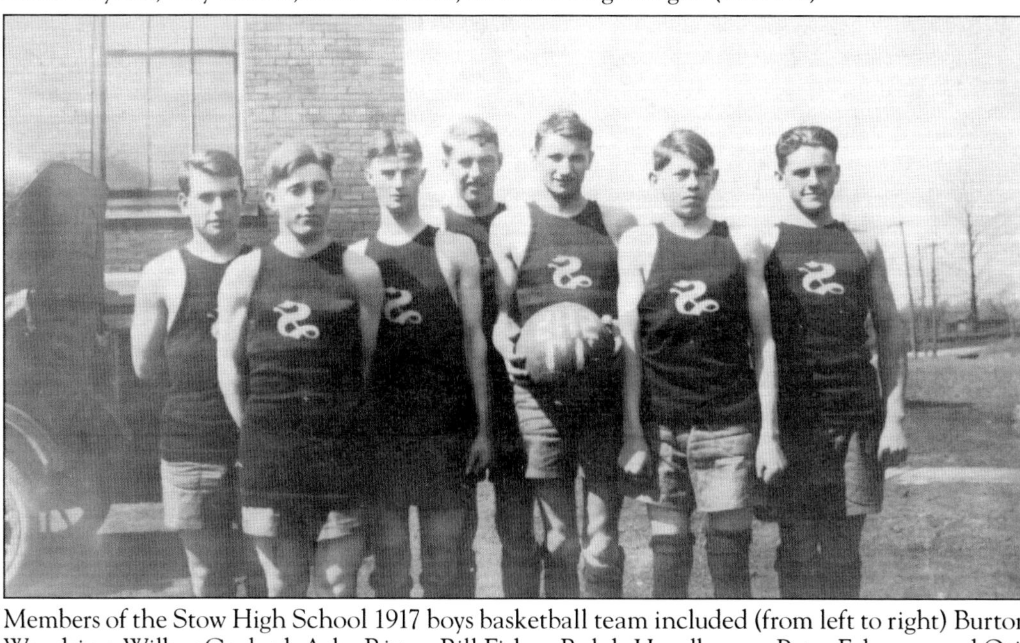

Members of the Stow High School 1917 boys basketball team included (from left to right) Burton Woodring, Wilbur Gaylord, Arba Ritter, Bill Fisher, Ralph Hagelbarger, Peter Fahrney, and Otis Hibbard. The back of this photograph states that Mr. Williams's car is in the background. Milton S. Williams was the principal of Stow High School. (FL.)

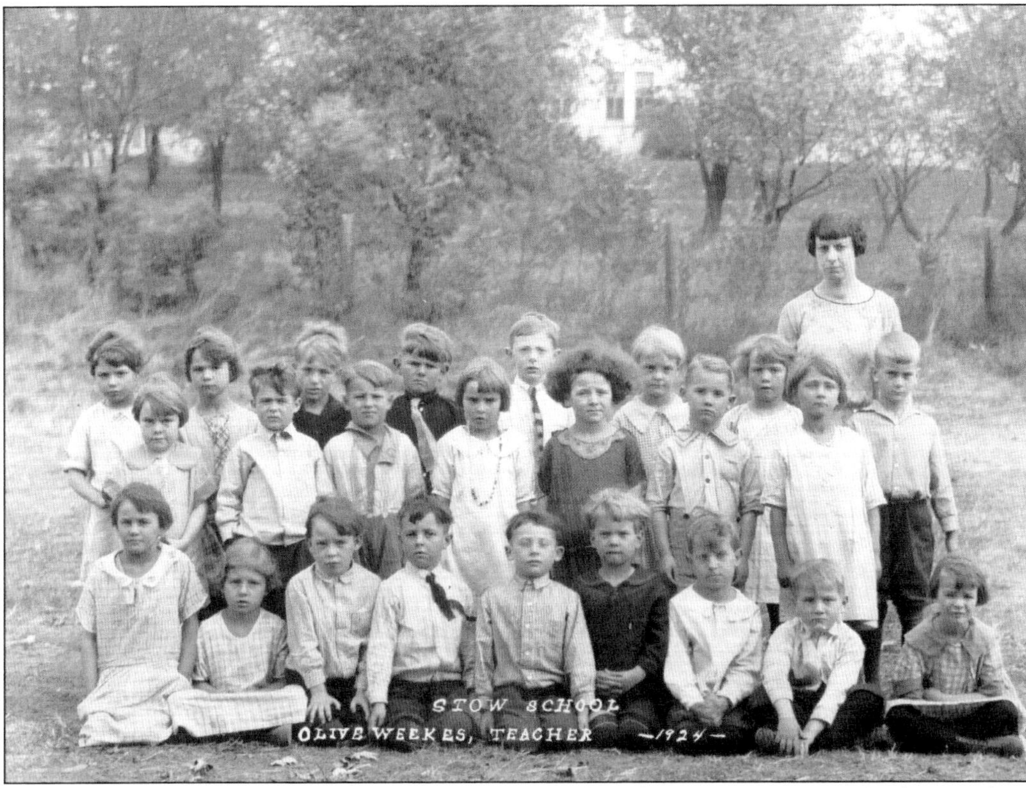

Olive Weeks was the teacher for this young group of students in 1924. In 1907, the people of Stow voted to centralize their school district. The 10 one-room schoolhouses were sold, and all the children in Stow then attended the new centralized school, which held both elementary and high school students. By 1924, when this photograph was taken, a new high school across the street from the centralized school had been built. (SMFPL.)

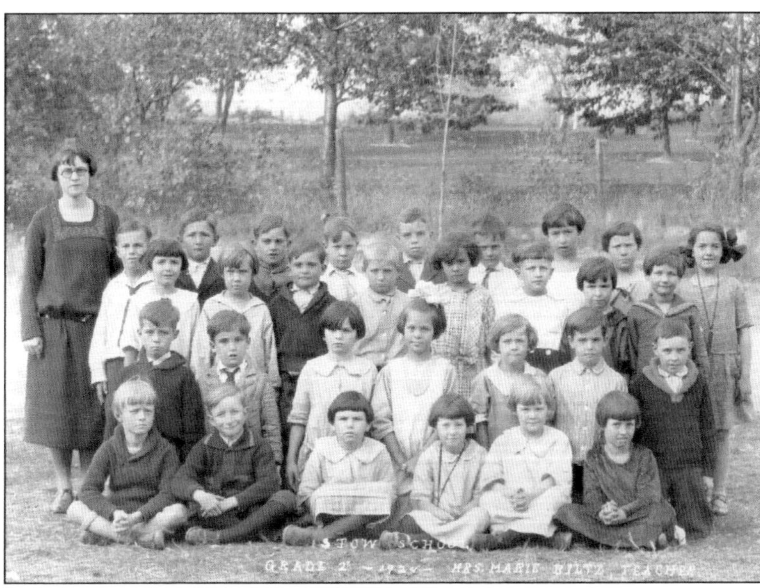

Marie Biltz was the teacher for this group of Stow second graders in 1924. A new high school was completed in 1924, but younger students remained at Stow Centralized School. Because of overcrowding, "portable" classrooms were set up outside Centralized School in 1925 to accommodate the number of students. (FL.)

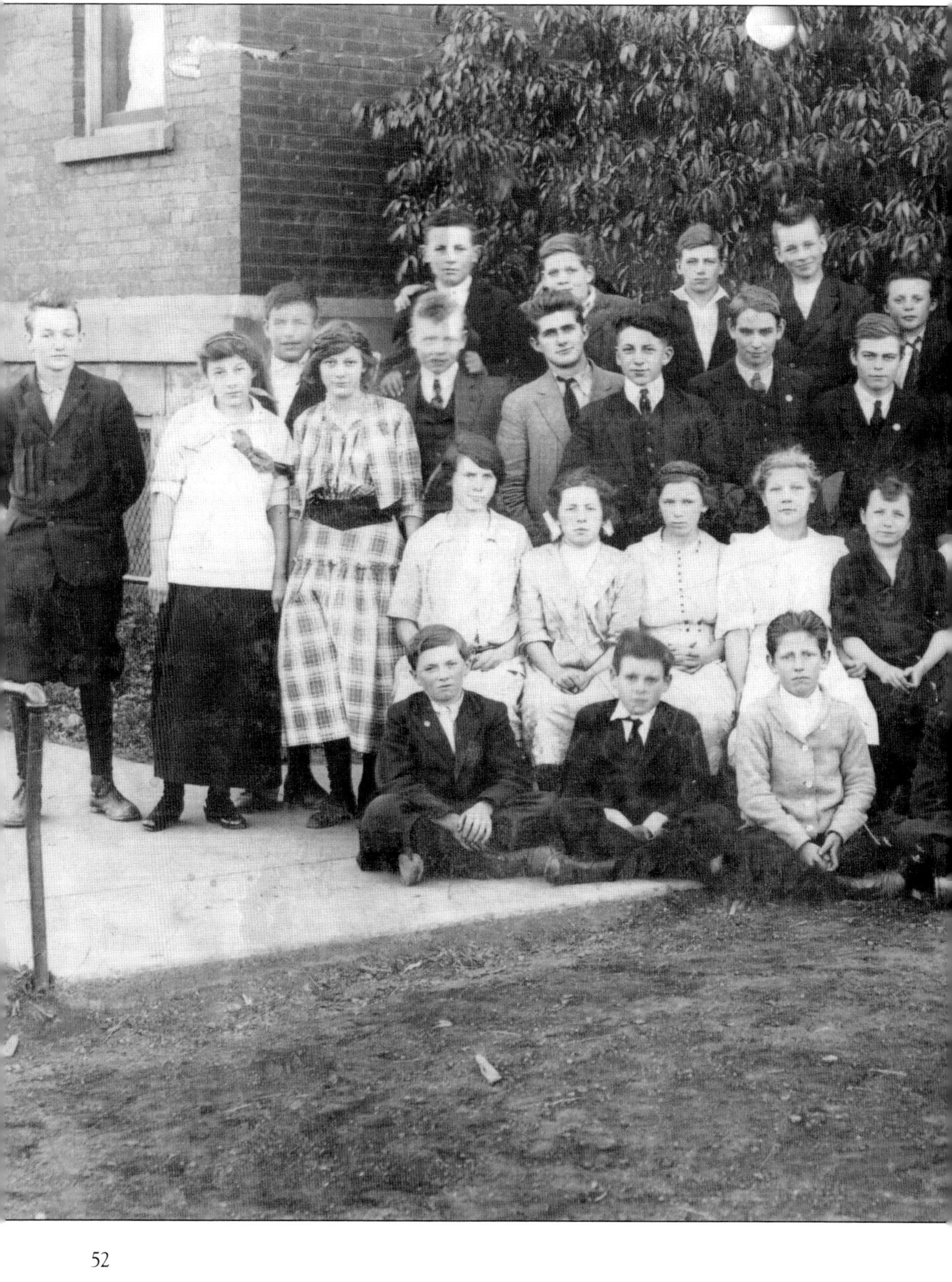

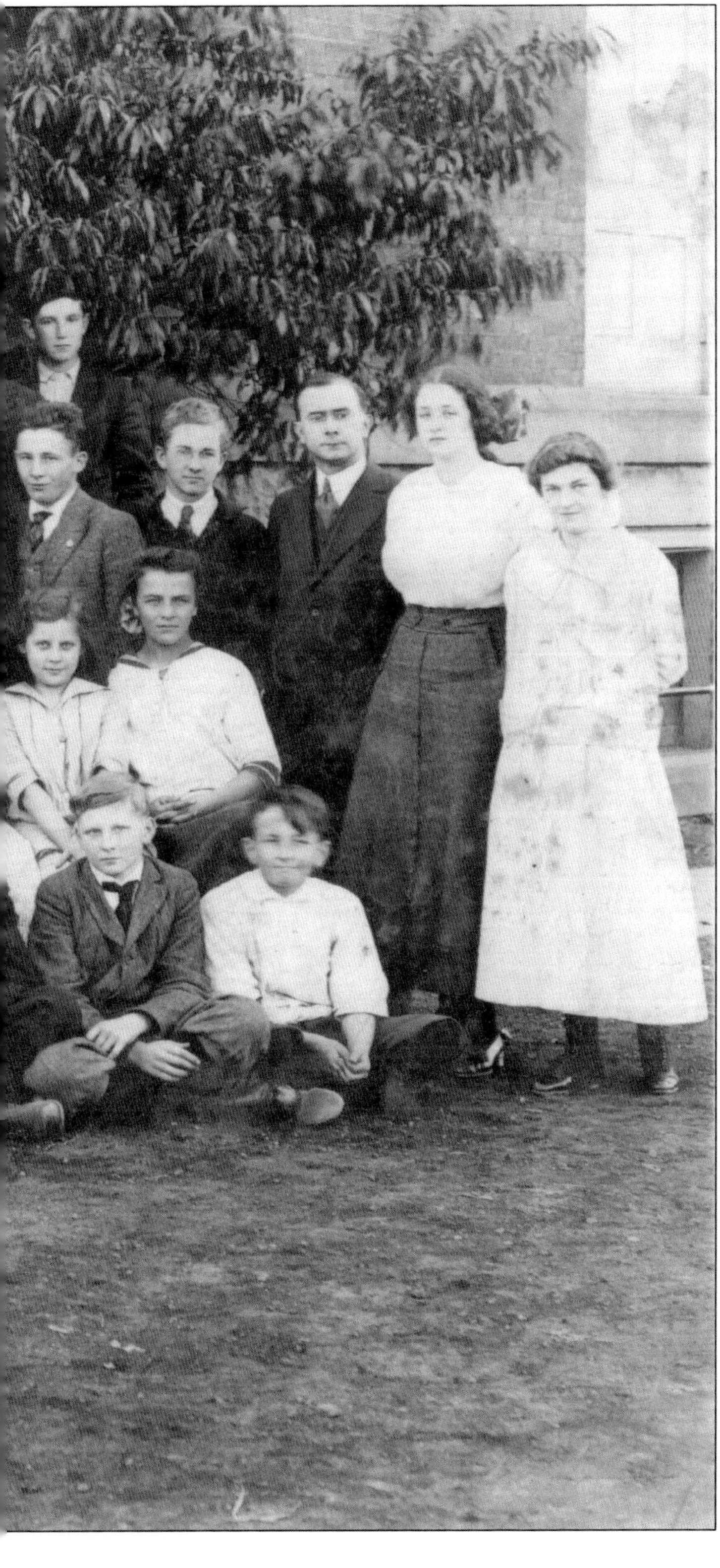

Students pictured in front of the Stow Township Centralized School in this undated photograph are, from left to right (first row), John Watson, John Marhofer, James Hibbard, Marian Smith, Gordon Grubb, and Howard Keener; (second row) ? Hoy, Mildred Smith, Vera Whitting ?, Helen Olson, Hester Hutchison, Gladys Appleton, Eleanor Witsaman, and Loretta Miller; (third row) Charles Pardee, Ruth Collier, Walter Augenstine, Amy Ripley-Fisher, Harley Judson, Earl Warner, Lloyd Hodgeman, Henry Howe, George Thomas, Howard Thompson, and Richard Butler; (fourth row) Evan Keener, Boyd Bridgewater, Albert Hoy, Harold Pardee, Harold Hites, Julius Williamson, unidentified, Clark Ritchie, unidentified, Valda Williamson (Hamilton), and Florence Lind (Croy). (SMFPL.)

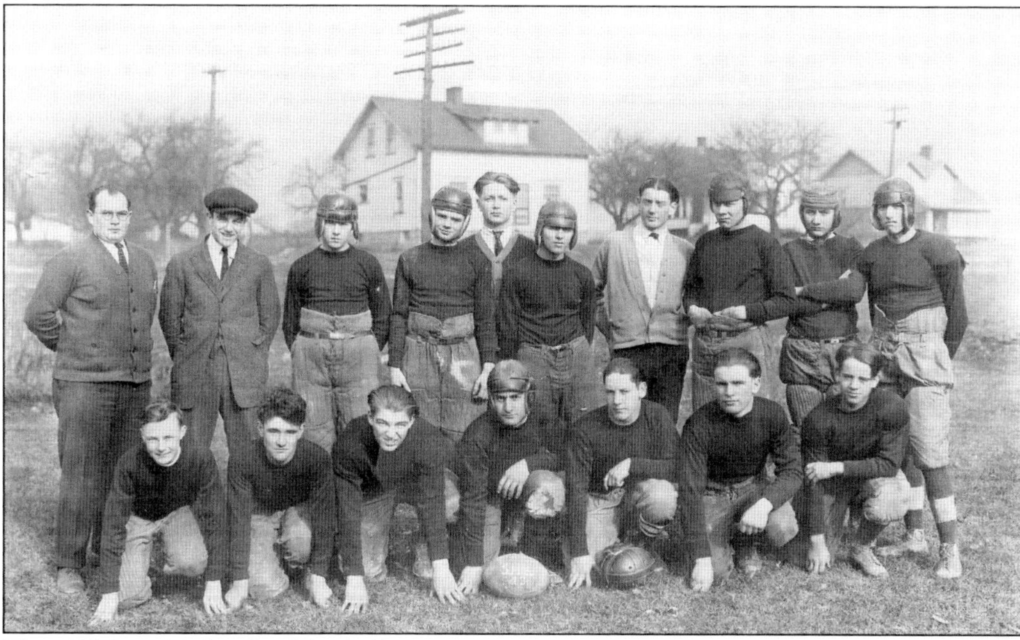

The 1923 Stow High School football team poses for the team photograph. Team members include, from left to right, (first row) Chip Dunn, Les ?, two unidentified, Leo McCracken, Frank Schlarb, and Ted Housley; (second row) Coach Ganyard, Ike Williamson, Robert Gaylord, Edward Lodge, unidentified, Castle Shakespeare, Paul Leonard, Elmer Kelborne, unidentified, and Kenneth Chacey. Because of overcrowding, a new high school was being built during this time. (FL.)

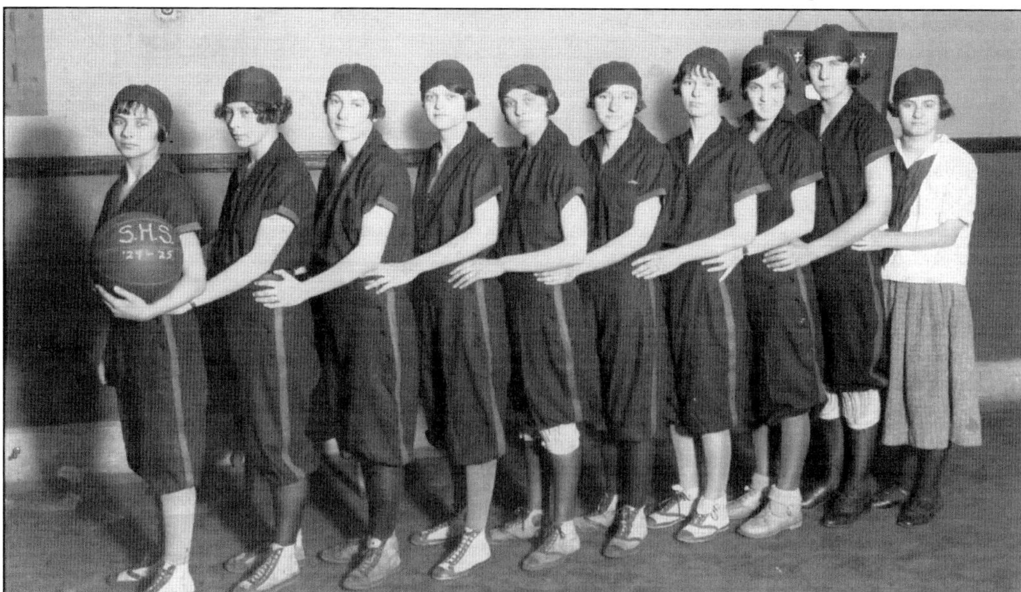

In 1916, the Stow High School girls decided to create a basketball team. They joined the Stow Athletic Association and English teacher Ruth Raw acted as coach. The first game against an outside team was with the Cuyahoga Falls High School sophomore team. Stow won that game with a score of 11 to 9. According to the 1915–1916 Stow High School annual, "The future for Stow basketball girls looks very good." The girls in this photograph formed the 1924–1925 team. (FL.)

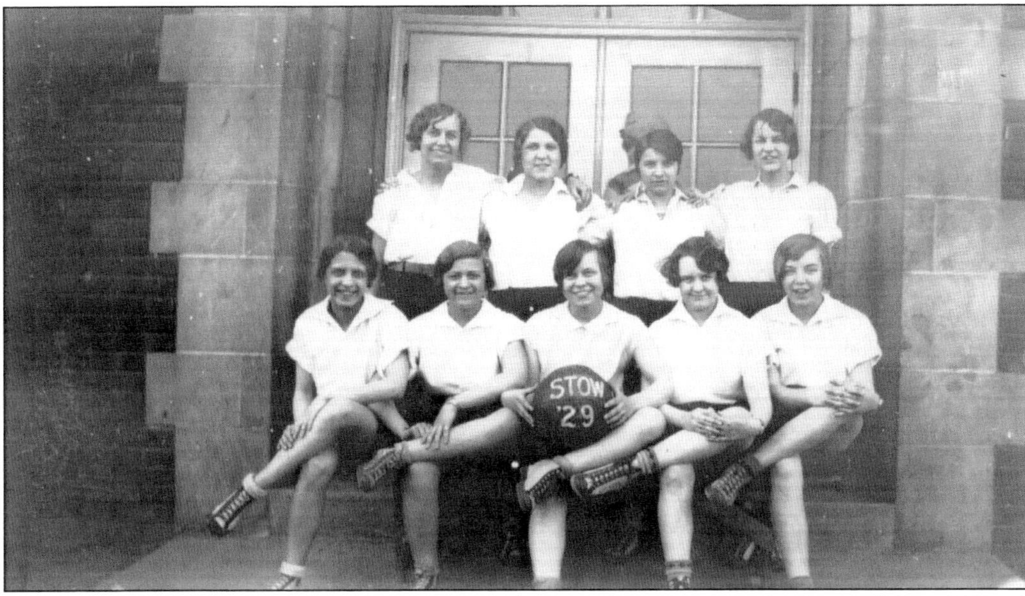

Girls basketball has been popular at Stow High School since 1916. Members of the 1929 girls basketball team pictured here are, from left to right, (first row) Jean Eader, Harriet Franklin, Mary Lou Haines, Lucy Gaylord, and Elizabeth Green; (second row) Mary Ann Whitecotton, Louise Grove, Marian McFee, and Ethel Klesa. (FL.)

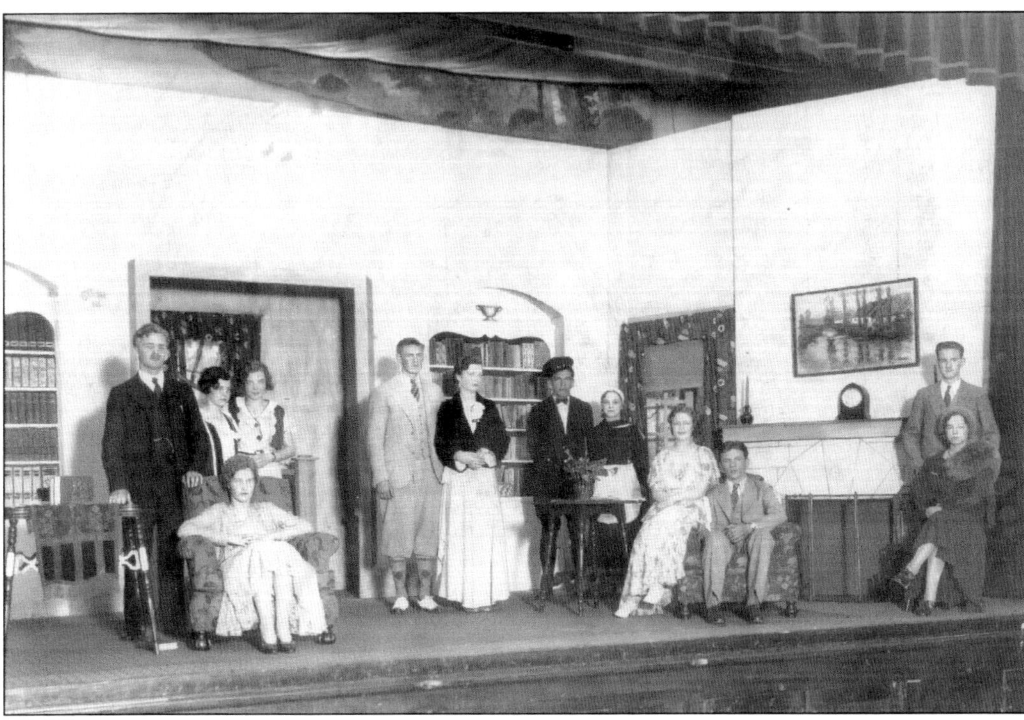

The Stow High School 1931 senior class play was held in the gymnasium of Stow High School. Voters had approved an addition to the high school after it was built in 1924, resulting in a gymnasium and more classrooms. The class of 1931 had 38 students: 19 girls and 19 boys. (SMFPL.)

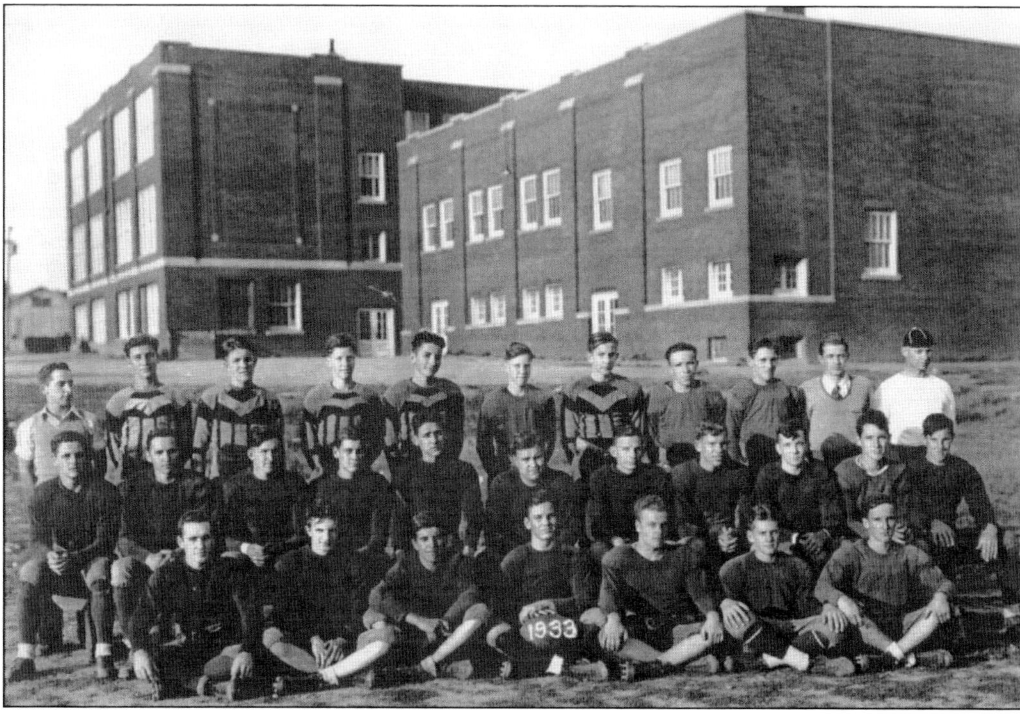

Members of the 1933 Stow High School football team were, from left to right, (first row) three unidentified, ? Coleman, ? Edwards, Wayne Carlson, and Cyril McCloskey; (second row) Hugh Nickerson, unidentified, Richard McCloskey, two unidentified, Paul Bishop, Otto Cobb, Don Traxler, Eddie Palmer, unidentified, and Wayne Dietz; (third row) Carl Arnold, Keith Spriggle, Norm Kempel, Bill Brown, Paul Weygandt, Bob Brown, Paul Monteith, Jim Anderson, Bob Long, Dick Schnee, and coach William Barr. (SMFPL.)

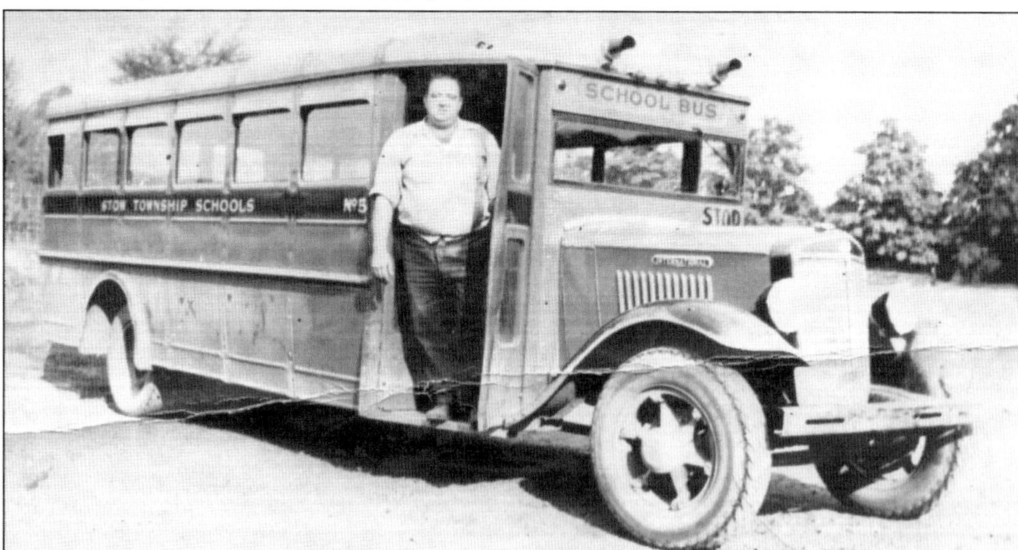

Stow Township school buses had progressed from horses and carts to motor vehicles by October 1936 when this photograph was taken. Driver Kenneth Deacon stands in the doorway of Stow Township Schools bus No. 5. (FL.)

Four high school students consult with their teacher in her classroom at Stow High School sometime in the 1930s. Typewriters on the desks and the Royal keyboard poster on the chalkboard indicate that this was a business class. This photograph is from the June Lorene Mowry Collection at Stow-Munroe Falls Public Library. (SMFPL.)

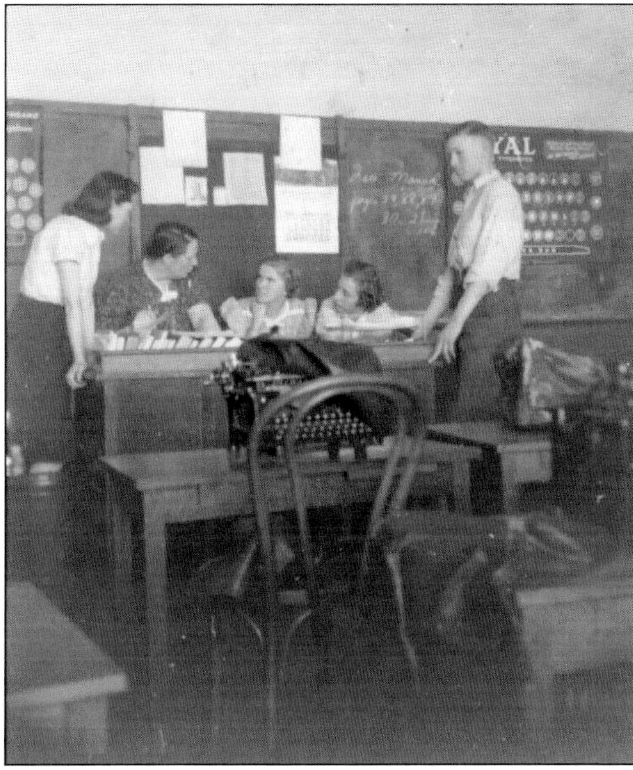

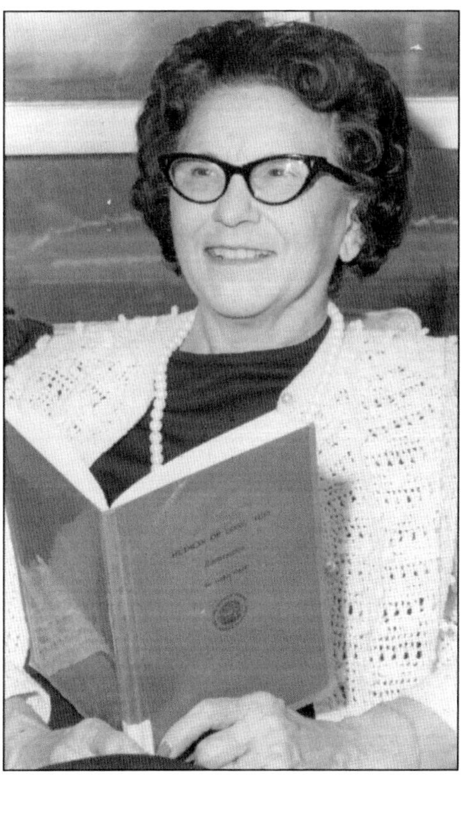

Elno Palmer Ackworth was a well-liked, longtime teacher in Stow. In the 1930s, she taught first grade and was an inspiration to her students. Ackworth's parents, Lewis and Almeda Palmer, were large land owners in the area, occupying a farm at the corner of Marsh and North River Roads where the Summit County Fishcreek wastewater treatment plant is now located. They had eight children. (FL.)

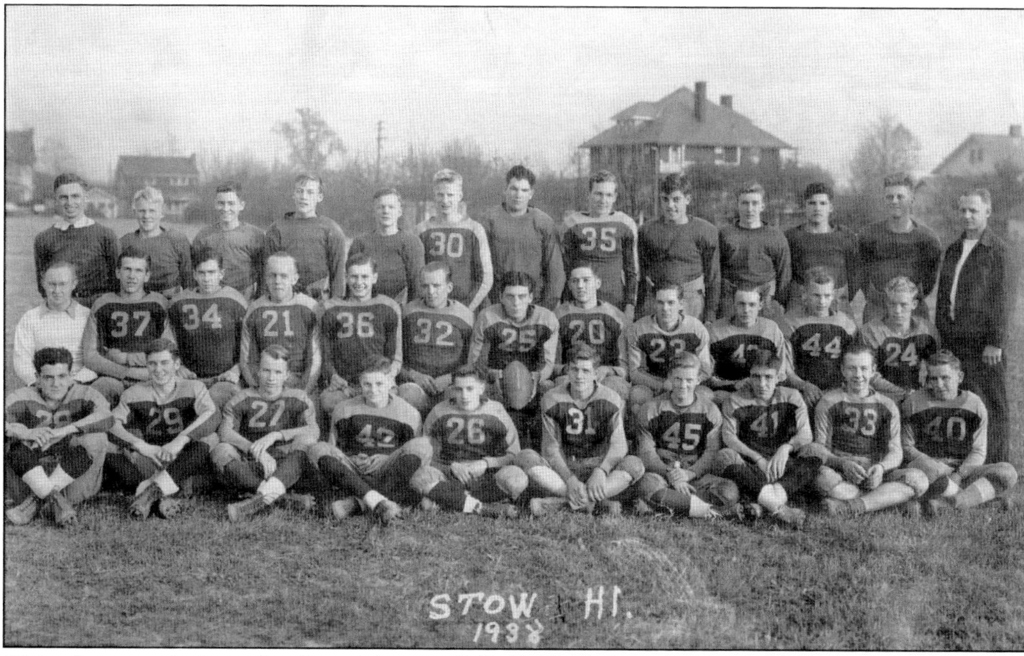

This photograph from the Stow-Munroe Falls Public Library Stow High School Class of 1940 collection shows the football team with Darrow Road homes in the background. At this time, the school system was known as the Stow Township Rural School District. The 1938 team won one game, lost five, and tied three. (SMFPL.)

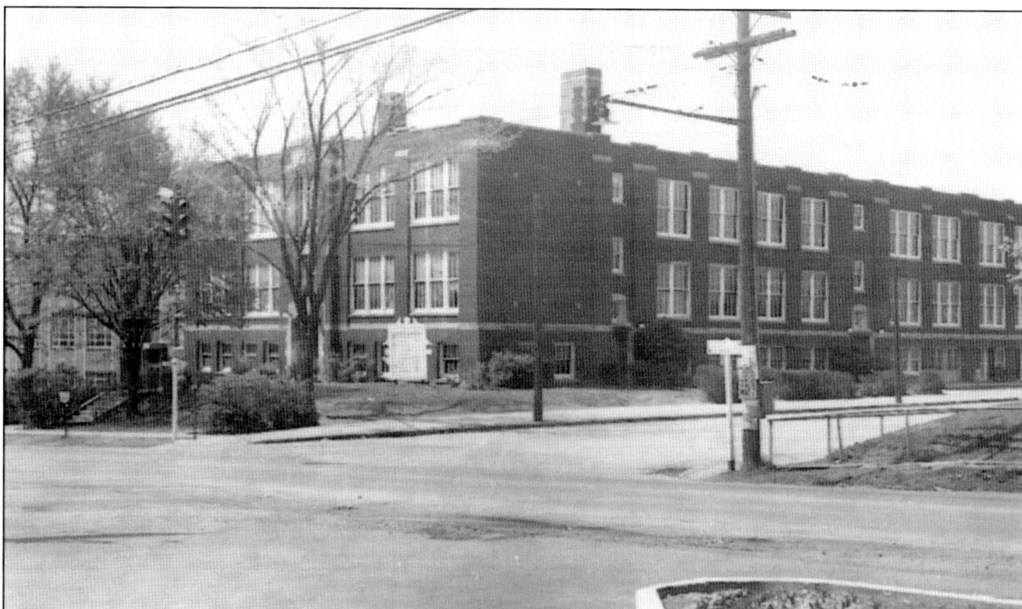

Located at the southwest corner of Graham and Darrow Roads, Stow High School was opened in 1924. It served the students of Stow Township, which included children in Stow and Munroe Falls. When Silver Lake merged with the Stow school system in 1926, it was then called the Stow Township Rural School District. This building, renamed Workman High School in 1968 after Stow teacher Velma Workman, was razed in 1989 to make way for a shopping plaza. (FL.)

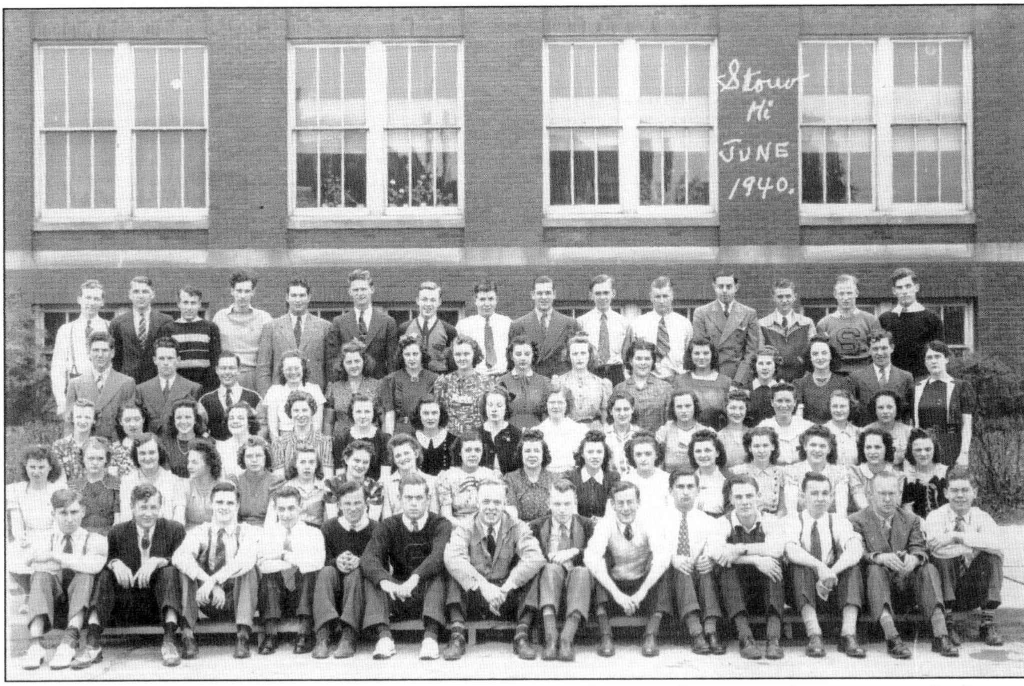

The Stow High School class of 1940 was the largest graduating class up to that point in the history of the school. Seventy-eight seniors received their diplomas in the school auditorium on June 5, 1940, at 8:00 p.m. Speakers at commencement included Betty Monteith ("Why I am Glad I am an American") and Don Becker ("How to Preserve Our Democracy"). The class address was given by Dr. Kenneth I. Brown, president of Hiram College. (SMFPL.)

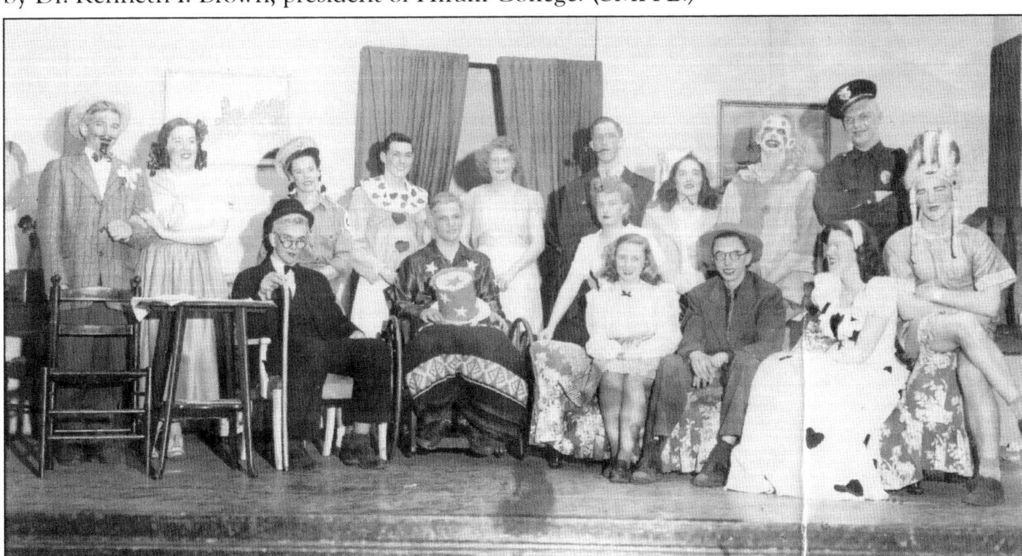

Stow High School class of 1945 presented *Spring Green* as their senior class play. Here students pose in their costumes on the high school stage. Cast members included Nancy Hale, Elaine Cooper, Colleen Fairbee, Charles Hall, Barbara Karch, Marilyn Kirkland, Roger Howard, Phil Wilbur, Marjorie Kirkhart, James Weldon, James Schaer, Jean Blackwelder, Dick Howell, Bill Hosfield, Bill Knowlton, and Bob Carlson. (SMFPL.)

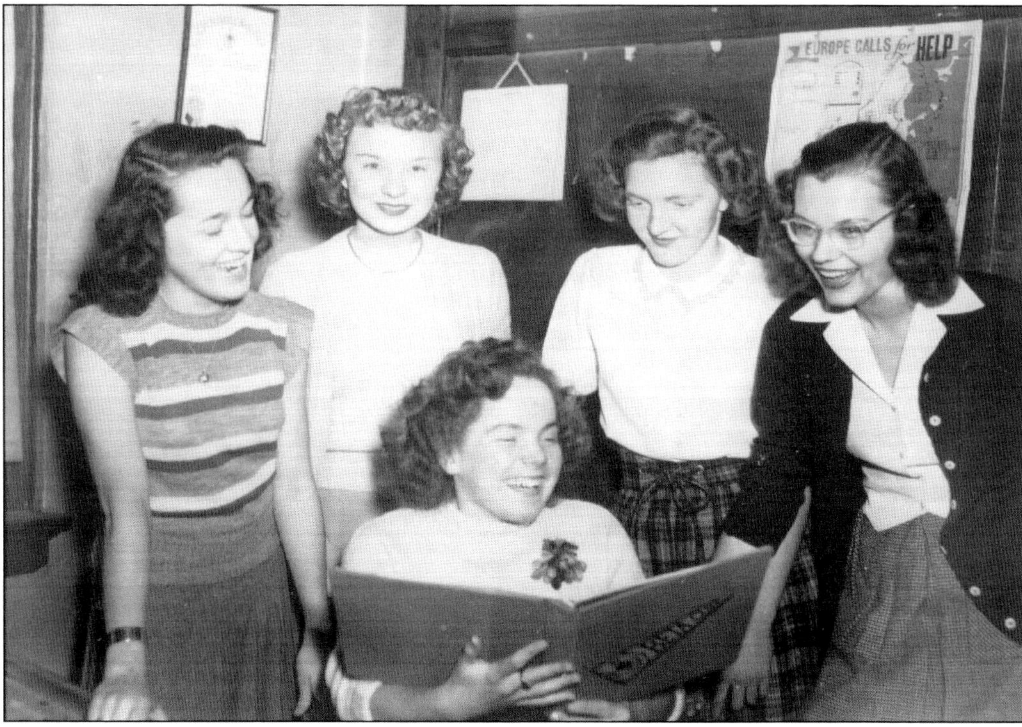

Kathryn McGrail (far left) and Mary Zimmerman (standing, second to left) are among these five students looking at a Beta Club album at Stow High School sometime in the 1940s. The other three students are unidentified. McGrail and Zimmerman were both in the Stow High School class of 1949. Beta Club was started in 1946 with Velma Workman as an advisor. The poster in the background states, "Europe Calls for HELP." (SMFPL.)

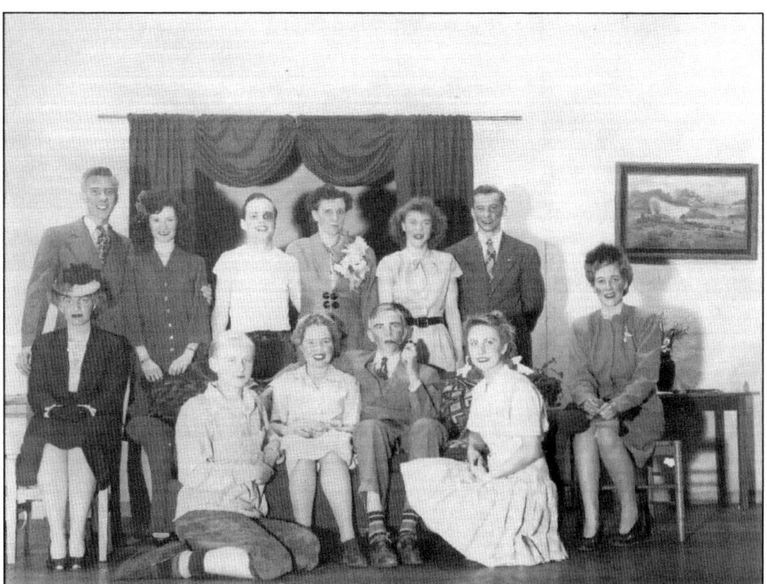

The Sunshine Twins was the name of the 1946 Stow High School senior class play. Performed on April 12, 1946, Maxine Simison and Huston Morgan starred as the mischievous twins. Stow High School teacher Bernice Brenizer is seen in the center of the back row. Approximately 800 people enjoyed seeing the "SST" play on a Friday night. (SMFPL.)

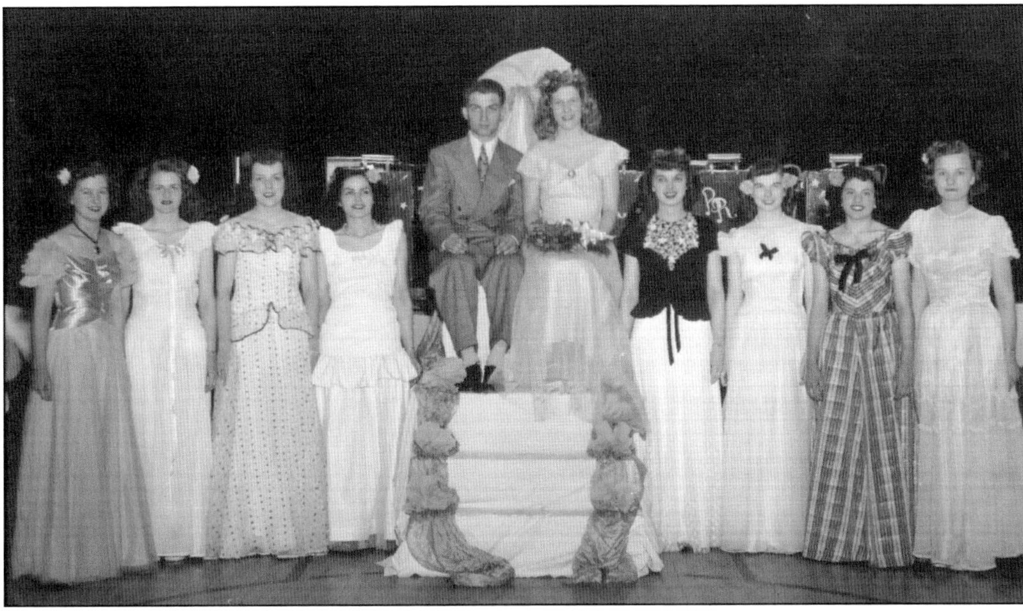

The Stow High School May Queen of 1946 is pictured here with her court. Commencement week activities for the Stow High School class of 1946 included the junior-senior dance, baccalaureate services, commencement, and a dinner. The 77 graduates included several returned service men. (FL.)

Doree Ernst was crowned Stow High School's Homecoming Queen at the pregame ceremonies before the Stow-Coventry football game on November 9, 1946. Her attendants were senior Mary Ann Yeager, junior Ruth Capra, sophomore Nancy Lou Nellis, and freshman Joyce Ewing. Senior Charles Ross was named "Football King." Ross and Ernst were in the class of 1947. (SMFPL.)

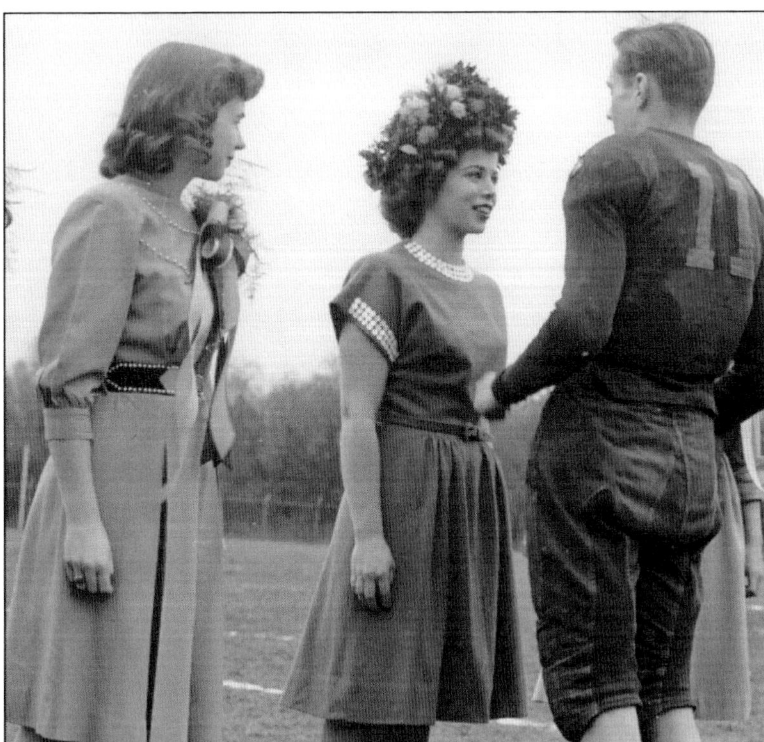

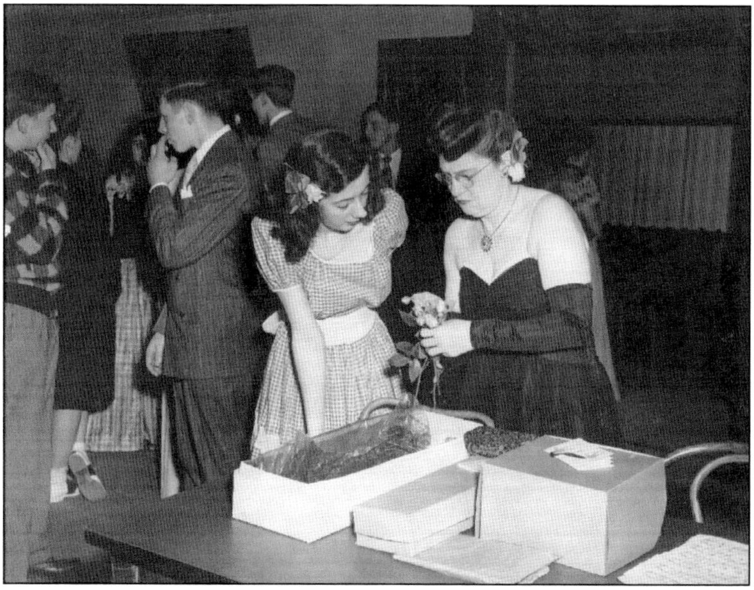

Velma Workman assists Phoebe Myers with her corsage at a Stow High School dance in 1947. Workman, a social studies teacher of American history and American government, was the class advisor and was involved in many extracurricular student activities. (SMFPL.)

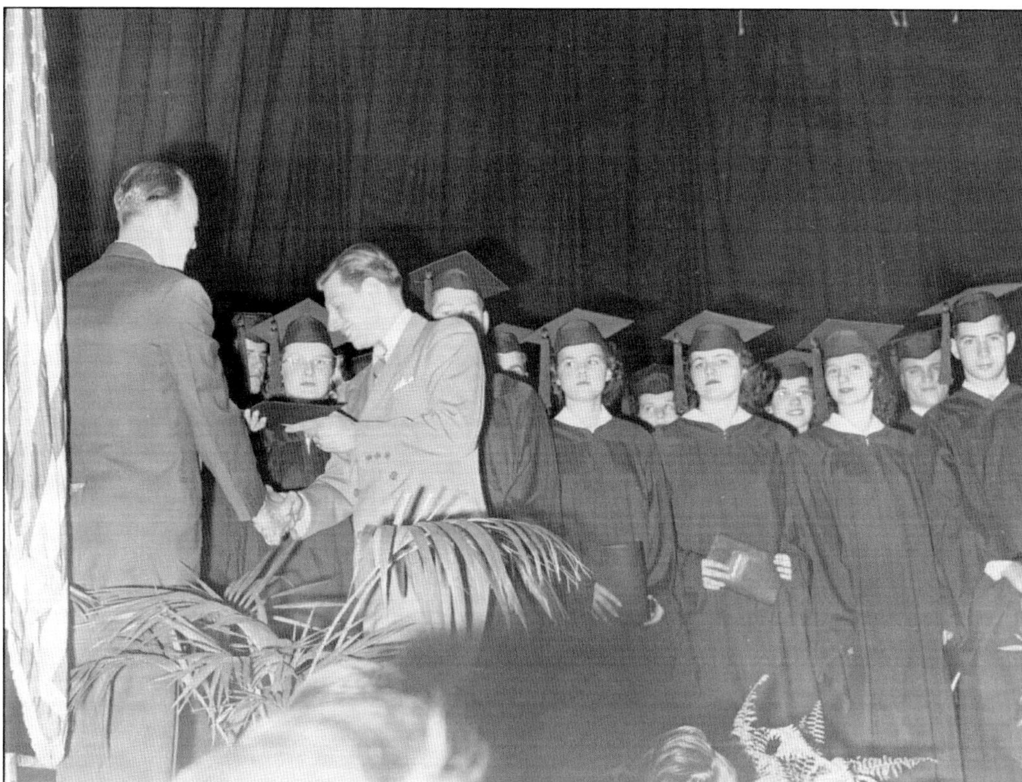

Judson Russell presented diplomas to the Stow High School class of 1947 at the commencement ceremony held on May 27, 1947. Several returned servicemen completed the requirements for graduation and received their diplomas at the ceremony as well. Two seniors, Doree Ernst and Charles Ross, received citizenship awards based on their scholastic standing and other qualities voted by the faculty. (SMFPL.)

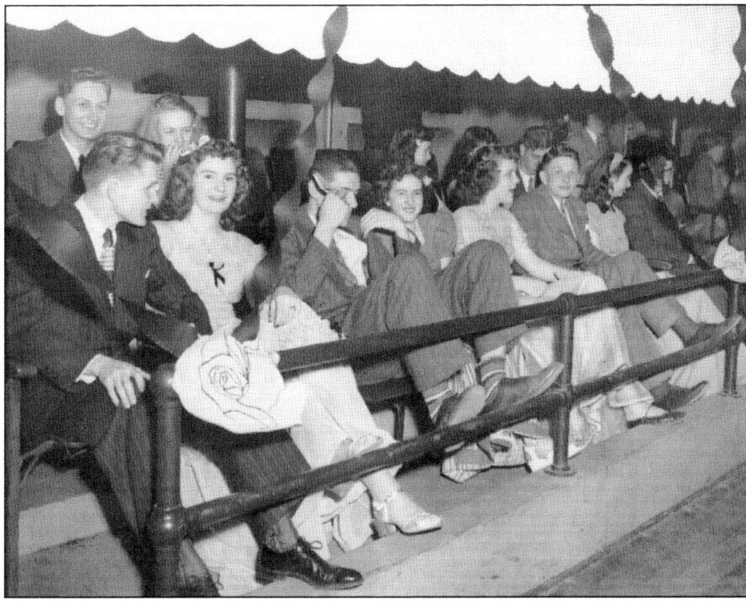

Stow High School students are seen socializing and watching the activities at a Stow High School homecoming dance in this late 1940s photograph. Charles Henault is at the far left, and Robert Gleason is third from the left in the first row. (SMFPL.)

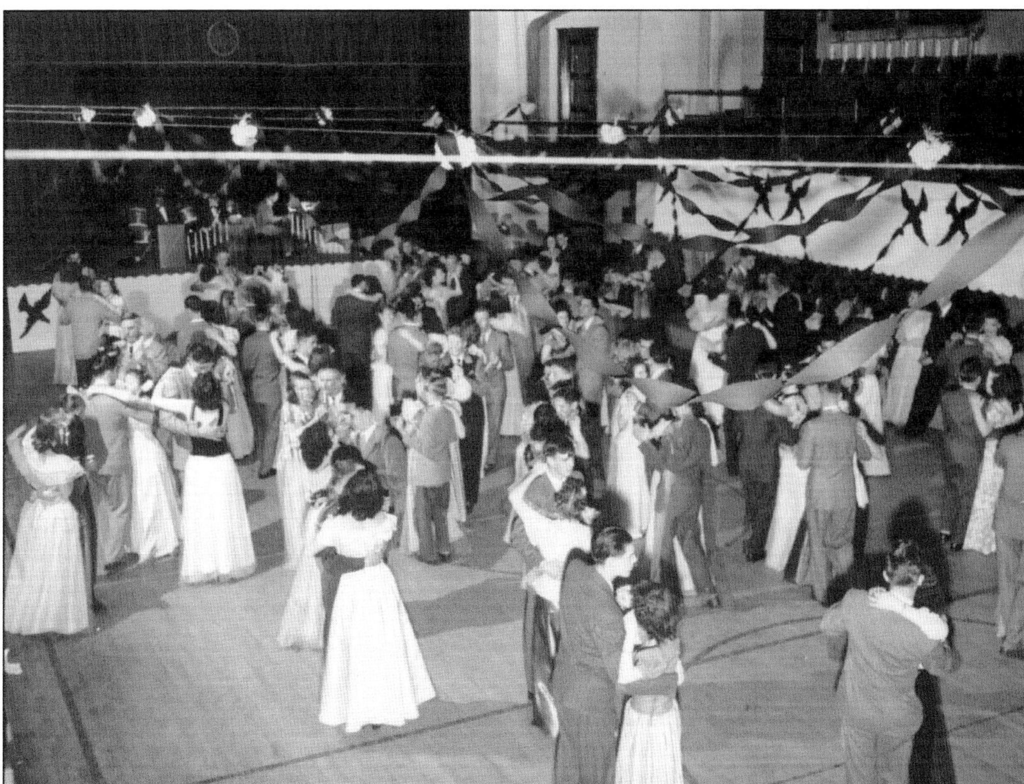

Students are seen here dancing in the gymnasium at the Stow High School 1950 homecoming dance. The high school at this time was on the southwest corner of Graham and Darrow Roads in the building later to be named after Velma Workman. (SMFPL.)

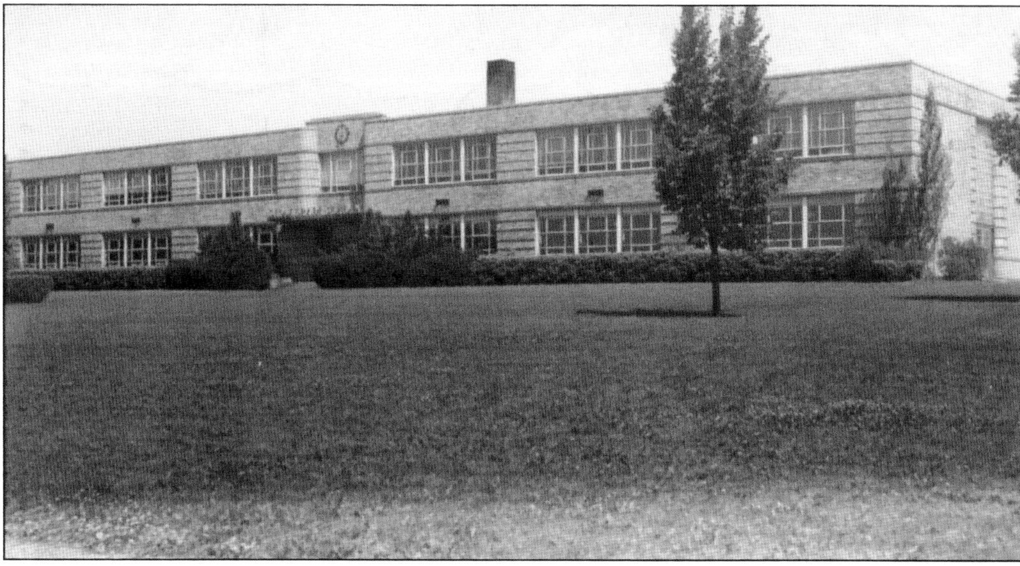

This postcard of Stow Grade School (now called Highland Elementary School) was mailed on January 28, 1952, with a 2¢ stamp. Stow Grade School was built in 1939 at a cost of $145,453. At that time, students in grades one through six were moved from Stow Centralized School to the grade school, and grades seven and up went to the high school built in 1924. (FL.)

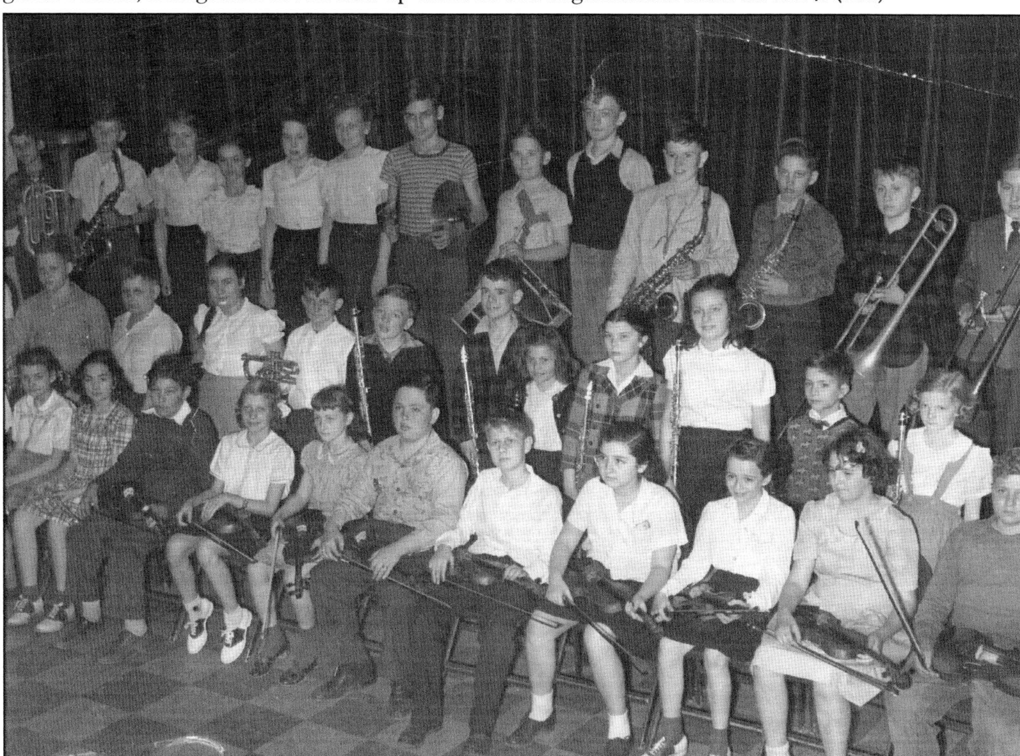

The Stow School's band program began sometime in the 1930s. This group of Stow Grade School students was in the 1946–1947 band directed by W. Russell Gray. Gray taught the band from 1939 to 1949. (FL.)

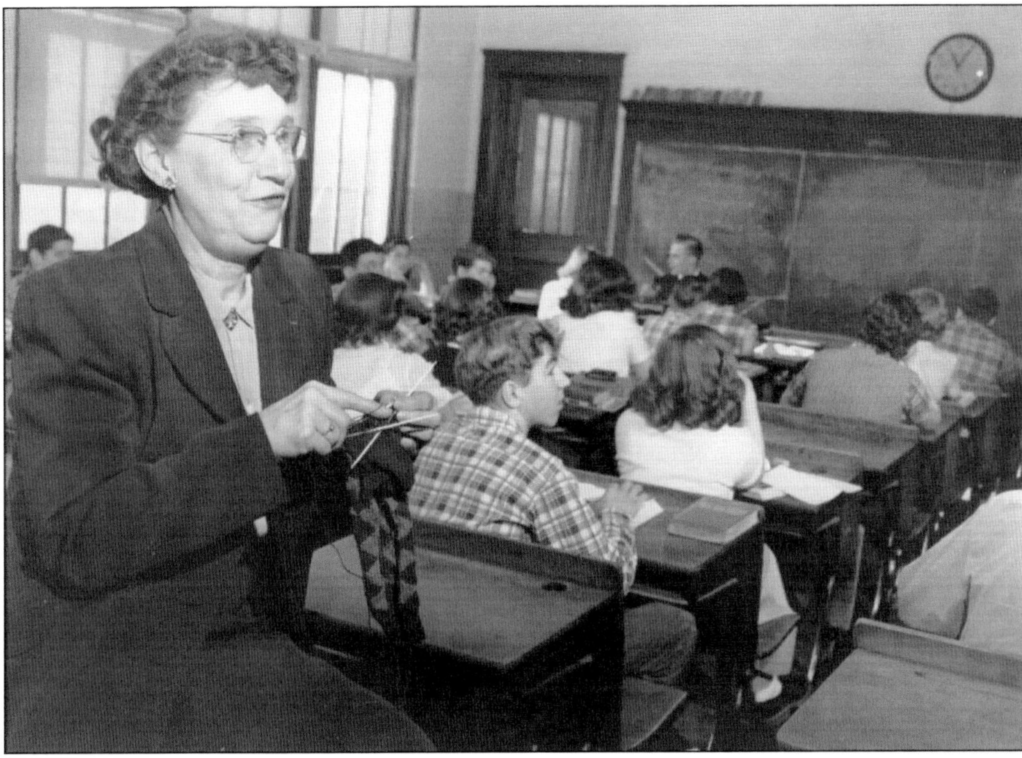

Velma Workman sits knitting in her classroom in this 1951 photograph. Identified students are Fred Long, Donald Sampson, and Robert Conley, all part of the class of 1954. Charles "Chick" Ewing (class of 1951) is the boy seated at the desk directly in front of Workman. Workman and W. W. Bloor were advisors to the class of 1951. (SMFPL.)

Ruth Patterson, the Stow High School music teacher, is seen playing the piano while student Jeannie Marino (standing) sings. William J. Barr was principal of Stow High School, and Walter B. Kimpton was superintendent in 1951. (SMFPL.)

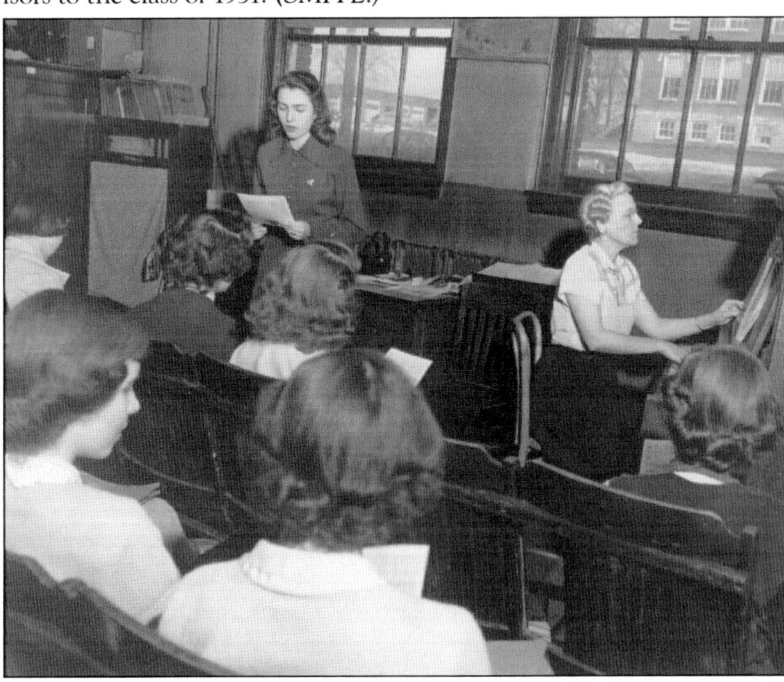

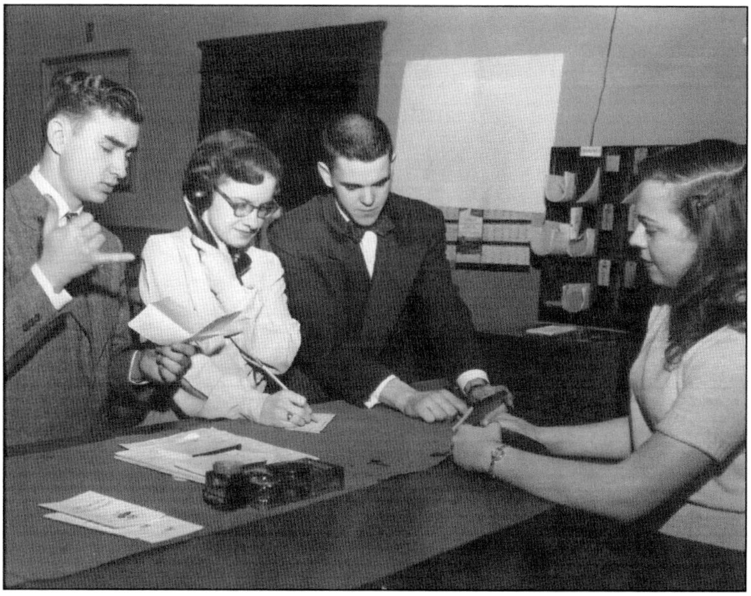

Students are seen here in the Stow High School office in this 1951 photograph. Both boys, Ted Milliken (on left) and Jim Horst (on right), were in the class of 1951. The two girls are unidentified. (SMFPL.)

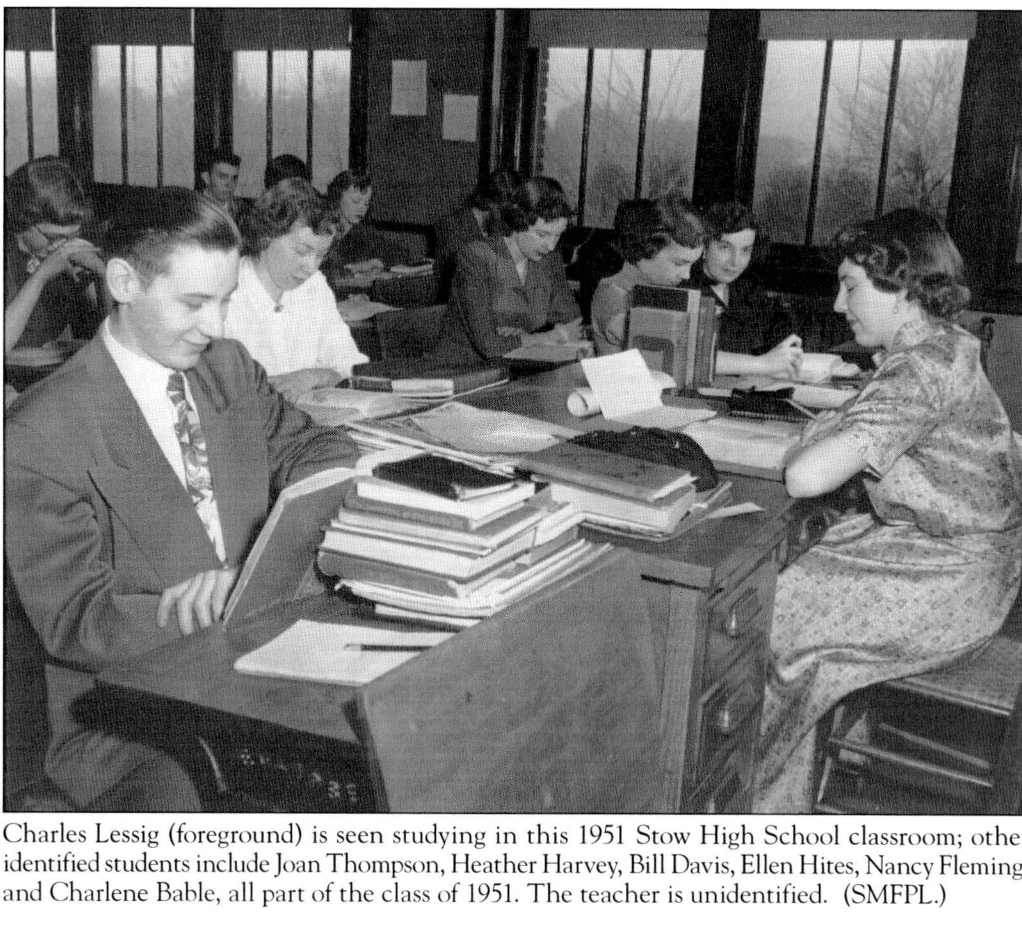

Charles Lessig (foreground) is seen studying in this 1951 Stow High School classroom; other identified students include Joan Thompson, Heather Harvey, Bill Davis, Ellen Hites, Nancy Fleming, and Charlene Bable, all part of the class of 1951. The teacher is unidentified. (SMFPL.)

Students are receiving safety instructions in this 1951 photograph of the Stow High School shop class. Pictured from left to right are Richard Phillips (class of 1954), Miles Lovingood (class of 1951), Frank Wetmore (class of 1954), Charles Meador (class of 1954), and Paul Phillips (class of 1954). (SMFPL.)

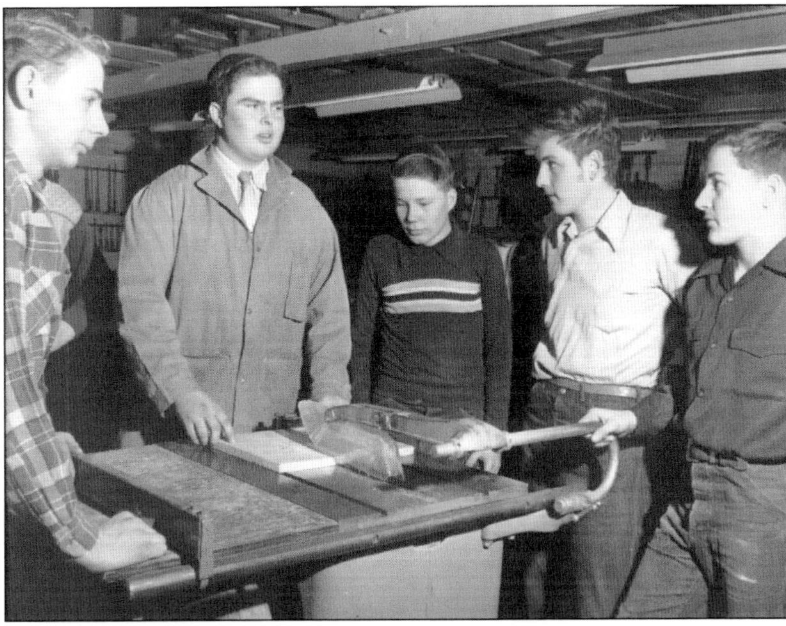

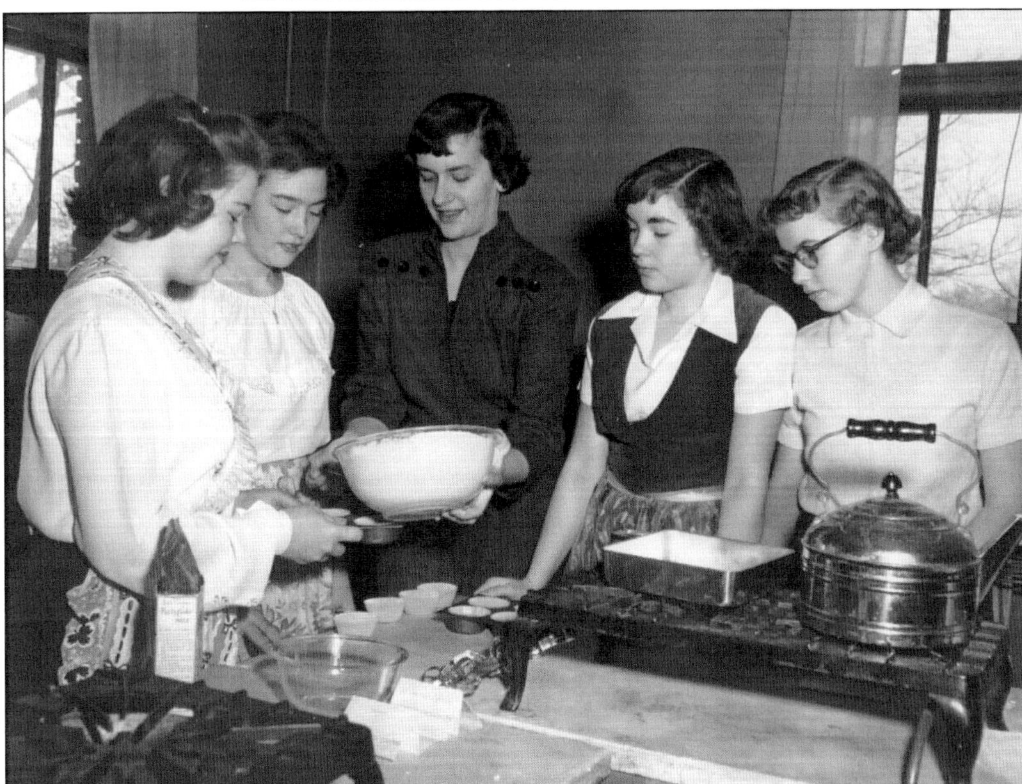

Girls at Stow High School learned how to cook, sew, and manage a home in home economics classes. These five students are learning how to bake cupcakes in a 1951 class. Pictured from left to right are Patricia Bee (class of 1954), Nancy Trego (class of 1954), Alice Conder (class of 1951), Jean Arnold (class of 1954), and Wanda Shaffer (class of 1954). (SMFPL.)

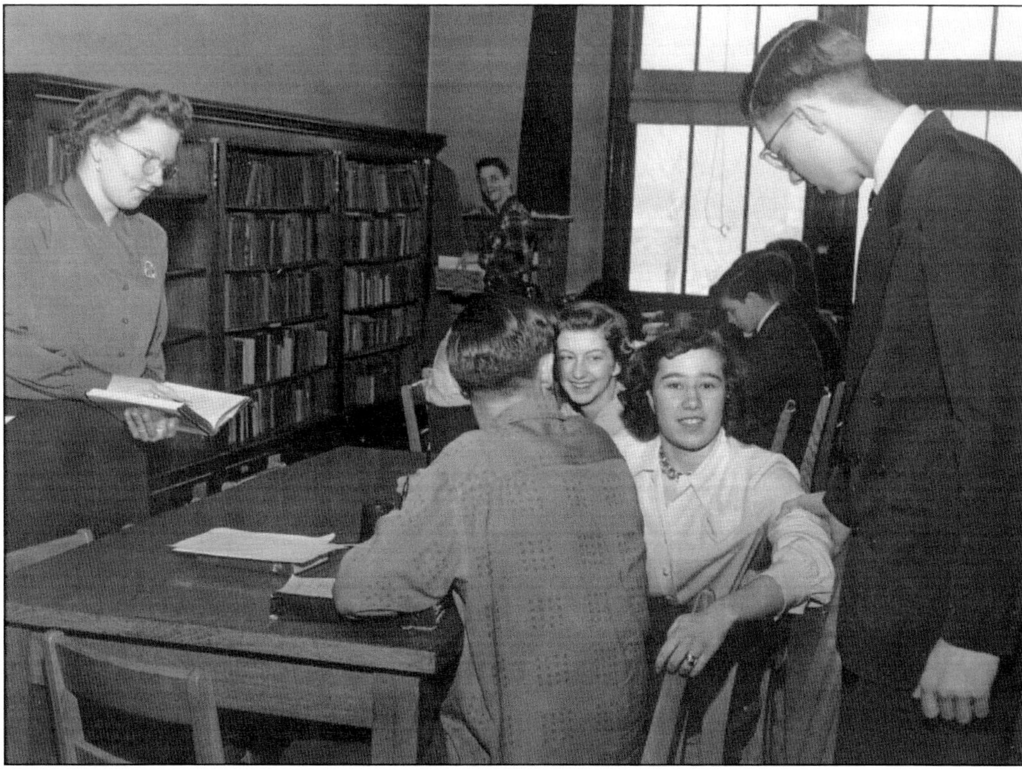

Students have gathered in the Stow High School library in this 1951 photograph. Pictured from left to right are (standing) Sonia Durant (class of 1951), Earl Jones (class of 1953), and Wesley Farrell (class of 1951); (girls sitting at the table) Marjory Koehler (class of 1951) and Carolee Wegmiller (class of 1952). In 1951, Stow Public Library still provided reference books and books for circulation to the school. (SMFPL.)

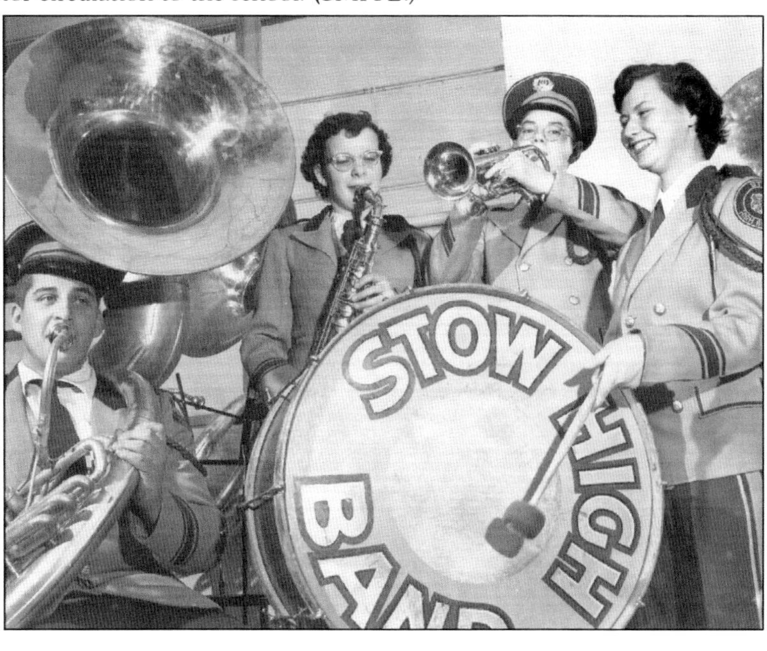

Pictured from left to right, Fred Long, Bonnie Marhofer, Tim Antes, and Beverly Willoughby play in the 1953 Stow High School Band. The director for this group of students was Dale Stanford, who led students from 1950 to 1954. The Stow-Munroe Falls High School Band continues its tradition of excellence that began in 1939 with director W. Russell Gray. (FL.)

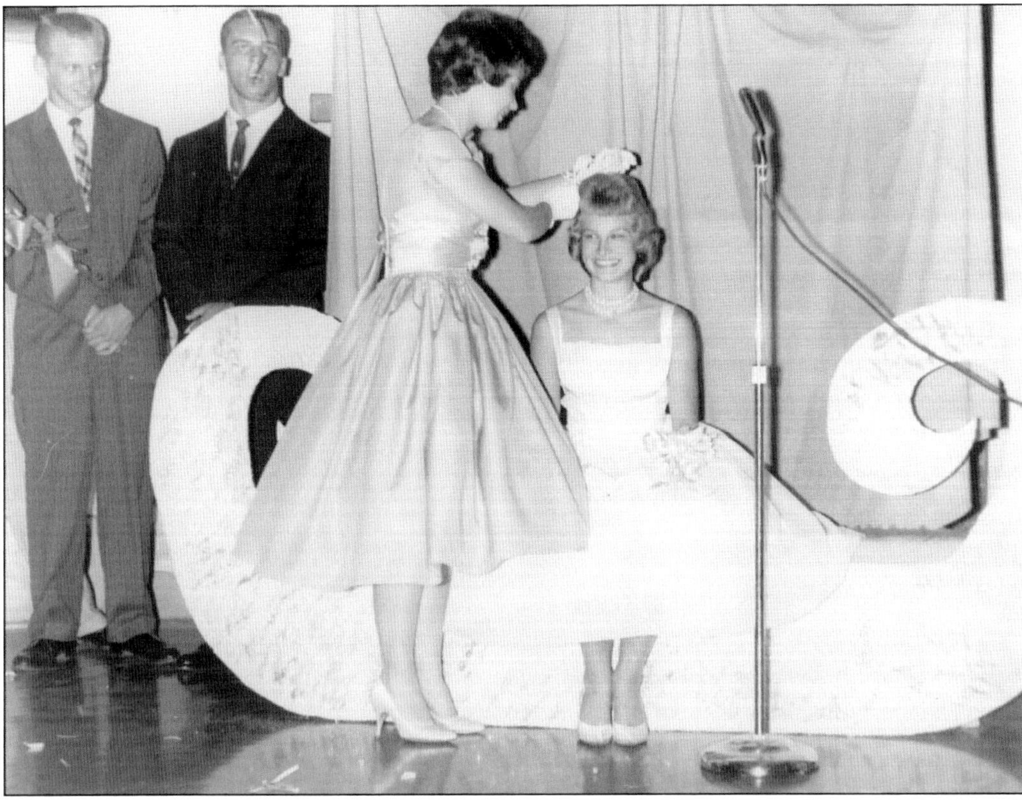

Class of 1961 Stow High School homecoming queen Judy Thomas receives her crown from Linda Henderson. Standing to the left of Henderson is Lynn Jackson, the leading man of the class of 1961. Thomas was a cheerleader and was involved in Y-Teens. (SMFPL.)

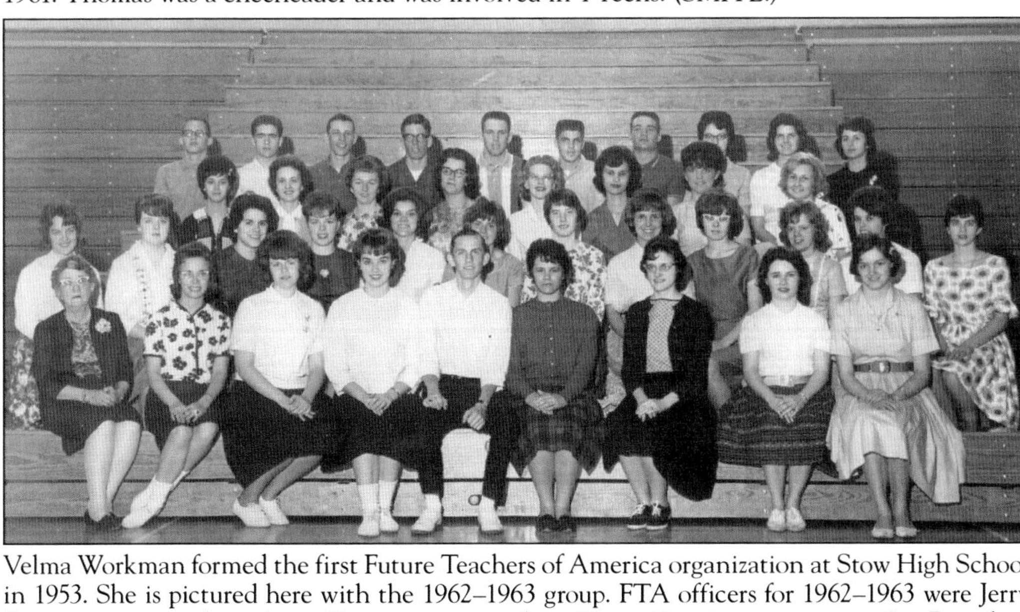

Velma Workman formed the first Future Teachers of America organization at Stow High School in 1953. She is pictured here with the 1962–1963 group. FTA officers for 1962–1963 were Jerry Zimmerman, president; Anita Brower, vice president; Diana Gretsinger, secretary; Sue Braucher, treasurer; Karen Donaldson, historian; and Velma Workman, advisor. (SMFPL.)

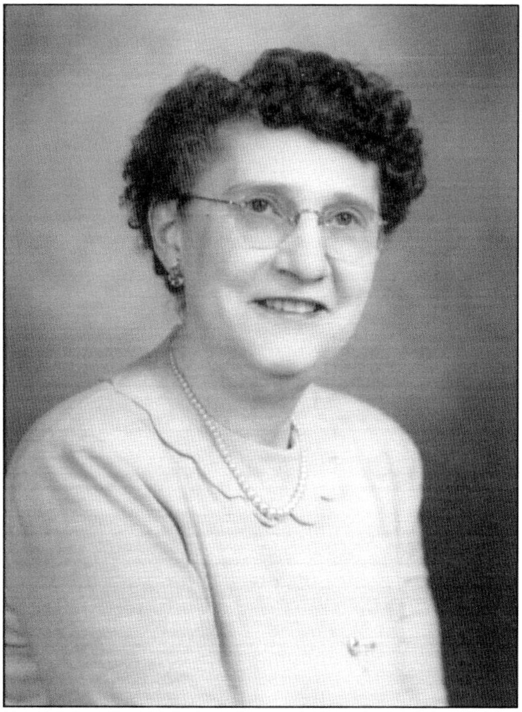

Velma Workman, shown here in a *Stoanno* (Stow High School yearbook) photograph, began teaching at Stow High School in 1930 and retired in 1967. She was a teacher of social studies, business, and government. The 1967 *Stoanno* was dedicated to Workman: "We cannot help but know that those coming after us will miss out on something that could have been a meaningful part of their education by not having Miss Workman." (FL.)

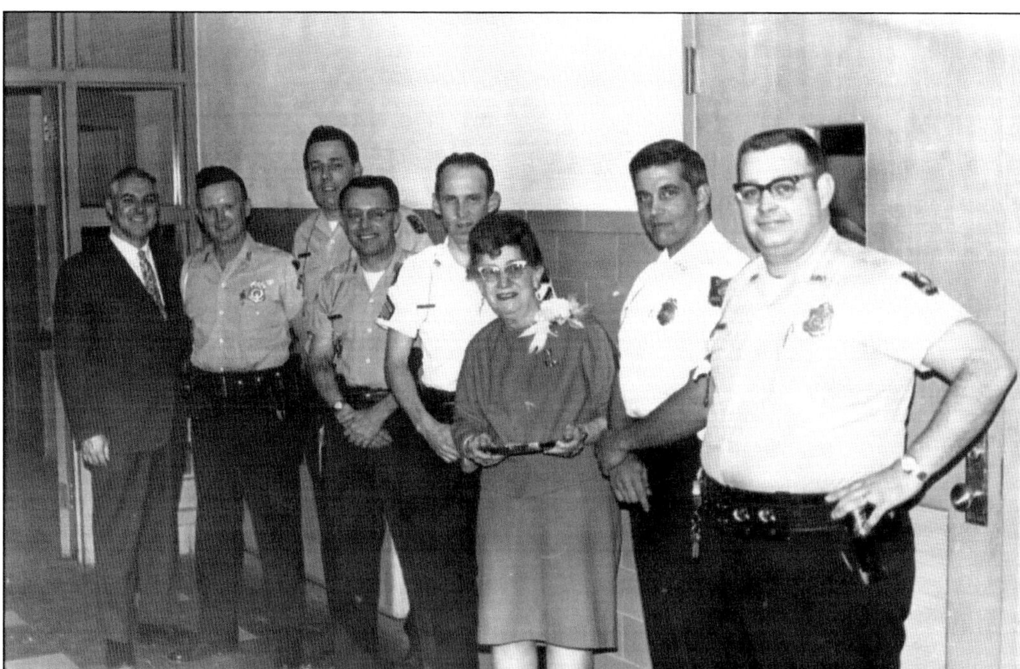

This photograph was taken at the retirement of Velma Workman in 1967. Among her former students were these men who worked for the City of Stow. Pictured, from left to right, are Mayor Roger Howard (class of 1945), patrolman William Hites (class of 1943), patrolman Robert Brisbin (class of 1955), patrolman Phil Large (class of 1944), Sgt. Dick Saxe (class of 1952), Sgt. Fred Long, and patrolman Duane Wood (both class of 1954). (FL.)

Four

NEIGHBORHOOD CLUBS AND ORGANIZATIONS

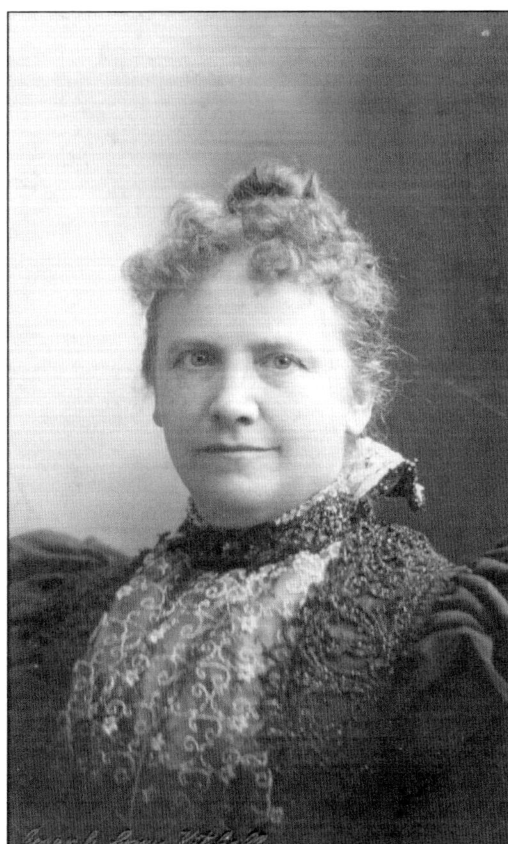

Charlotte Gaylord Banning (Mrs. James H.) was the first president of the Stow Self-Culture Club, formed in 1902. The organization was established for the development of culture and refinement within the community. The Self-Culture Club became the Stow Culture Club in 1924 and the Stow Woman's Club in 1964. Banning was born in Munroe Falls in 1847 and was the youngest daughter of Sylvester and Julia North Gaylord, pioneers of the Western Reserve. (SMFPL.)

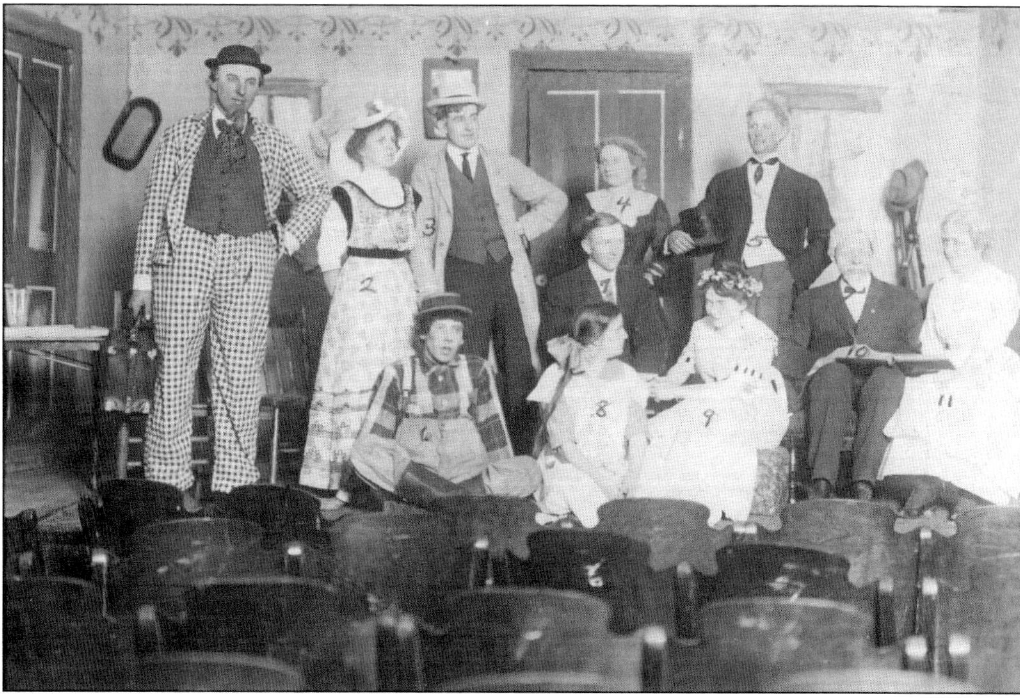

The original Stow Players' (also known as the Stow Dramatic Club) first production was in 1911. This 1913 production of *Country Folks* featured Oakley Spaght, Ethel Grove, Loton Hartle, Nina (Ripley) Carlyon, Charles Wetmore, Joe Studt, Howard Call, Hallie Nickerson, Winfred (Scott) Thomas, Frank Hill, and Blanche (Mrs. Arthur) Wetmore. The players stayed together for six years, earning enough money to begin construction on an addition to the First Christian Church Ladies Hall. (SHS.)

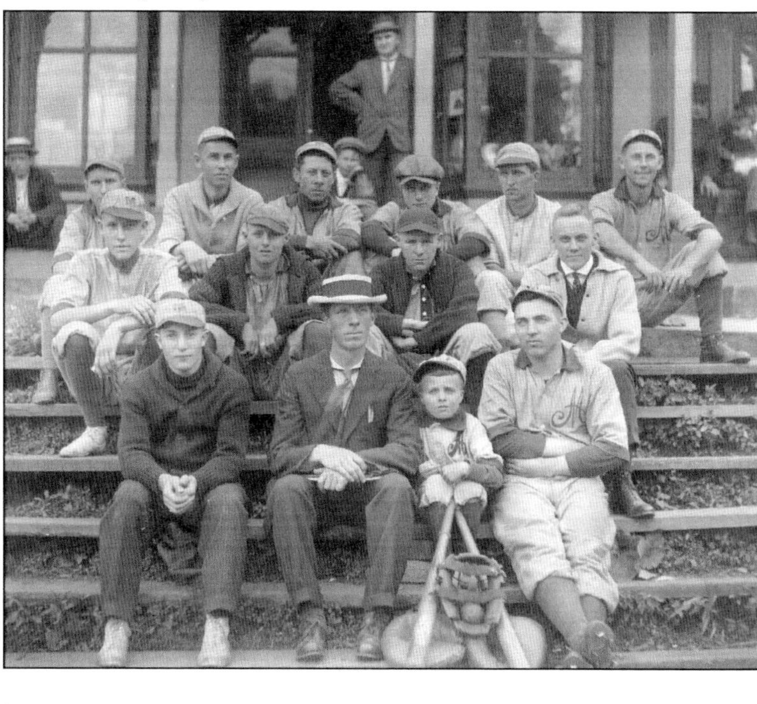

This photograph shows the Munroe Falls baseball team in 1915. According to the writings of Munroe Falls resident Keith Spriggel, the ball field was adjacent to the B&O Railroad tracks and near the river just east of U.S. Route 91 on the Munroe Falls Paper Mill property. Spriggel remembered that Lester North was the catcher on the baseball team in the late 1920s and early 1930s. (MFHS.)

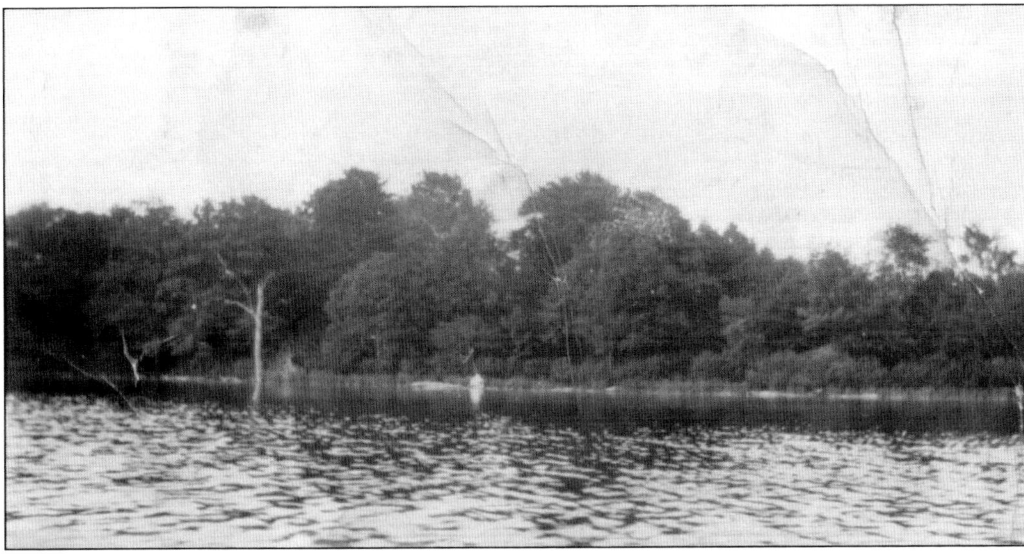

Meadowbrook Lake, pictured here in 1939, was once owned by the Hibbard family. It is situated in the area bordered by today's Hudson Drive and Darrow Road. Sometime in the 1920s, the Summit Development Company of Akron planned exclusive homes, a golf course, and a recreational area to be called Borough of Meadow Brook. Although advertised as "Akron's newest and greatest suburb," the development never came to fruition because one of the company officers absconded with the funds. (SMFPL.)

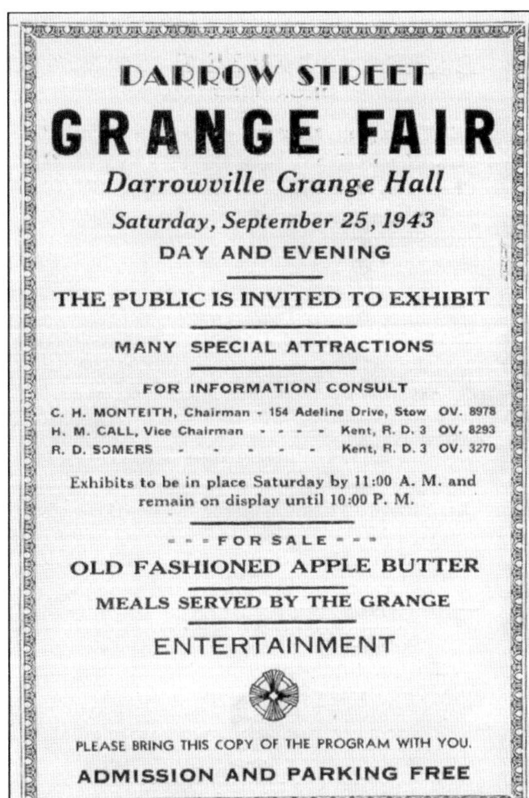

This program from the Darrow Street Grange Fair, held at Darrowville Grange Hall, is dated September 25, 1943. Some of the exhibits included flowers, needlework, canned goods, fruits, and vegetables. Lunch and dinner were served cafeteria style, and baked goods were for sale. Program advertisers included Lawson Milk Company, Ritchie Meat Market, Munroe Falls Square Deal Store, Marhofer Chevrolet, and Isaly's Dairy. Darrowville is on the border of Stow and Hudson. (CJC.)

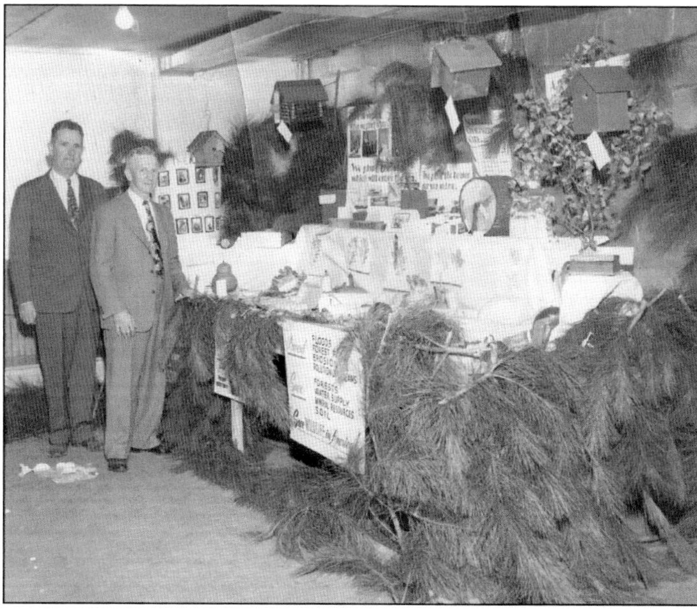

Joe Mitten (left) and Howard Call look at a 4-H display about forestry at the Darrowville Fair sometime in the 1940s. Call, owner of Call's Farm in Stow, spent his lifetime involved in forestry. He organized the Ohio Forestry Organization and had an ongoing interest in the Ohio Tree Farm System. Mitten, the principal of Lincoln Elementary School in Cuyahoga Falls, lived in Stow and owned tree farms in Glenmont, Ohio. (CJC.)

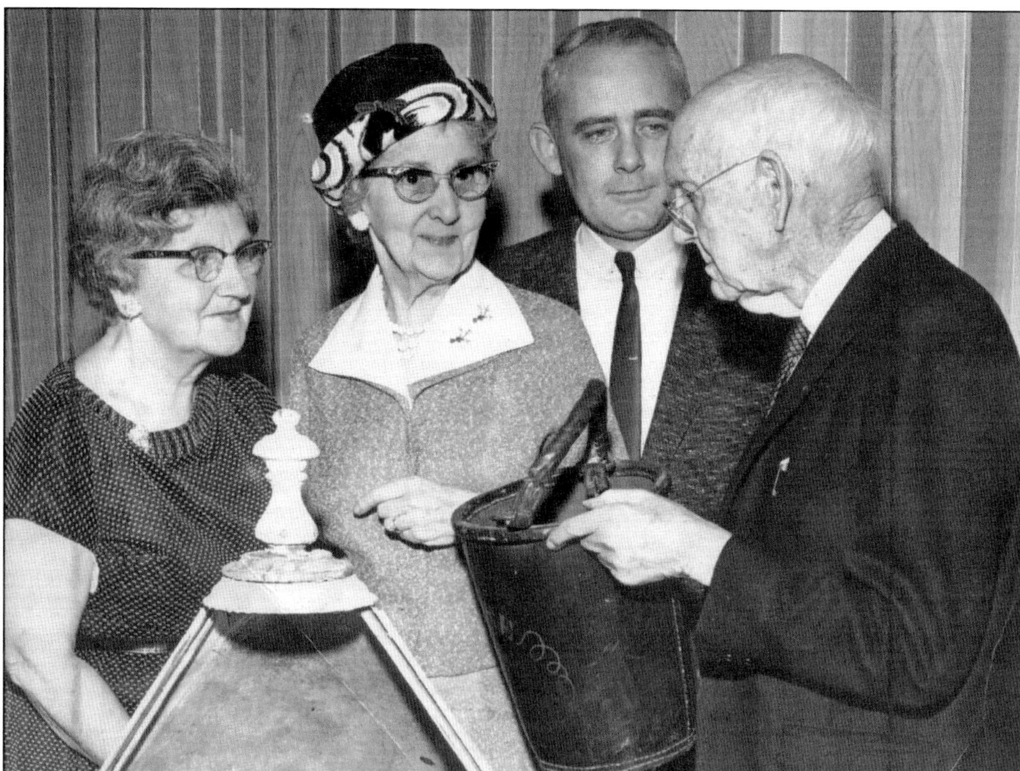

On November 15, 1949, a group of citizens residing in Stow met in the Stow Township Hall for the purpose of forming a historical society. The objectives of the Stow Historical Society were to gather and record historical data pertaining to the development of Stow Township and to obtain relics that have a historical value to Stow Township. Sarah Amlung (far left) and Frank Green (far right) are shown here with two other members. (SHS.)

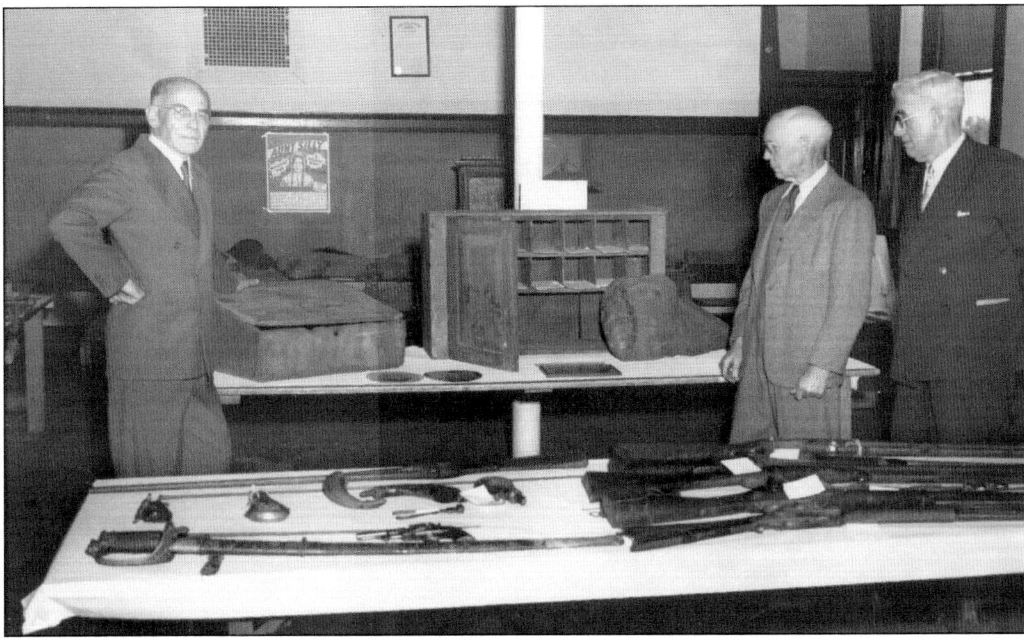

This photograph was taken on June 4, 1950, at the Stow Historical Society Antique Show. Joseph Studt (hand on the desk), Frank Green (second to right), and J. Frank Hartle are standing at an 1834 post office desk used by Stow's first postmaster, Titus Wetmore. The letter pigeonholes were where each family's mail was deposited. The saddlebags on the table were used to deliver the mail to Cuyahoga Falls and Akron. (FL.)

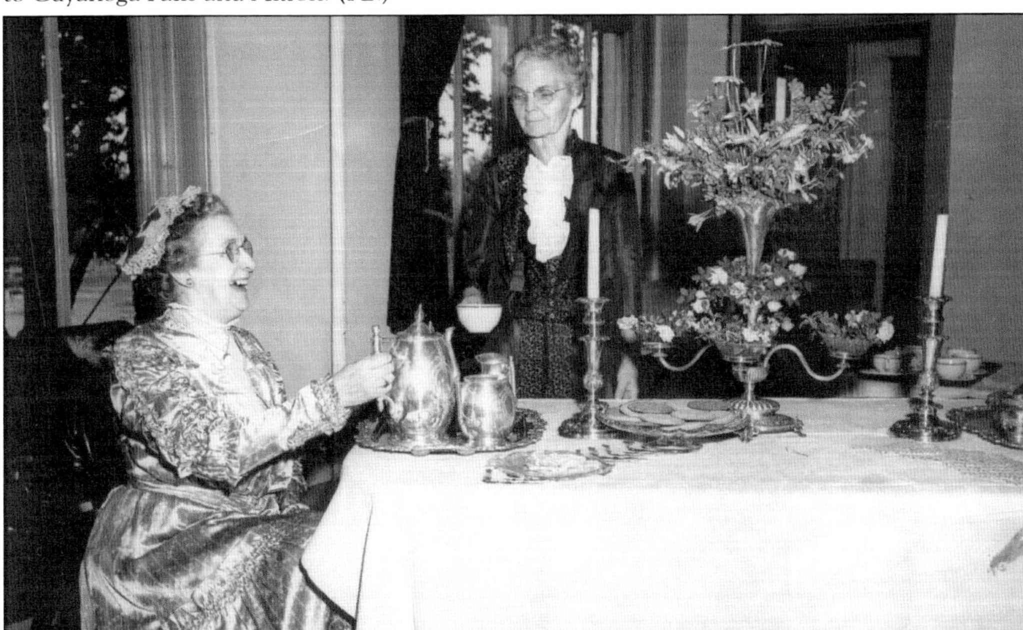

May (Mrs. Frank) Hartle serves tea to Mary (Mrs. Iru) Wetmore Palmer at the Stow Historical Society Antique Show held June 4, 1950. Both ladies and their husbands were charter members of the historical society, which was first organized in 1949. (FL.)

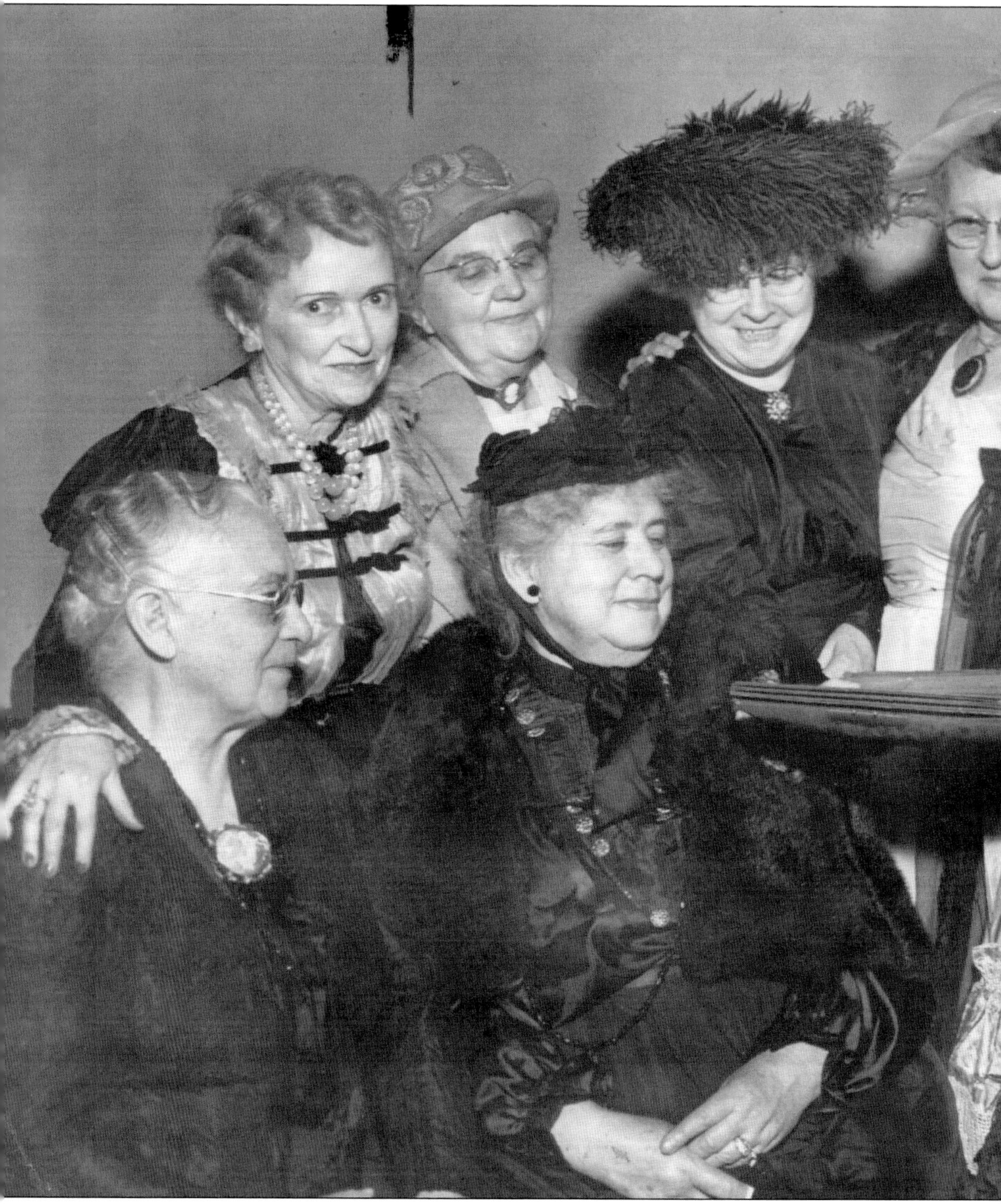

Members re-created 50 years of Stow Culture Club in November 1952. Listed here are the members and those they portrayed: pictured from left to right are (seated) Mrs. Oakley Spaght—Mrs. Julia Wetmore, Mrs. J. A. Studt—aunt Velonia Wetmore, Mrs. Grace E. Samuels—Mrs. Ralph Lodge, and Mrs. J. G. Lichty—Mrs. Blanche Wetmore; (standing) Mrs. Harold Thomas—Mrs. Lottie

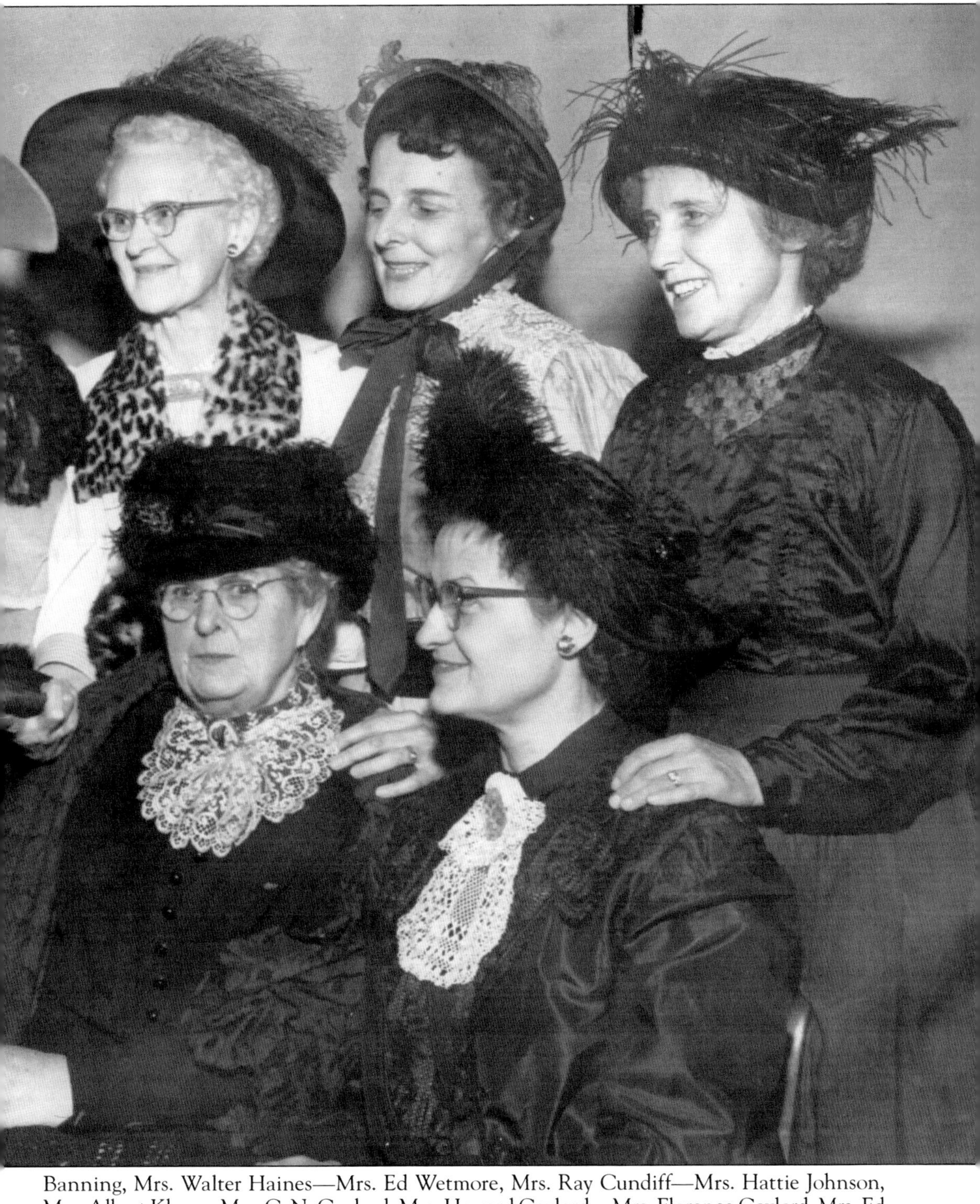

Banning, Mrs. Walter Haines—Mrs. Ed Wetmore, Mrs. Ray Cundiff—Mrs. Hattie Johnson, Mrs. Albert Klesa—Mrs. C. N. Gaylord, Mrs. Howard Gaylord—Mrs. Florence Gaylord, Mrs. Ed Mackey—Mrs. Rose Hale, and Mrs. F. S. Grubb—aunt Anna Grubb. (SMFPL.)

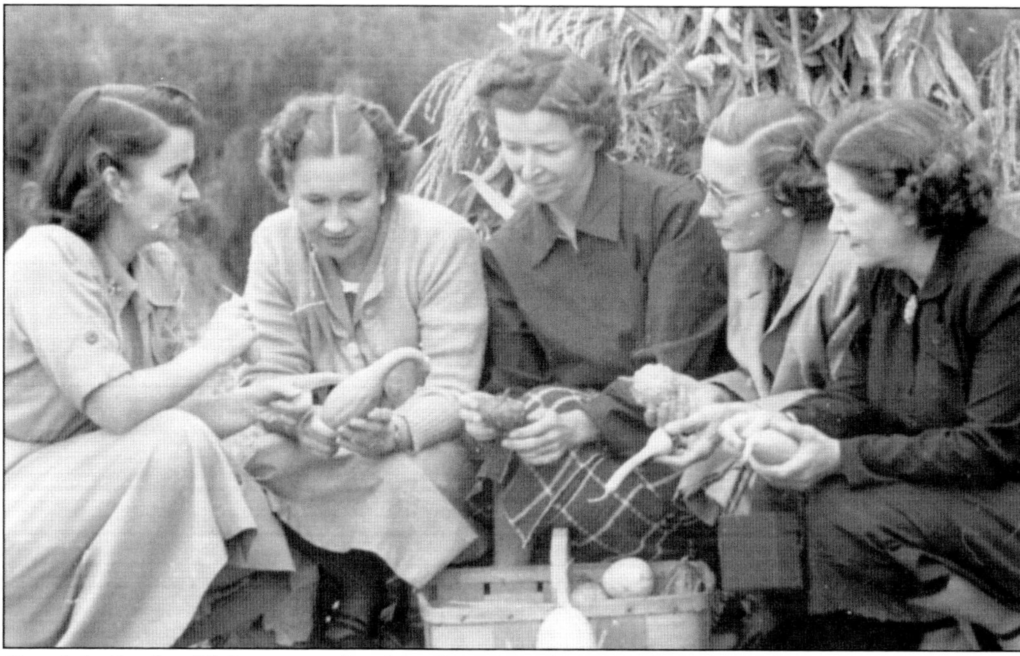

Overdale Garden Club organized in March 1951 with 17 members; four officers were elected. Here the four club officers and a garden club member examine vegetables. Pictured from left to right are Mrs. Pierre Verheyden (secretary), Mrs. Bump (member), Mrs. John Long (president), Mrs. F. W. Hoff Jr. (treasurer), and Mrs. W. C. Rosenberger (vice president). (SMFPL.)

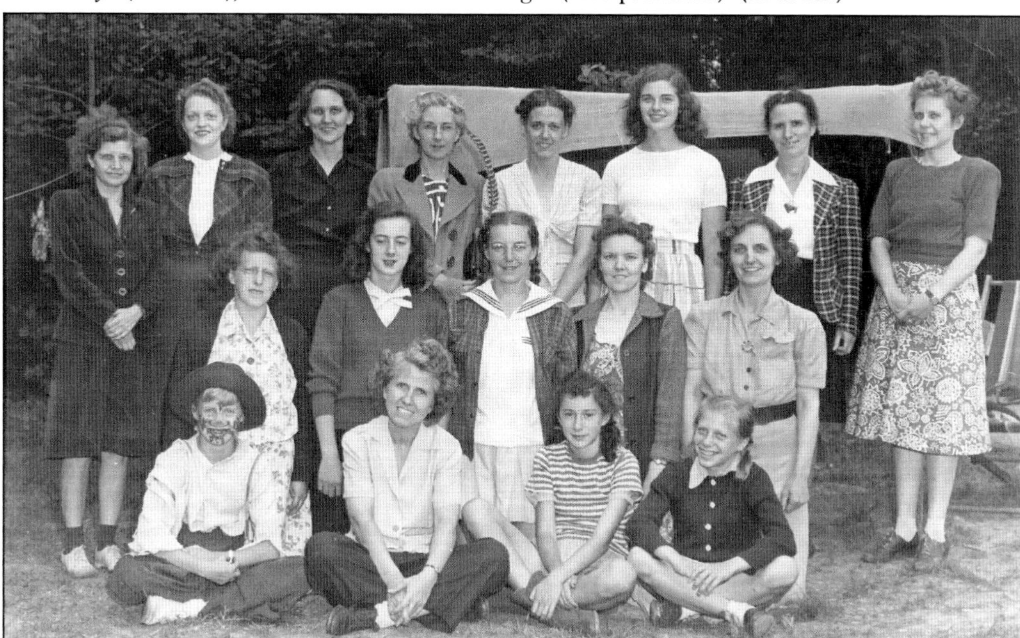

This group of local Girl Scout leaders met at Adell Durbin Park in the early 1950s. Listed on the back of the photograph in no particular order are Terry Partridge, Clara Gillam, Ruby Clark, Mary Thompson, Loraine Lichty, Nina Parpart, Olive Gazdik, Phoebe Myers, Elizabeth Cowles, Ruth Godfrey, Sarah Smith, Ellen Patridge, Marilyn Biltz, and Carol Anderson. (FL.)

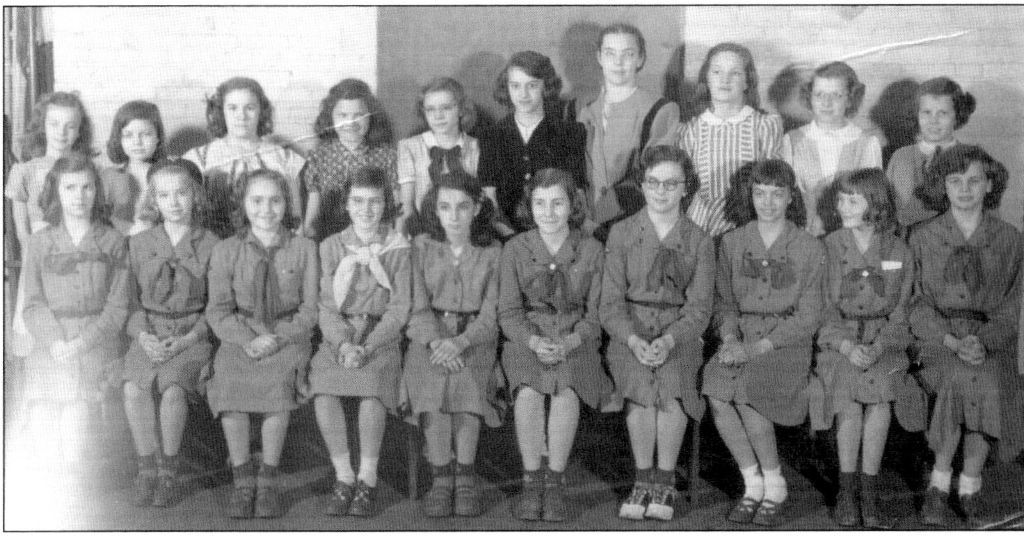

This *c.* 1950 photograph shows Elizabeth Stow Green Cowles with her Girl Scout troop. Cowles led a Girl Scout camp at Adell Durbin Park and felt that Girl Scouts was a great learning experience for girls. (FL.)

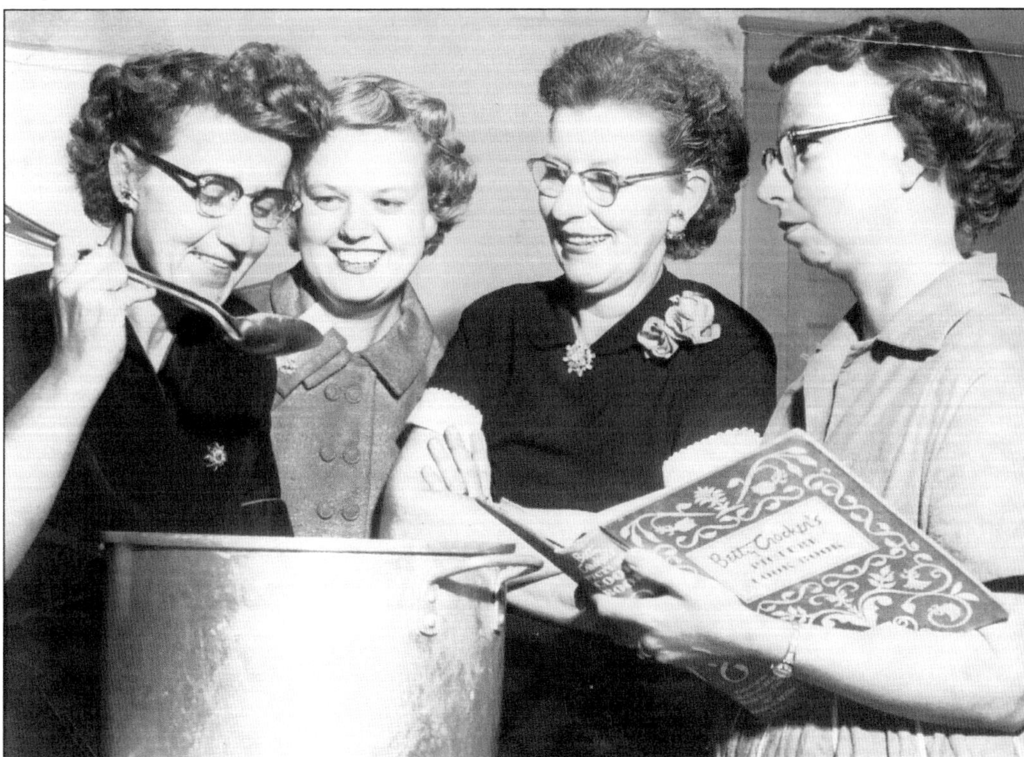

Members of the Stow Firettes, Mrs. James Hites, Dorothy Egger Olson, Mrs. James Thompson, and Betty Chipps McCloskey, prepare a batch of sloppy joes for the June 1955 Stow Volunteer Fire Department benefit carnival. Proceeds from the carnival were used to purchase equipment for Stow firemen. The Firettes, organized about 1955 as a social group open to wives of firemen, were active until 1963 when the firefighters came under civil service. (FL.)

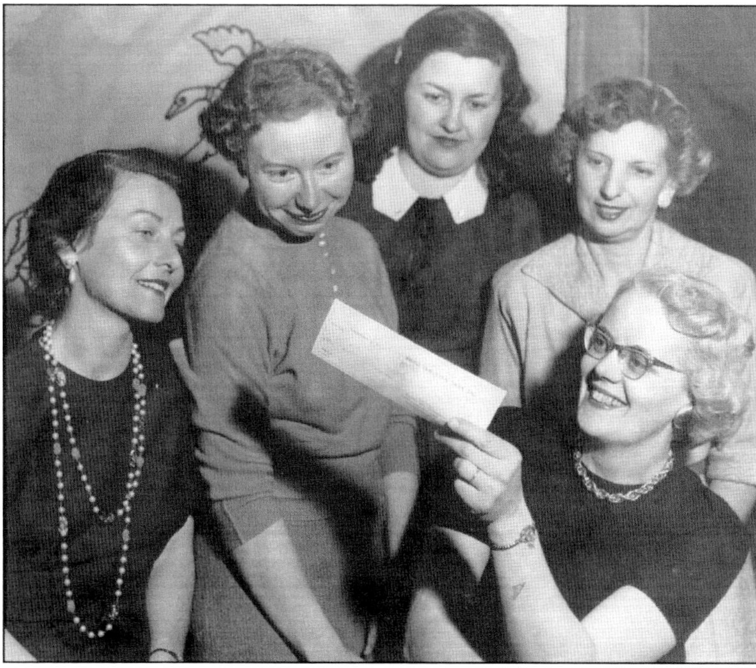

Mrs. Donald Stein, president of the Stow Child Study Club, displays to other club members the $300 grand prize awarded in the 1957 WCUE Community Club award contest. Others in the picture are, from left to right, Mrs. R. J. Anderson Jr., chairwoman of the Ways and Means Committee; Mrs. Charles Haury, secretary; Mrs. Wilbur K. Gosnell, vice president; and Mrs. Edward L. Koffroth, treasurer. (SMFPL.)

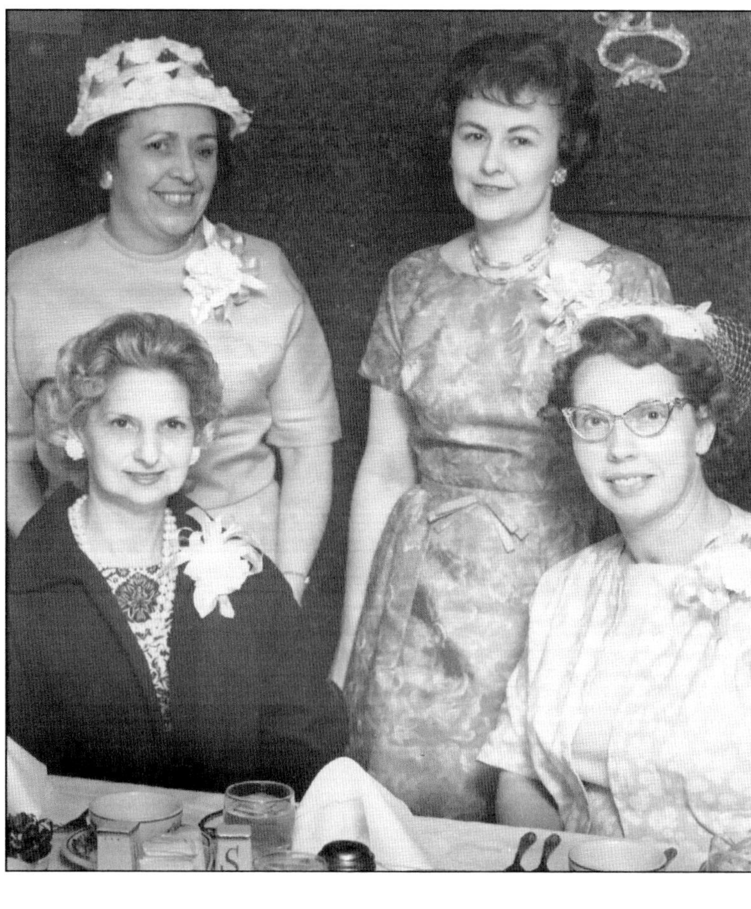

Members of the Stow Study Club gather at the 1964 spring dinner in this photograph. Originally known as the Stow Child Study Club, the organization was formed on May 22, 1941. The club was known for its many philanthropic interests, including sponsoring the Stow Dental Health Care Program for children in the Stow Public Schools and Holy Family School. (SMFPL.)

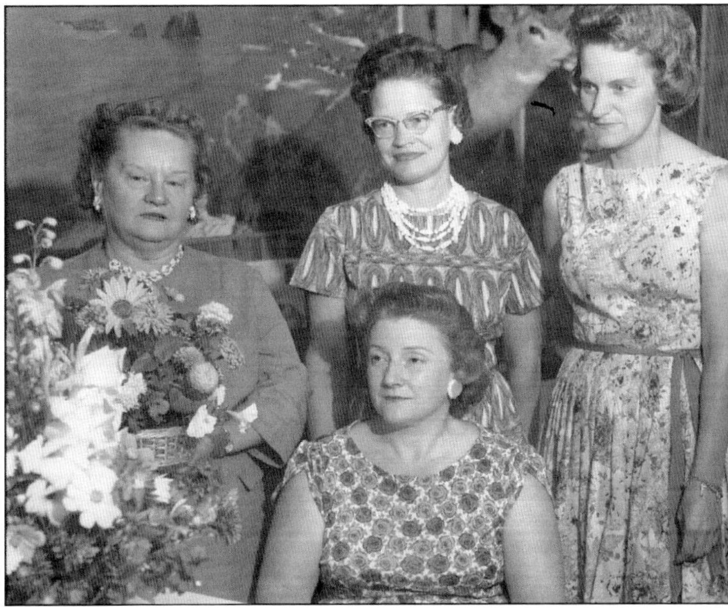

"September Song" was the theme of the Stow Home and Garden Club's eighth annual flower show in 1963. Looking at an arrangement by Mrs. Wayne Barr are (seated) Mrs. C. E. Olson, chairwoman of the show committee and hostess for the affair; (standing, from left to right) Mrs. K. T. Ritterbusch, Mrs. Ralph Nelson, and Mrs. Frank Wooley. Mrs. Barr and Mrs. R. V. Nelson were awarded best of show for their entries. (SMFPL.)

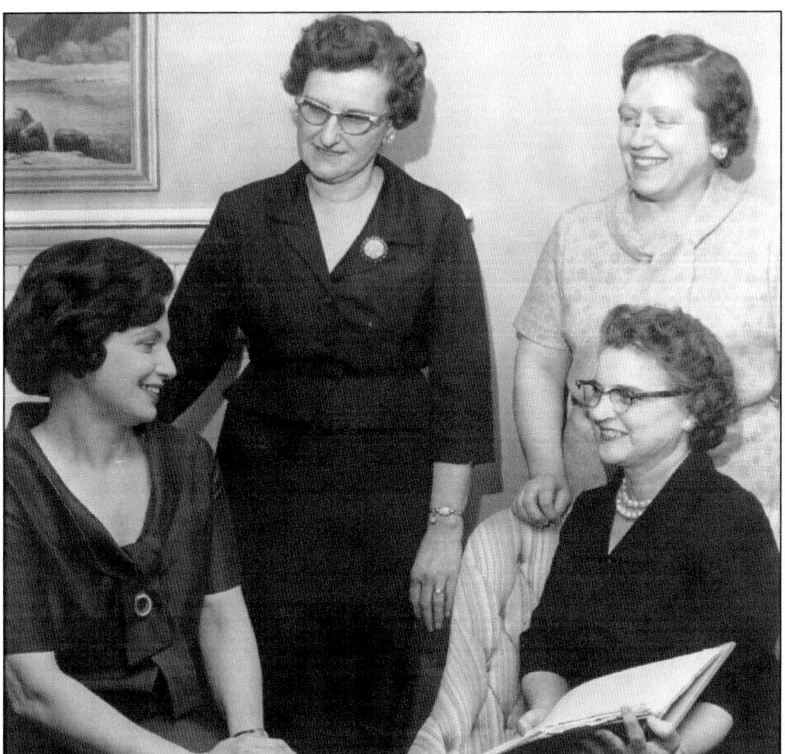

In 1964, the Charring Cross Garden club officers were installed at a meeting at the home of Mrs. Earl Bush. Pictured from left to right are (seated) president Mrs. Richard O'Barski and retiring president Mrs. Allan Ely; (standing) treasurer Mrs. William Kimball and vice president Mrs. Robert Dyke. Mrs. Robert Kuchner (not pictured) was the installing officer. (SMFPL.)

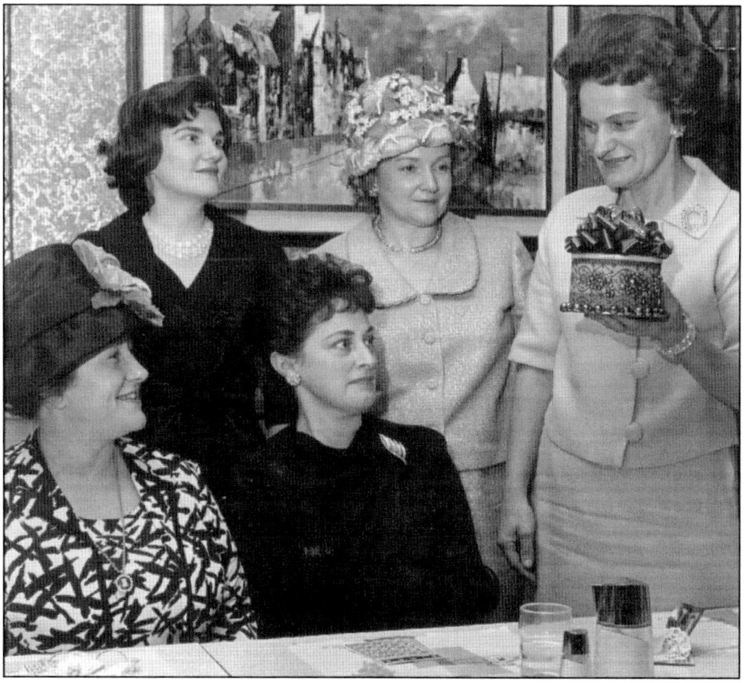

Members of the Stow Home and Garden Club celebrated the group's 10th anniversary on March 4, 1965, at Sperry's Restaurant in Tallmadge. Following dinner, charter member and past president Mrs. C. E. Olson spoke on "Home and Gardeners," a history of the club. Pictured are, from left to right, (seated) Mrs. A. J. Alexander and Mrs. Charles Tritle; (standing) Mrs. M. E. Rossman, Mrs. Olson, and Mrs. Fran Wooley. (SMFPL.)

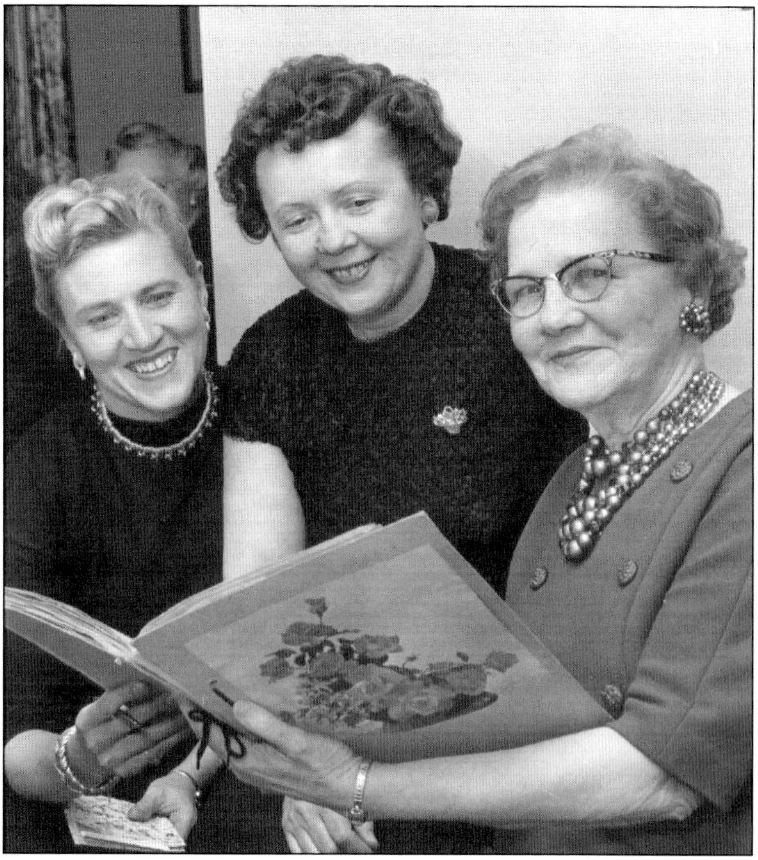

Stow Garden Club held a Valentine luncheon at the home of club president Mrs. Carl McElroy of Munroe Falls on February 15, 1966; the cohostess was Mrs. Effie Deen. The guest speaker of the event was Lilliane Hanni from Geneva, Switzerland, a foreign exchange student attending Stow High School. Pictured admiring the club scrapbook display are, from left to right, Lee Casey, Ann Czartoski, and Vi Bullock. The Stow Garden Club was organized in 1929. (SMFPL.)

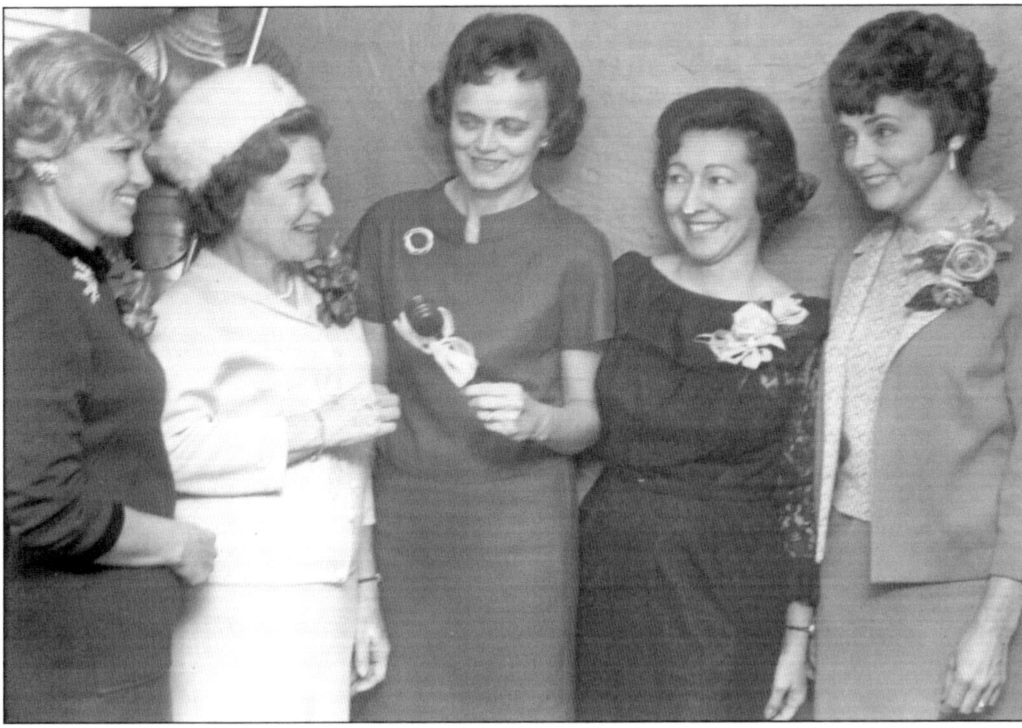

The Stow Garden Forum installation of officers was held at Robin Hood Restaurant in Kent, Ohio, in 1967. Pictured from left to right are vice president Mrs. William Davis (Charring Cross Garden Club), president Mrs. Harvey Greer (Stow Home and Garden Club), Mrs. Wayne Barr (with gavel), treasurer Mrs. Robert Reider (Silvercrest Garden Club), and secretary Mrs. Robert Henning (Overdale Garden Club). (SMFPL.)

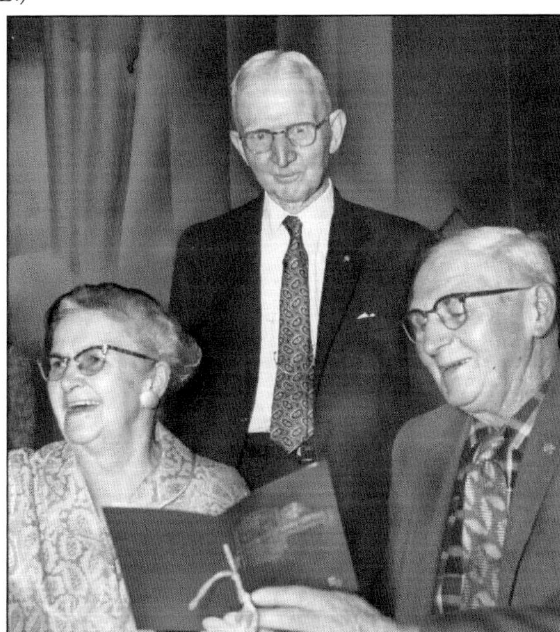

Howard M. Call (standing) looks over the program with Laura Call and Edward C. McCauley at a Darrow Street Grange anniversary celebration in 1967. Summit County Darrow Street Grange (No. 751) was organized on March 26, 1874, with 31 charter members. The fee to join was 50¢ for women and $3 for men. As the Grange grew, a building site was purchased and a building was dedicated on July 2, 1875. The Grange is still active. (CJC.)

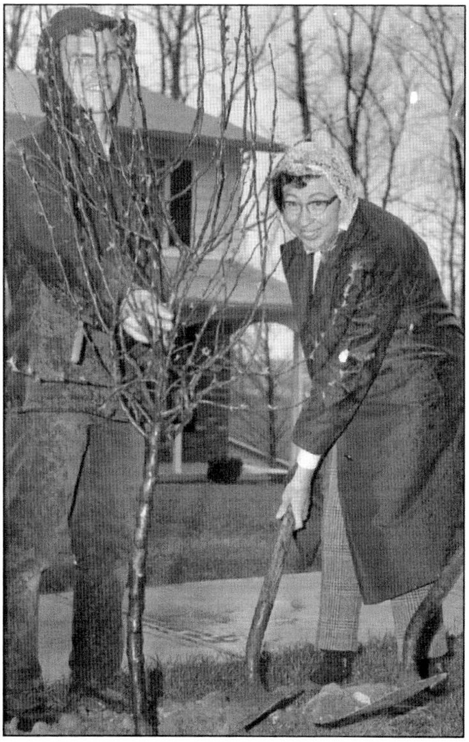

Wyoga Lake Women's Club was formed in 1968 as an organization for residents of Wyoga Lake Estates to promote the growth and beauty of their neighborhood. Officers elected were Mrs. George Marquis (president), Mrs. Charles Meier (vice president), Mrs. John Pastor (secretary), and Mrs. Raymond Walter (treasurer). This photograph, dated April 1969, shows Dick Wise and Mrs. Pastor planting 1 of the 50 trees purchased by residents of the neighborhood. (SMFPL.)

This aerial view looking east from west shows the Wyoga Lake Estates development in northwest Stow about 1970. Wyoga Lake became a stop on the Akron-Bedford-Cleveland (or ABC) Rapid Transit electric train station in the late 1800s when the Jotham Potter family from Cleveland purchased the lake and surrounding property. The ABC line ran east of the lake along what is now the Summit County Metro Parks Bike and Hike Trail. (FL.)

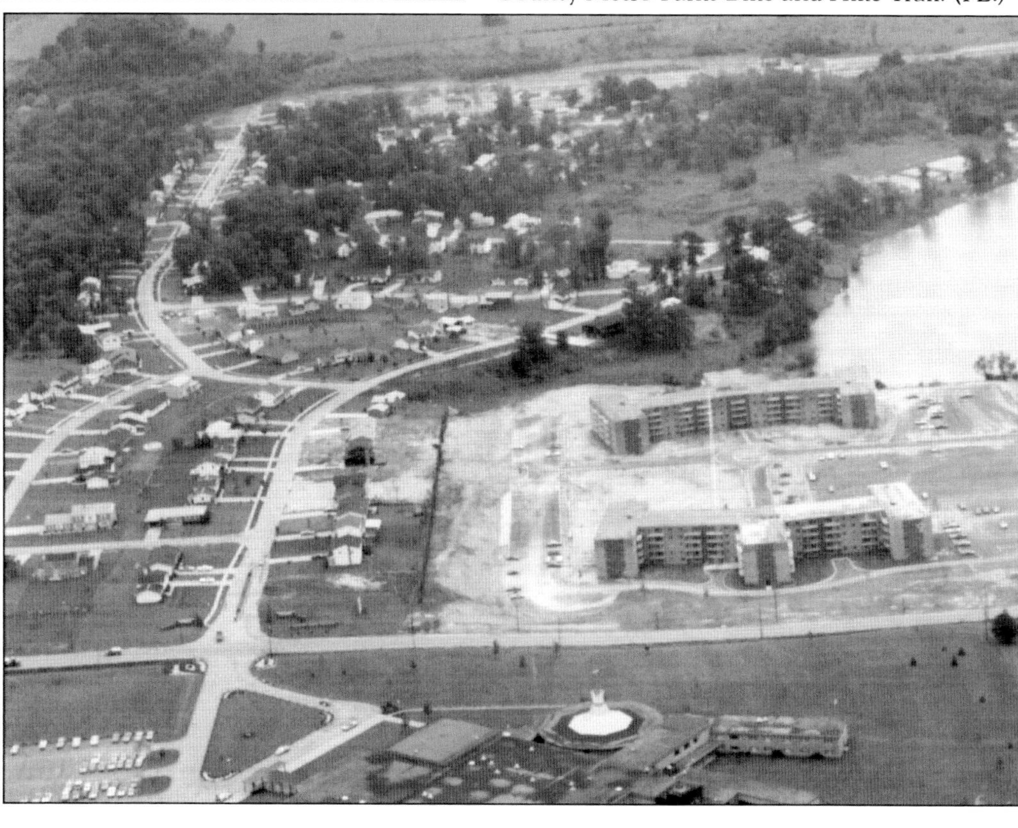

Five

Worshipping, Shopping, and Doing Business

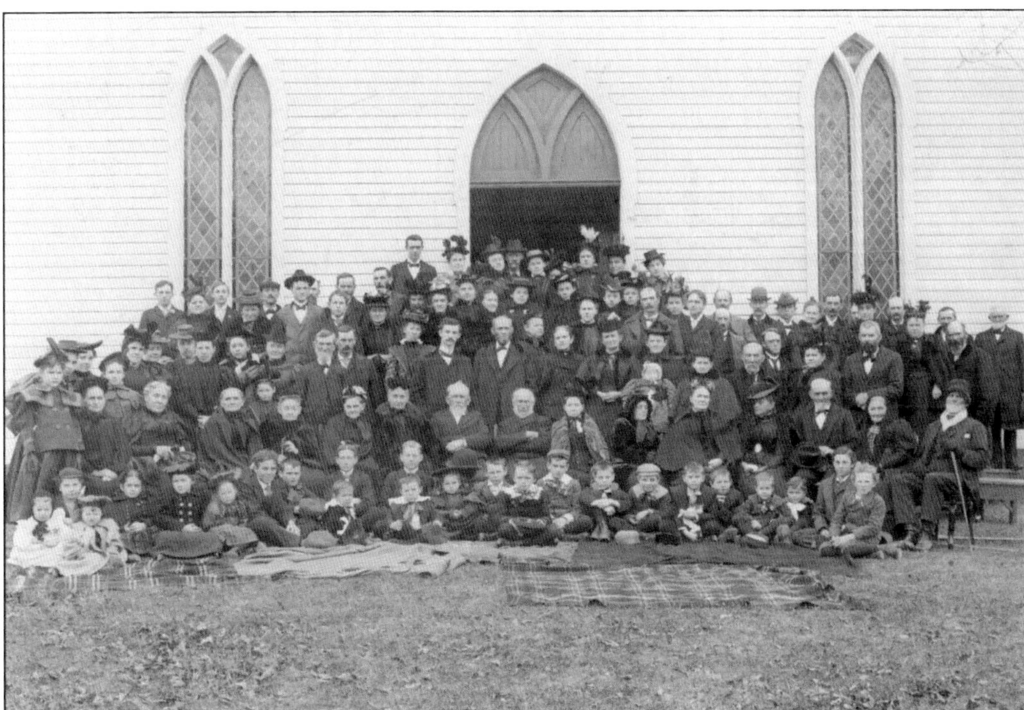

The Disciples of Christ trace their formation in Stow back to 1831, with preacher William Hayden. Members first met in homes, then in a small wooden meetinghouse next to Stow Cemetery. In 1876, the congregation moved into a new church located on 2 acres just north of Stow Corners on Darrow Road. The congregation has gathered in front of the church for this 1897 photograph. (FL.)

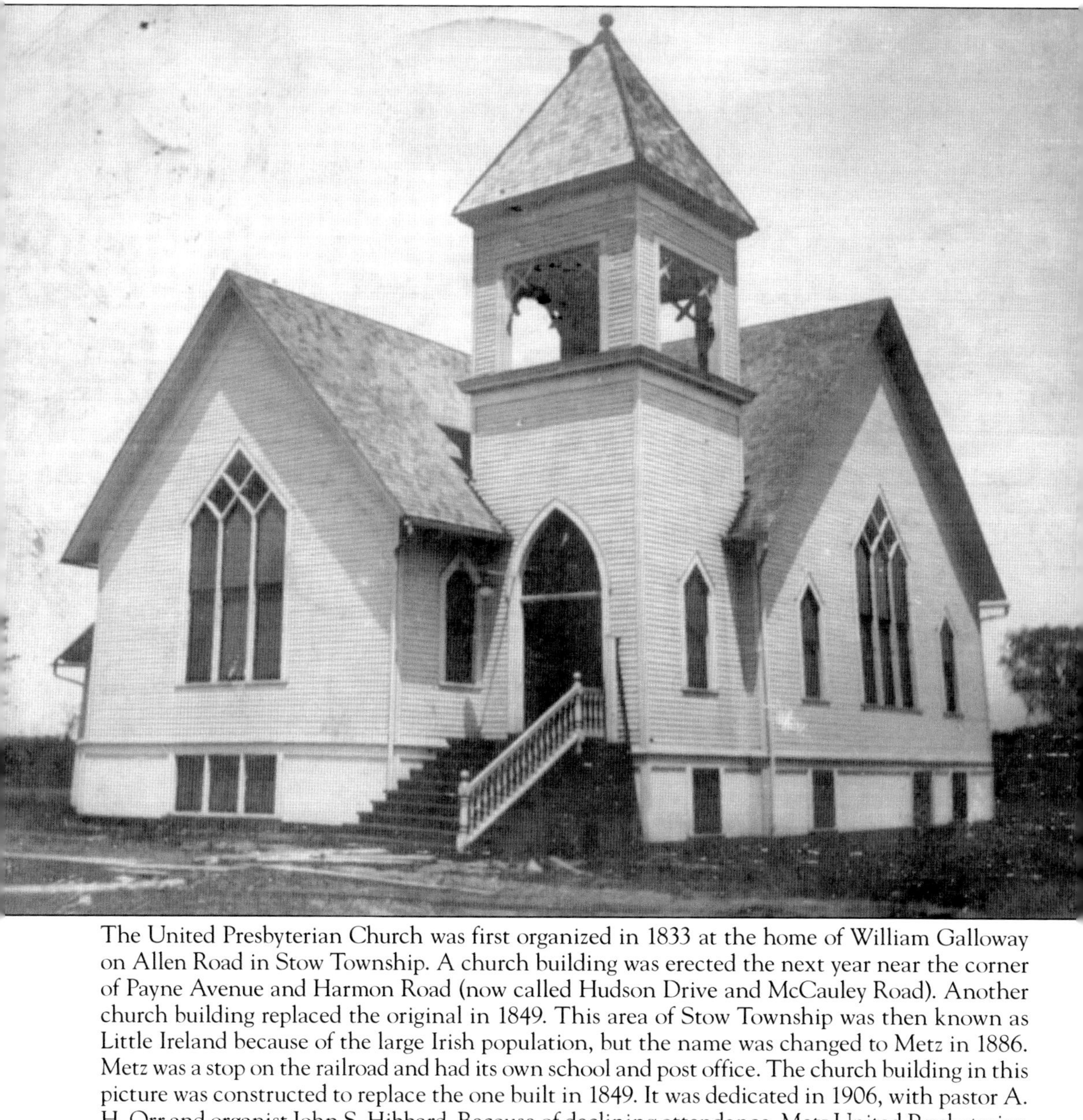

The United Presbyterian Church was first organized in 1833 at the home of William Galloway on Allen Road in Stow Township. A church building was erected the next year near the corner of Payne Avenue and Harmon Road (now called Hudson Drive and McCauley Road). Another church building replaced the original in 1849. This area of Stow Township was then known as Little Ireland because of the large Irish population, but the name was changed to Metz in 1886. Metz was a stop on the railroad and had its own school and post office. The church building in this picture was constructed to replace the one built in 1849. It was dedicated in 1906, with pastor A. H. Orr and organist John S. Hibbard. Because of declining attendance, Metz United Presbyterian Church was disbanded and the building sold to North Hill United Presbyterian Church in the early 1920s. The Metz Missionary Society was formed in 1885 by wife of the minister, Mrs. William Wallace. The society continued to meet even after the church was disbanded. It continued to serve the community until 1977. (FL.)

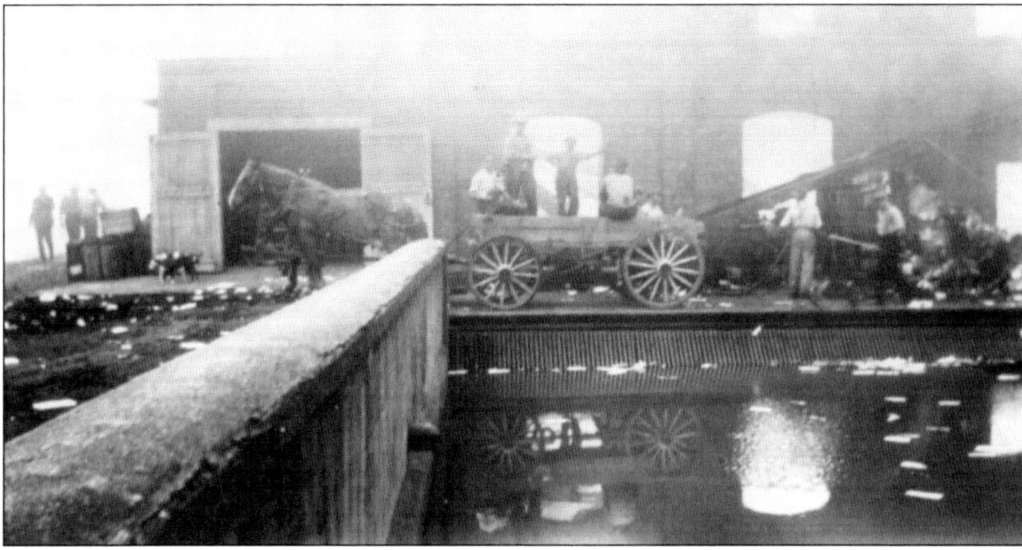

The Munroe Falls Paper Mill stood at the same location from approximately 1866 until its closing in the 1950s. Once the site of the town gristmill, the paper mill was rebuilt after at least two fires and operated under various owners. Sonoco Products purchased the property in 1960 and remained at 59 North Main Street until closing in 2001. This photograph is dated August 6, 1925. (MFHS.)

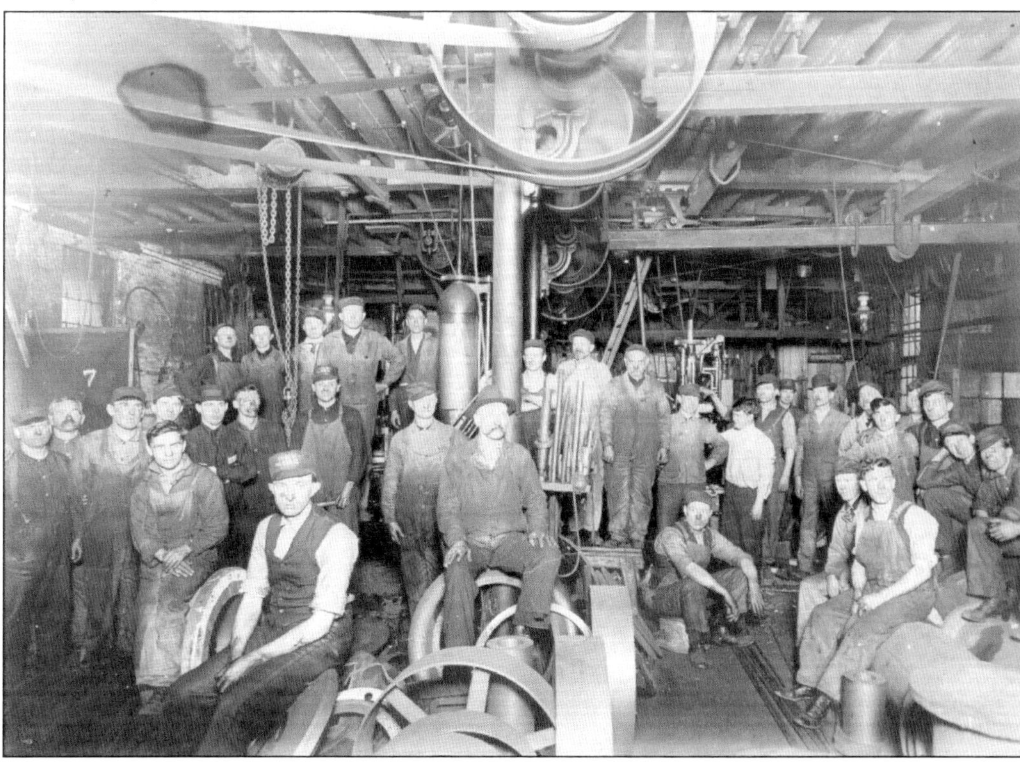

By the early 1900s, the employees of the Munroe Falls Paper Company were working double shifts. The 35 employees produced 12 tons of paper daily. Products shipped all over the country included light and dark rag wrapping paper, absorbent fly paper, felt paper, and carpet lining. (MFHS.)

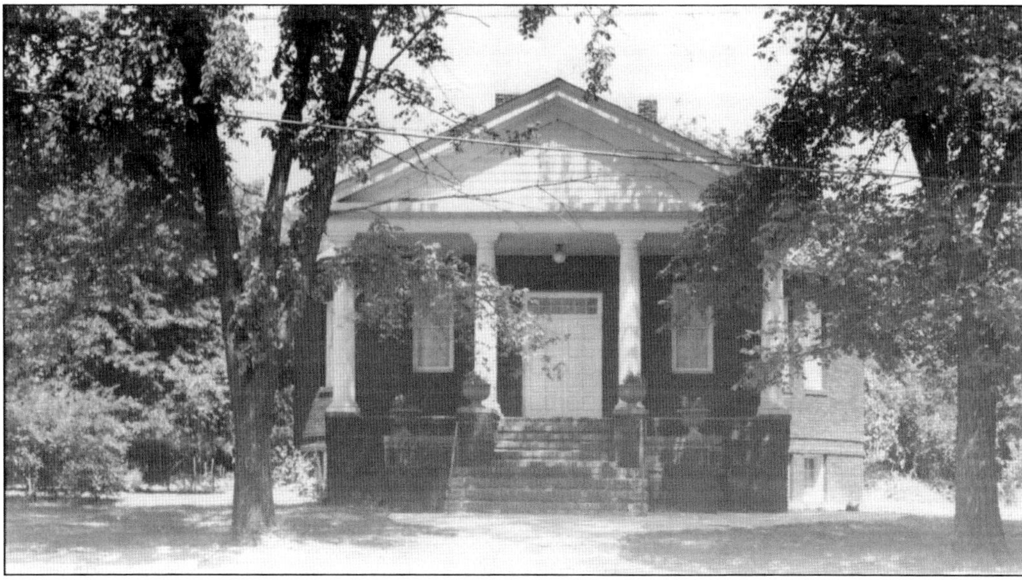

In 1917, a group of about 40 Stow residents met to organize a nondenominational church for those not affiliated with the Disciples of Christ. Services were held in Stow High School until William R. Lodge donated the old Silver Lake Park Aquarium to be used as the new church building. The aquarium building was hauled brick by brick to Elm Road in 1919 and rebuilt. The church was dedicated in September 1920. (FL.)

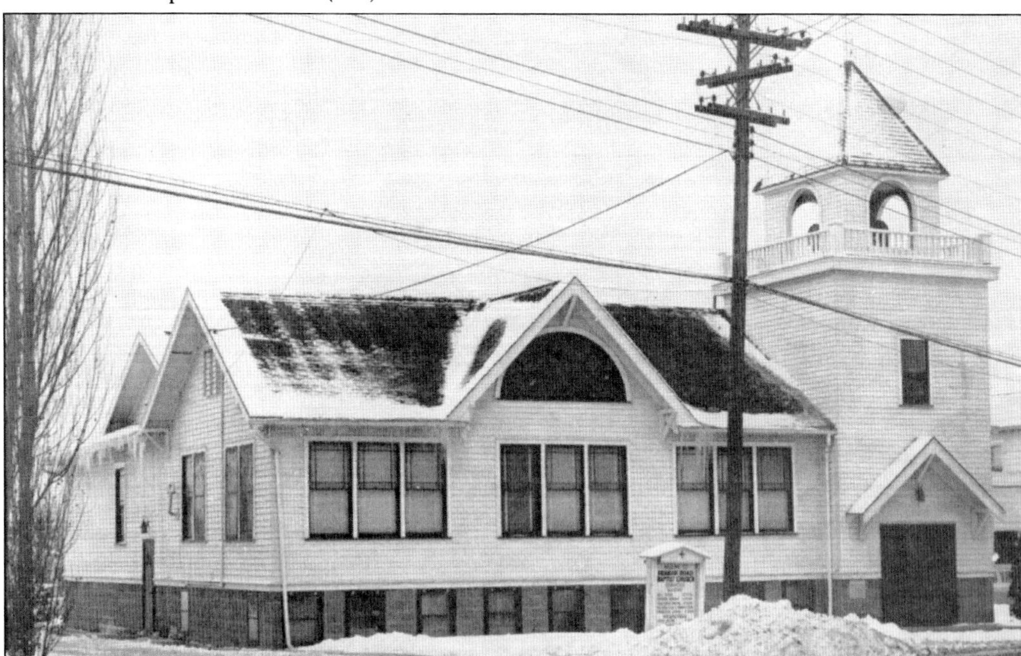

Graham Road Baptist Church, located at 705 Graham Road, was founded in 1926 and originally organized as a nondenominational Sunday school. Members later decided to organize as a Baptist congregation, and this church building was completed in 1927. The church had 23 charter members. An addition to double the size of the building was completed in 1940. The church pictured here was replaced by a new brick church in 1962 and has had two additions since. (HLC.)

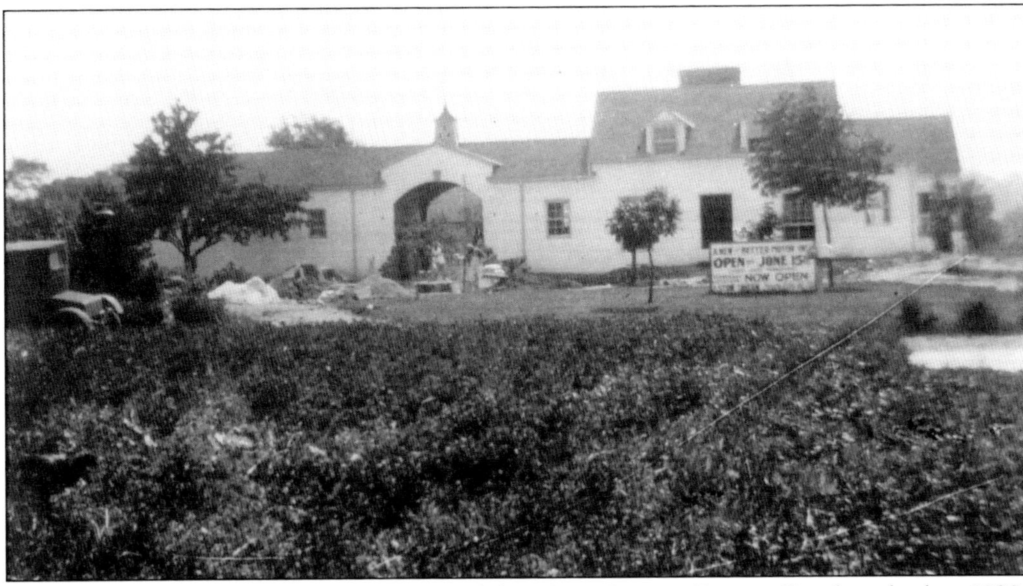

This photograph shows the construction of the Motor Inn on Darrow Road in the late 1930s. The Motor Inn later became the Stow Smorgasbord, widely known for its delicious food featuring Scandinavian specialties. Lena Osman, founder of Osman's Pies, worked at the Smorgasbord during the 1940s as the head chef. The Smorgasbord advertised in the October 1940 *Stohion* (Stow High School student newspaper) meals for 75¢ to $2. (FL.)

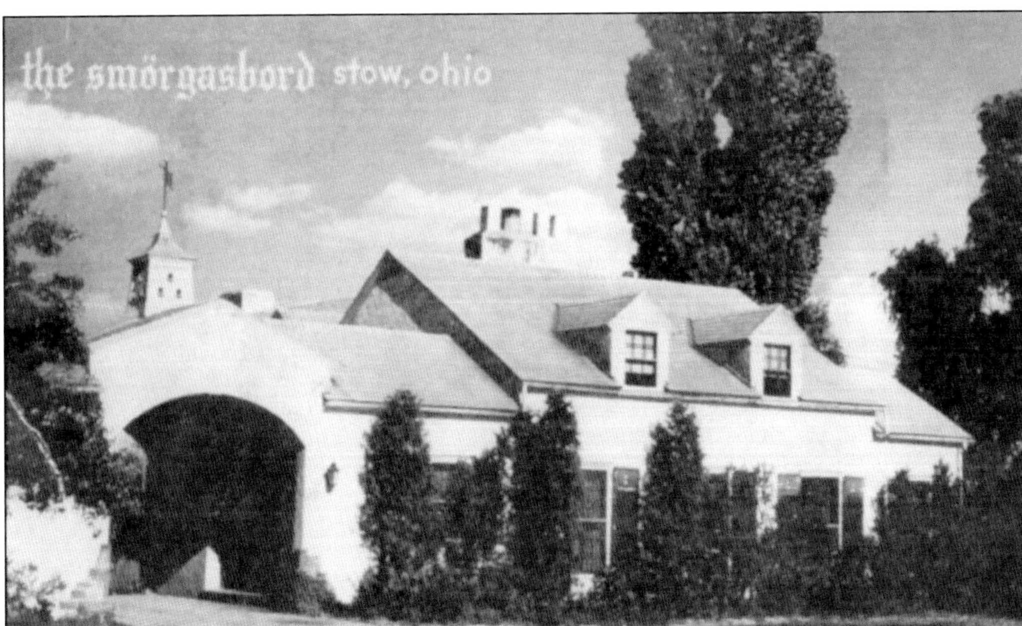

This postcard of the Stow Smorgasbord was mailed with a 1¢ stamp. The description on the back reads, "The Smorgasbord, located amid beautiful surroundings on Route 91 five miles south of Hudson, one mile north of Stow. From the people of Sweden we've borrowed a name; from the people of the Scandinavian countries, a custom; and from people all over the world, recipes for fine foods." Parasson's Restaurant is now located in the former Smorgasbord building. (SMFPL.)

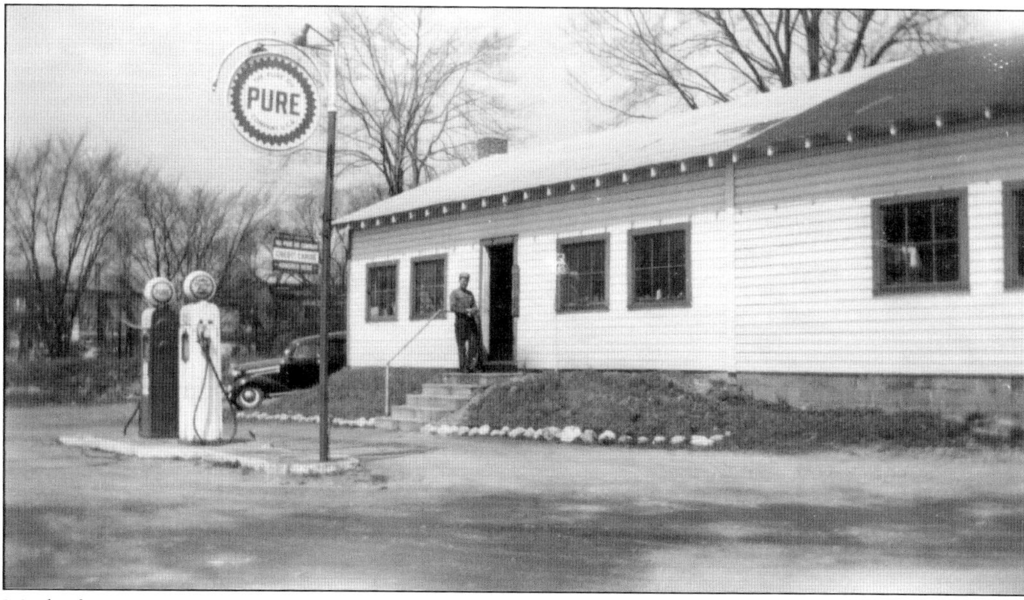

Marhofer Garage was opened in Stow in 1919 by Chester Marhofer, son of John and Leah Marhofer. The repair shop was located on property about 100 feet south of Kent Road (U.S. Route 59) near Stow Corners. At the time, Marhofer's younger brother, John, helped out in the garage. John Marhofer eventually took over the shop and it became Marhofer Chevrolet sometime in the 1930s. Thirty-six new cars were delivered in 1936. (SMFPL.)

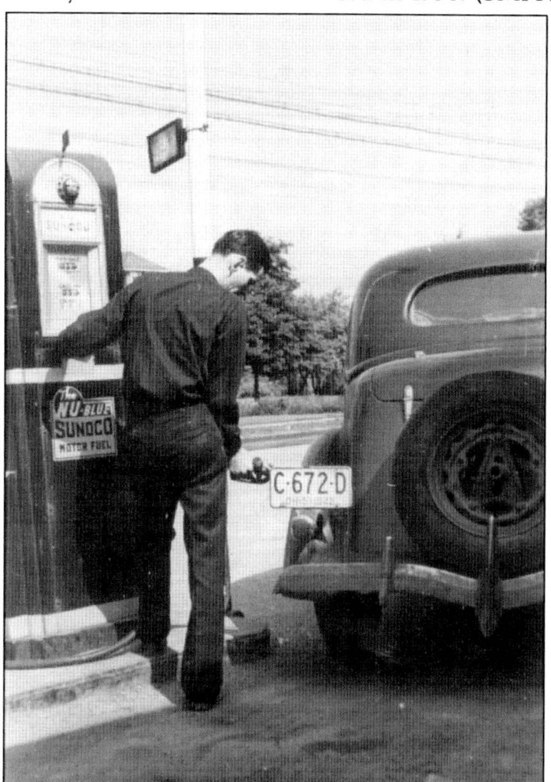

Clyde Gerber, pictured pumping gas, was the son of William C. Gerber, owner of W. C. Gerber and Son service station. Located at 201 Hudson Road (now Darrow Road) in Stow, Gerber's offered complete automobile service and repairs, Sunoco gas, and oil service. Shortly after this photograph was taken, the Sunoco station was sold, and Clyde entered the U.S. Army to serve in World War II. The license plate on this automobile is dated 1942. (FL.)

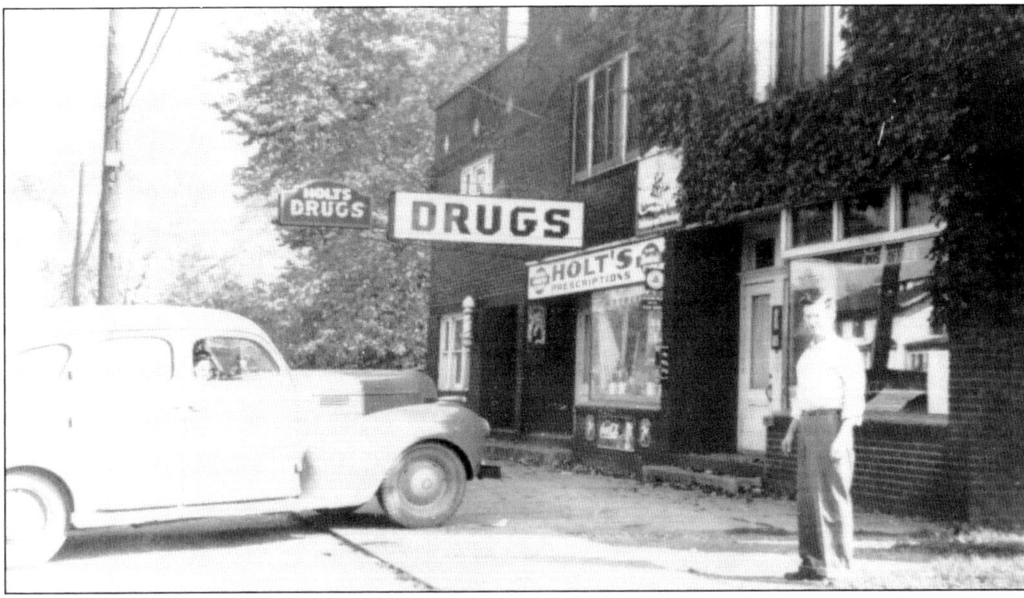

Chester Holt, pharmacist and owner of Holt's Drug Store (previously named Cut-Rate Drugs), stands in front of his establishment at 3310 Kent Road. Holt and wife, Helen, built the store in 1926. Living in the four rooms above, they kept the business open 365 days a year. Harold and Jacqueline Winkler bought the store in 1958 and operated Stow Pharmacy for 34 years, making it one of the longest running businesses in Stow. (SMFPL.)

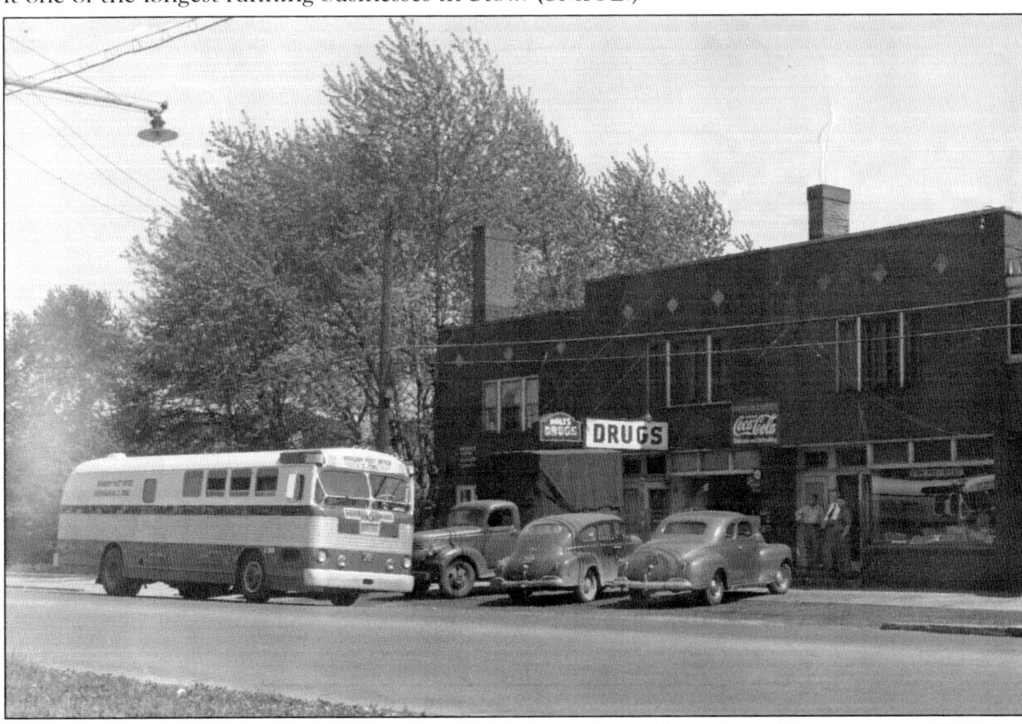

The Stow Post Office was located next to Holt's Drug Store (later Stow Pharmacy) at 3310 Kent Road for many years, making this building a hub of activity in Stow. The bus in this photograph was used primarily for rural mail delivery. (FL.)

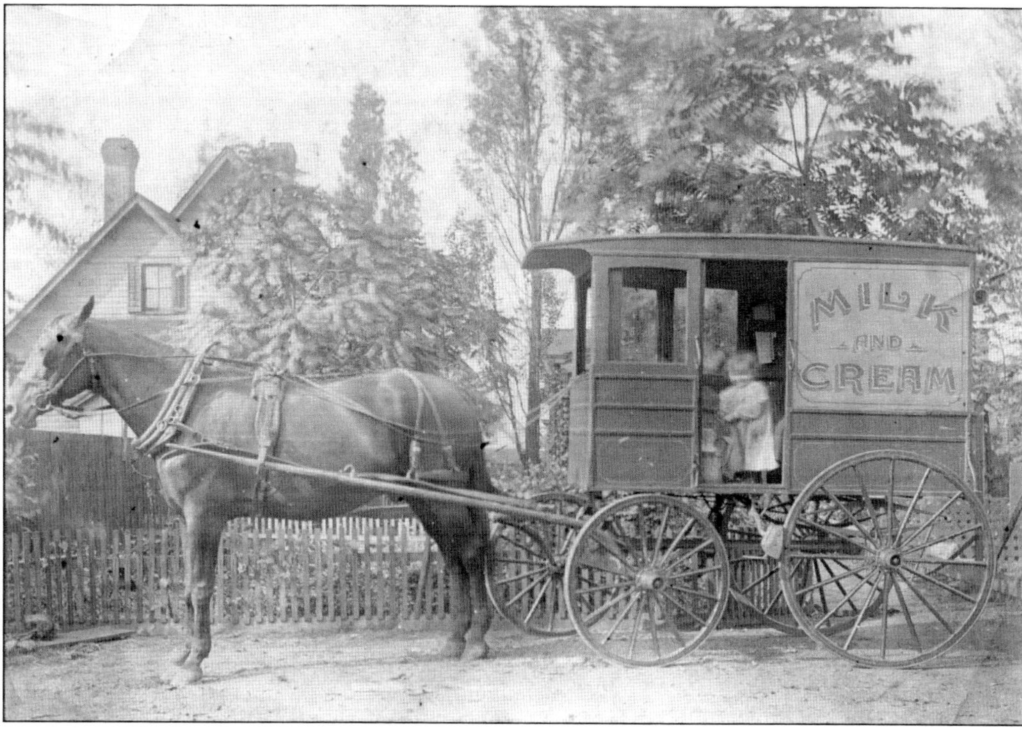

Described in the 1891 *Summit County Illustrated Atlas* as a dairy township, Stow was the home of several dairy operations well into the middle of the 20th century. Milk and cream were delivered by horse and wagon in the early 1900s. (FL.)

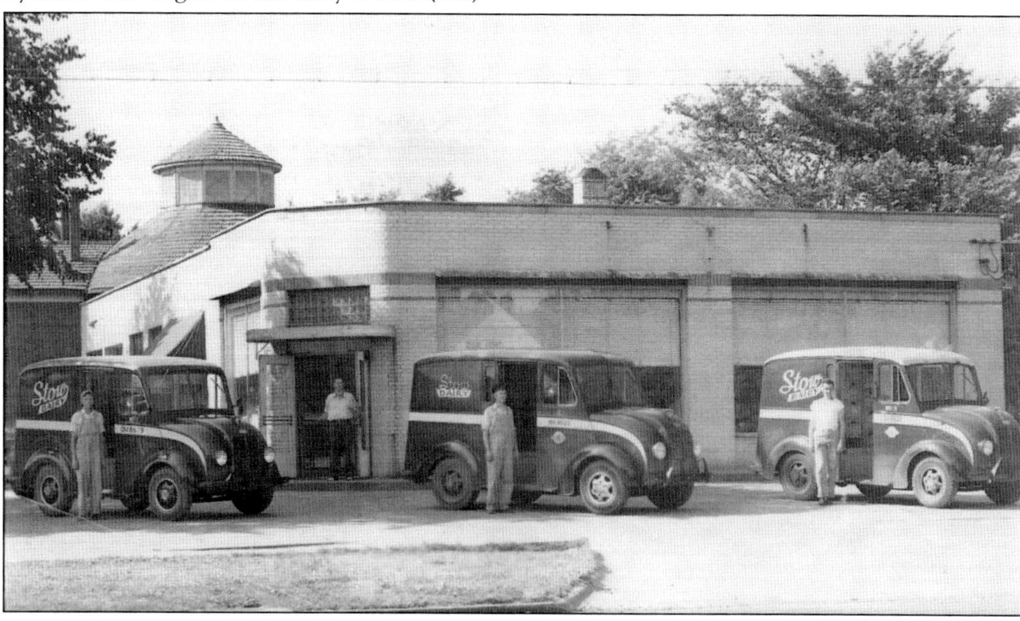

Stow Dairy, started in 1920 by Al Stein, processed milk provided by local farmers and also sold dairy products directly to the consumer. It was purchased by Lawson Milk Company in 1953 and designated as Plant No. 2 and was managed by Acton (Bill) Jones. Pictured standing by their trucks in this 1941 photograph are, from left to right, Carl King, Joe Micklic, and Jules Rank. (FL.)

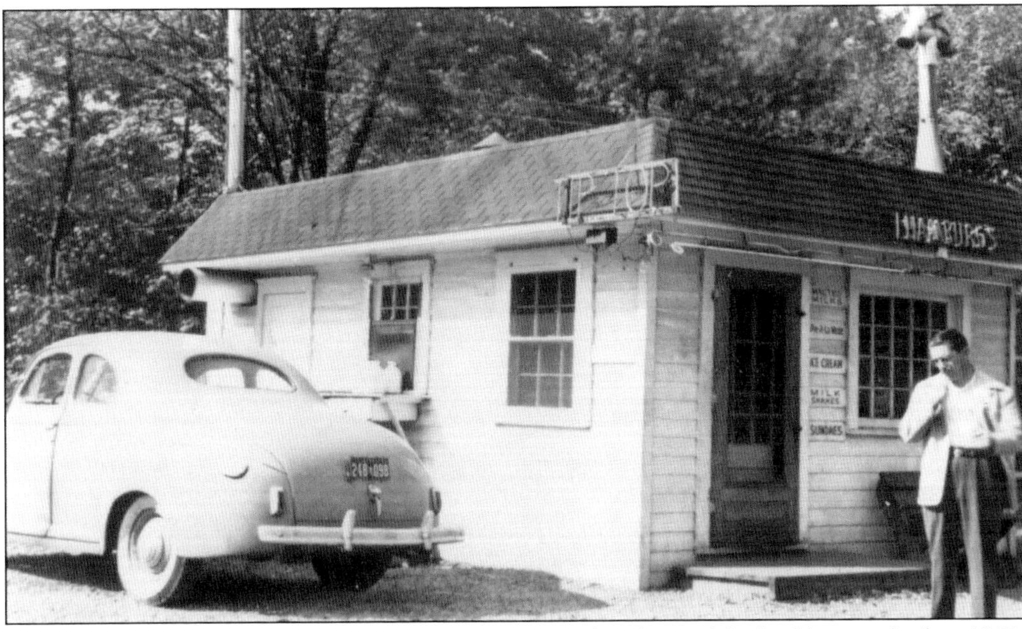

Leo Wagner, owner of The Tip Top Drive-In is pictured in front of the building in the late 1940s. Wagner purchased the restaurant from Eddie Bell. The Tip Top, also known as Hamburger Land, offered curbside service featuring malted milks, pie a la mode, ice cream, milk shakes, and sundaes. (SMFPL.)

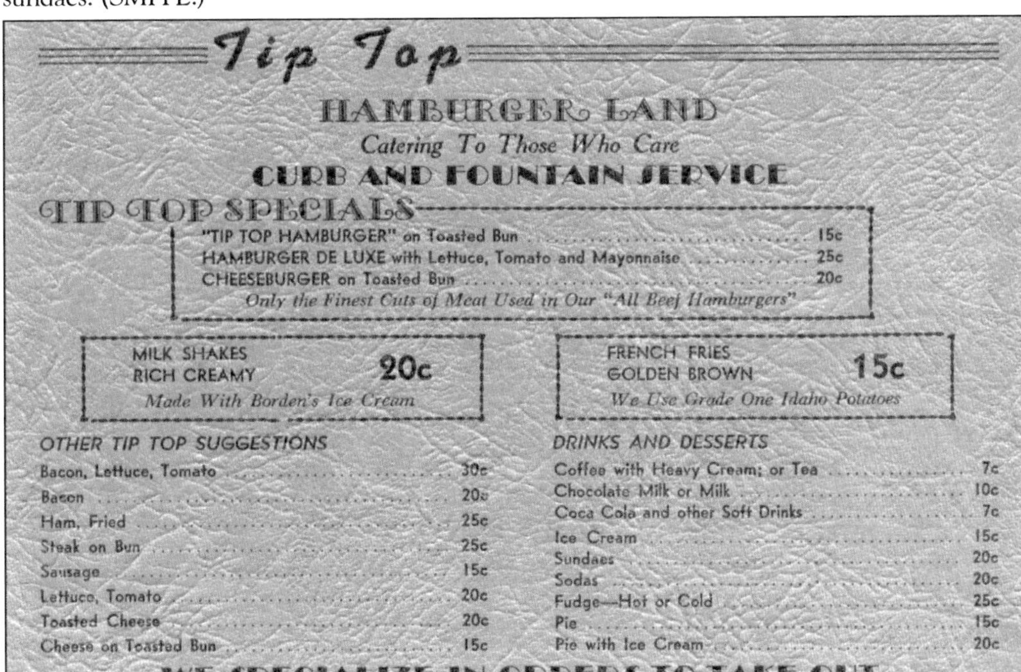

Tip Top

HAMBURGER LAND

Catering To Those Who Care

CURB AND FOUNTAIN SERVICE

TIP TOP SPECIALS

"TIP TOP HAMBURGER" on Toasted Bun	15c
HAMBURGER DE LUXE with Lettuce, Tomato and Mayonnaise	25c
CHEESEBURGER on Toasted Bun	20c

Only the Finest Cuts of Meat Used in Our "All Beef Hamburgers"

MILK SHAKES
RICH CREAMY 20c
Made With Borden's Ice Cream

FRENCH FRIES
GOLDEN BROWN 15c
We Use Grade One Idaho Potatoes

OTHER TIP TOP SUGGESTIONS

Bacon, Lettuce, Tomato	30c
Bacon	20c
Ham, Fried	25c
Steak on Bun	25c
Sausage	15c
Lettuce, Tomato	20c
Toasted Cheese	20c
Cheese on Toasted Bun	15c

DRINKS AND DESSERTS

Coffee with Heavy Cream; or Tea	7c
Chocolate Milk or Milk	10c
Coca Cola and other Soft Drinks	7c
Ice Cream	15c
Sundaes	20c
Sodas	20c
Fudge—Hot or Cold	25c
Pie	15c
Pie with Ice Cream	20c

WE SPECIALIZE IN ORDERS TO TAKE OUT

The Tip Top Drive-In Hamburger Land menu offered the best hamburgers in Stow and Munroe Falls. Specials included the "Tip Top Hamburger" on a toasted bun for 15¢, rich and creamy milkshakes made with Borden's ice cream for 20¢, and french fries for 15¢. Both curb and fountain service were available at the restaurant located on Darrow Road, south of Stow Corners. (FL.)

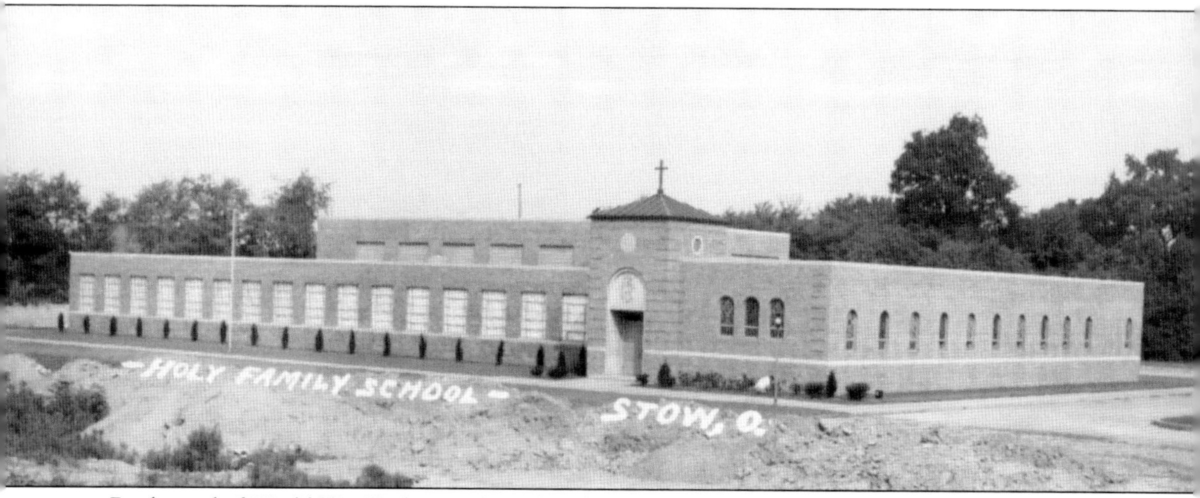

By the end of World War II, the number of Catholics in and around Stow had increased considerably. Under the authorization of Archbishop Hoban of the Cleveland diocese, Fr. John F. Gallagher, pastor of St. Joseph Church in Cuyahoga Falls, was directed to purchase property "for the organization of a Mission in the Village of Stow." In 1946, Gallagher purchased property across from Stow Cemetery consisting of 19 lots at Sycamore Drive and Kent Road. Fr. Howard E. Sammon was selected to lead the new parish to be known as the Parish of the Holy Family. The first Mass was celebrated on December 22, 1946, in the cafeteria of Stow High School in the presence of 68 parishioners. By the end of 1948, ground had been broken for the first church building, consisting of a chapel and offices, and for the Holy Family School. The Holy Family School opened in September 1949 with 100 students. (FL.)

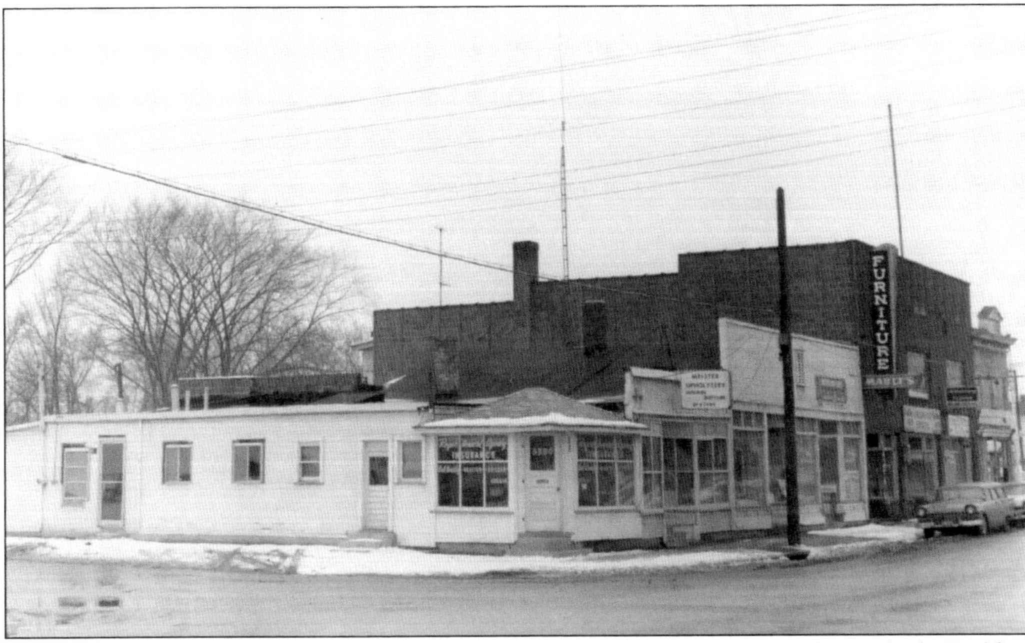

This photograph from the late 1950s shows some of the businesses occupying the Marhofer Building at 3390 Kent Road in Stow. Pictured are the Roger Howard Insurance Agency (previously the site of the George Thomas Tavern), Bob Beckley—Realtor and Developer, Meister Upholstery, and Mault's Furniture. During the 1930s, two of the businesses occupying the upstairs of the building at different times were a dance hall with a live orchestra and a roller-skating rink. (FL.)

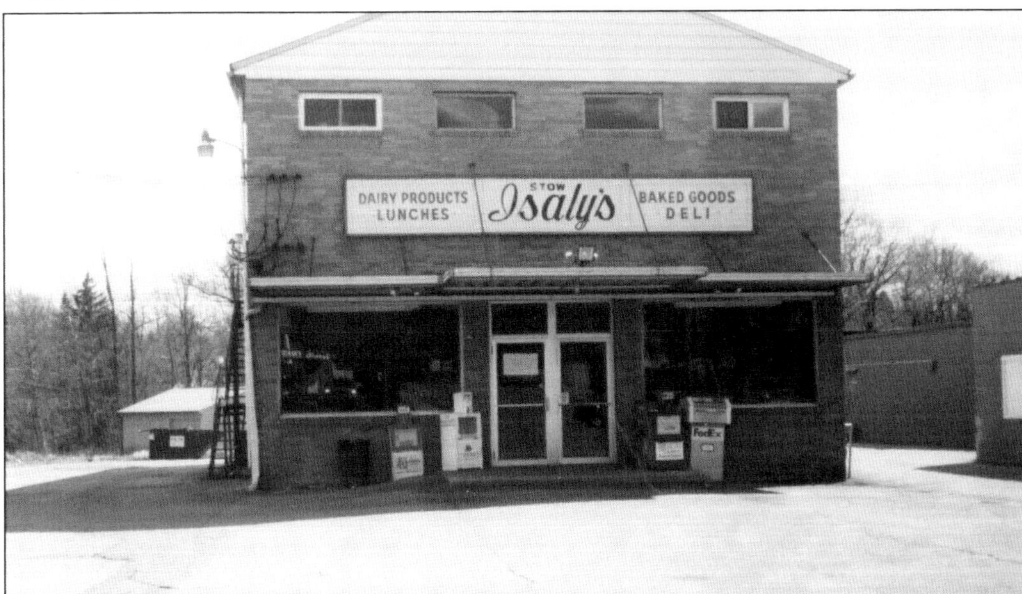

The Stow Isaly's was first opened by "Pop" A. J. Rearick about 1932. In 1952, Mr. and Mrs. W. D. Braucher purchased the store located in the 3390 building on Kent Road. In 1955, they moved their business into this new building at 3322 Kent Road. According to a 1955 news clipping, the lunchroom section had a "homey" atmosphere, with a *U*-shaped counter and new stainless steel equipment. Isaly's specialized in dairy products and light lunches. (SHS.)

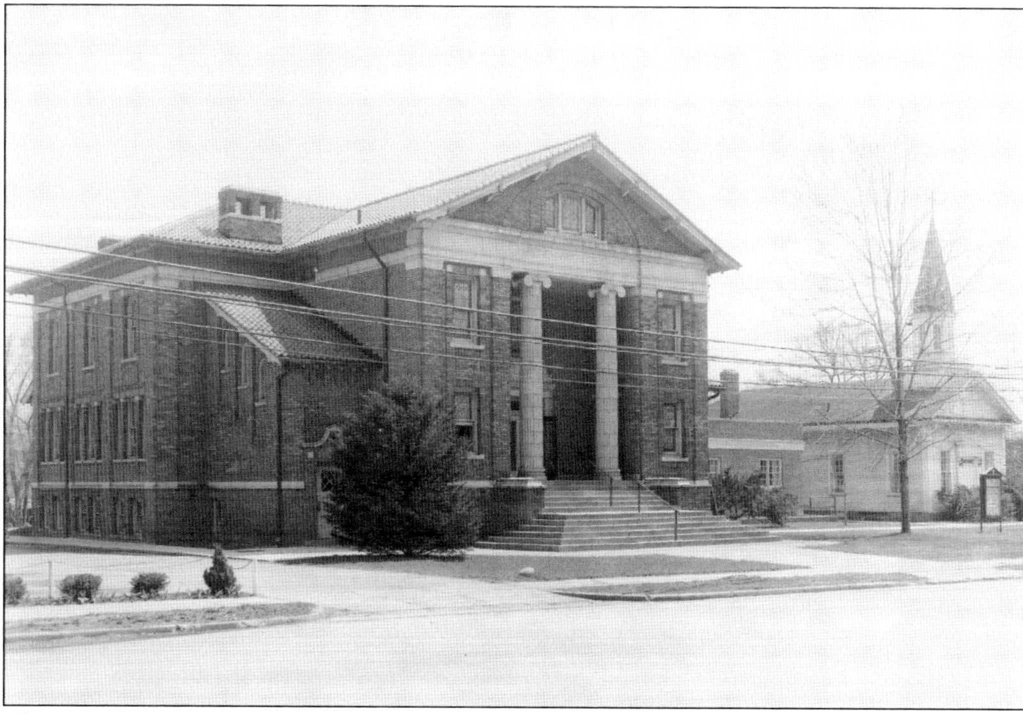

The Stow Disciples of Christ moved into this new brick building in 1922. Constructed at the cost of $87,000, it was incorporated under the name Church of Christ at Stow. The older church building remained standing just to the left of the new brick building until it was moved in 1925. Next to the church in this photograph is the Children's Chapel, which was not moved to this location until 1941. (FL.)

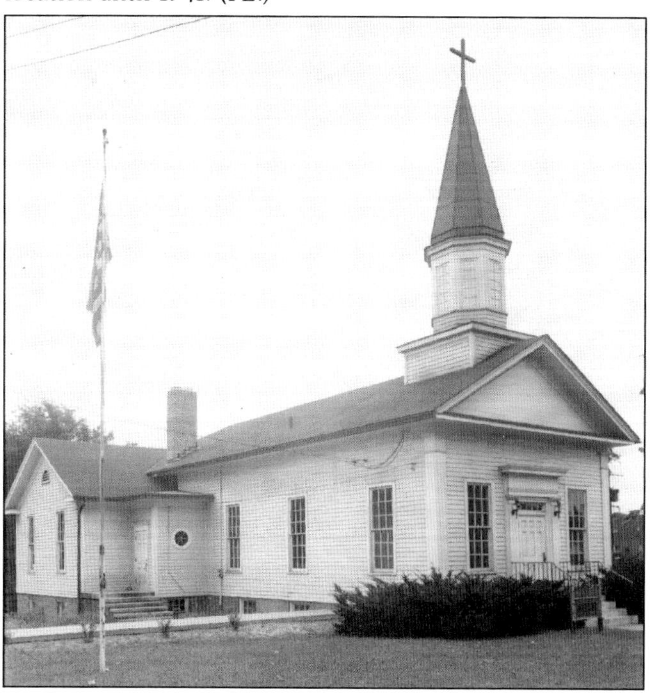

First constructed in 1868, this building served as the Stow Township Hall and as the Stow Public Library. In 1941, Rev. Leo Gregory of the Disciples of Christ purchased the building to be made into a special place for children to worship. It was purchased for $350 and moved next to the church. Due to materials shortages brought on by World War II, the children's chapel was not completed and dedicated until August 15, 1948. (FL.)

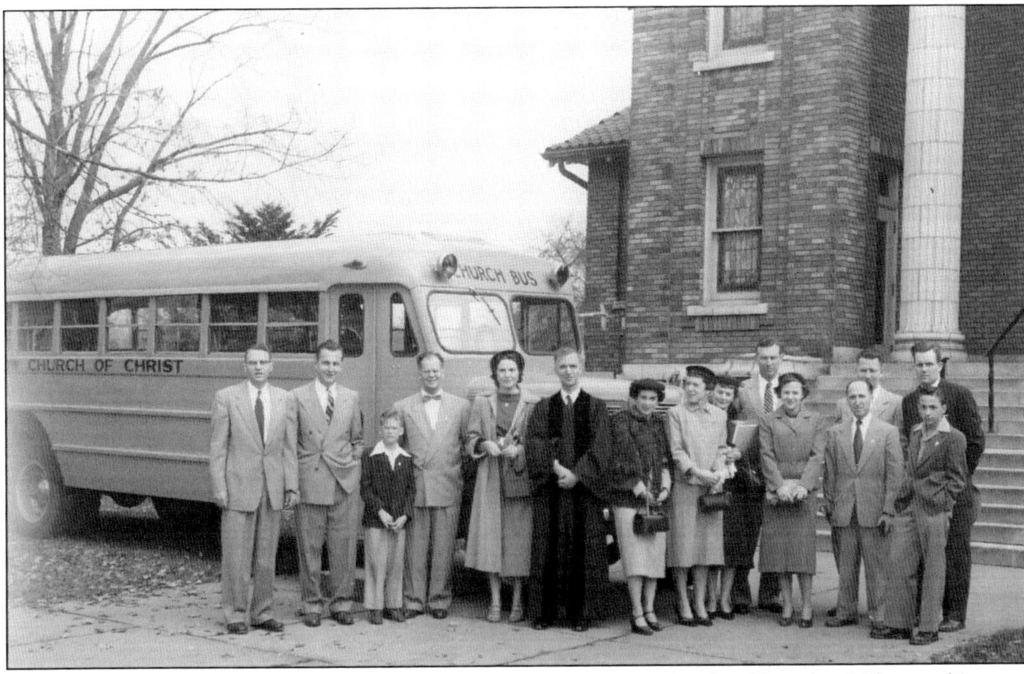

Pastor Theodore Cord was an active and evangelistic minister for the Church of Christ of Stow in the 1950s. He is pictured here with members of the congregation in front of the newly purchased church bus. Early in 1954, the 40-passenger bus was purchased primarily to be used for transporting the young people of the church. (FL.)

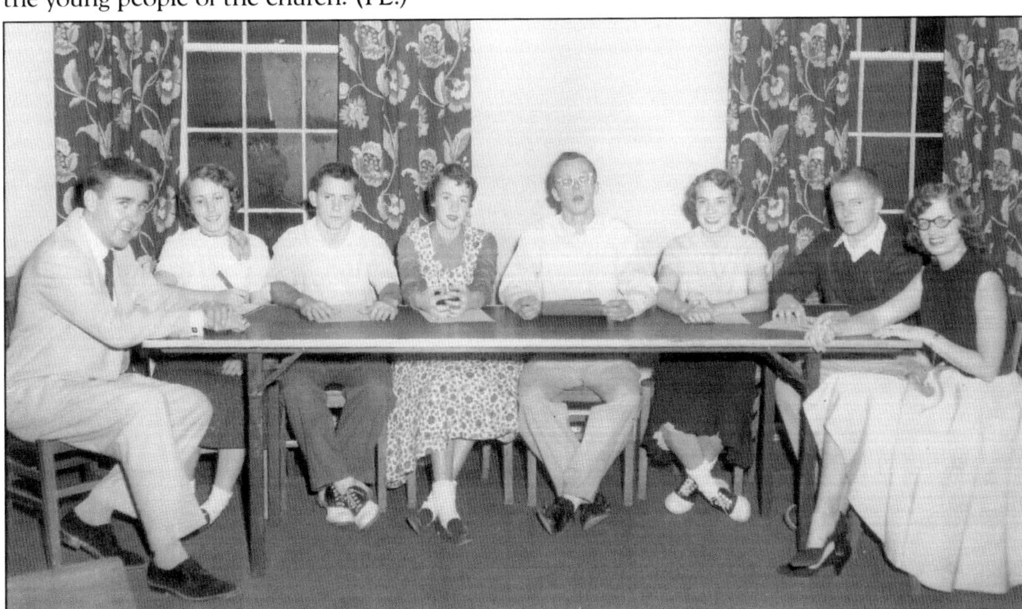

Stow Church of Christ Christian Youth Fellowship advisors and board members of 1955 included, from left to right, Robert Sandercox, ? Unk, David Mulvaney, ? Unk, William Stemple, Miriam Russell, Dennis Whalen, and ? Unk. In 1956, the youth fellowship started the tradition of being responsible for leadership of the Easter sunrise service. (FL.)

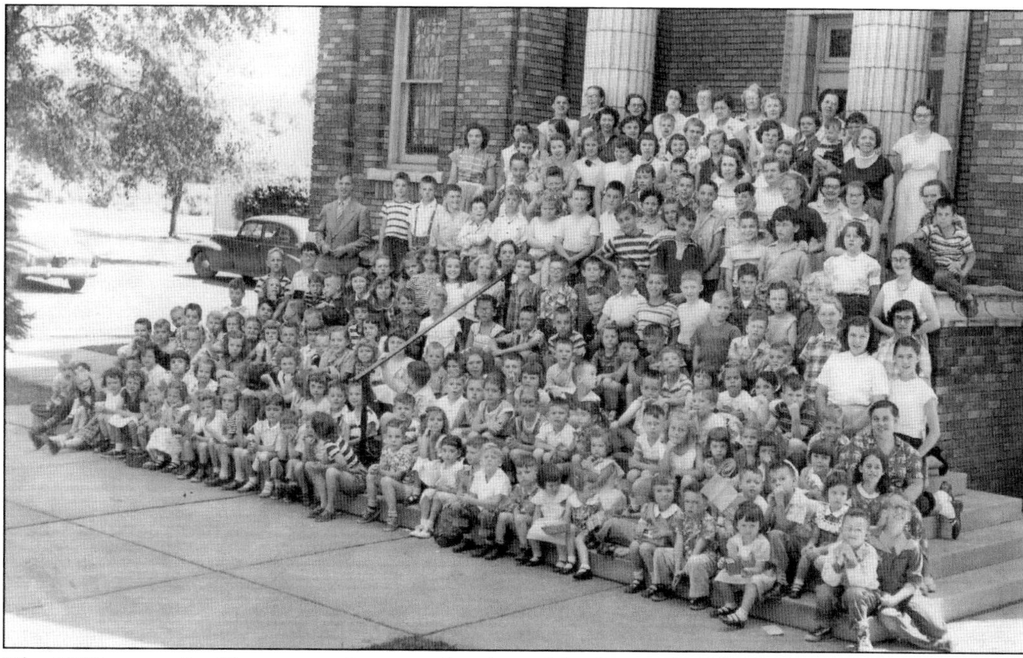

The 1950s saw a significant growth in membership of the Stow Church of Christ, particularly in the Sunday school. In 1957, the Church of Christ, previously known as the Disciples of Christ, officially changed the name of their congregation to the First Christian Church of Stow. Shown in this picture are all of the Sunday school groups in front of the church at 3493 Darrow Road. (FL.)

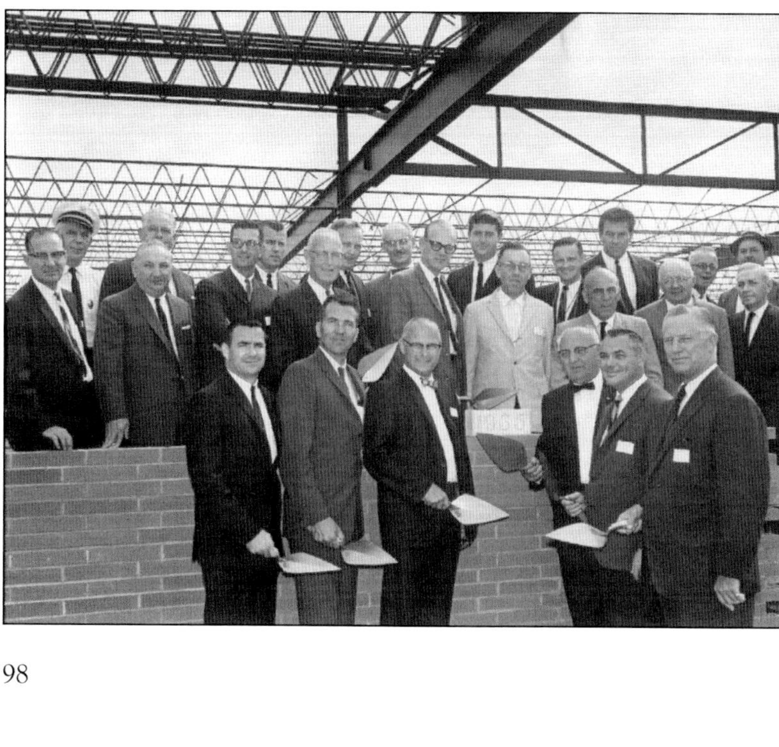

This image was sent to Mayor Roger Howard from Fred I. Albrecht, president of Acme Stores in Akron, Ohio. The photograph is of the cornerstone-laying ceremony for the Acme Click store on Kent Road in Stow in 1965. Mayor Howard is pictured second from the right in the first row. (SMFPL.)

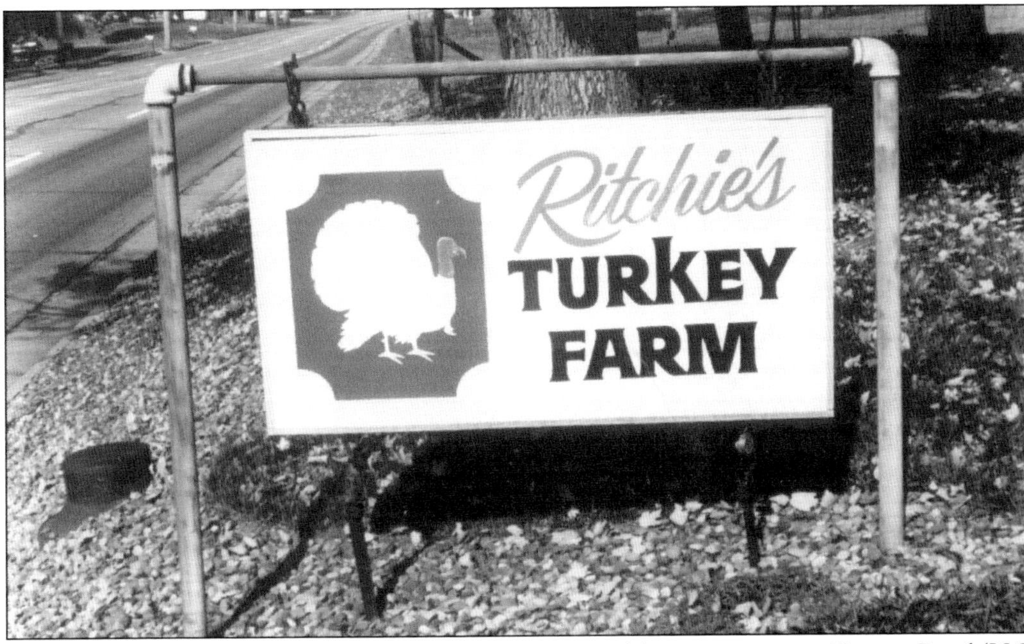

The Lawrence and Virginia Ritchie Turkey Farm operated for many years on Darrow Road (U.S. Route 91) in Darrowville (between Stow and Hudson). During the Thanksgiving and Christmas holiday seasons, the Ritchies processed thousands of turkeys with the help of hired hands, many of whom were Stow High School boys. The turkey farm operated from 1935 to 1986, at one time raising 11,000 turkeys a year. (FL.)

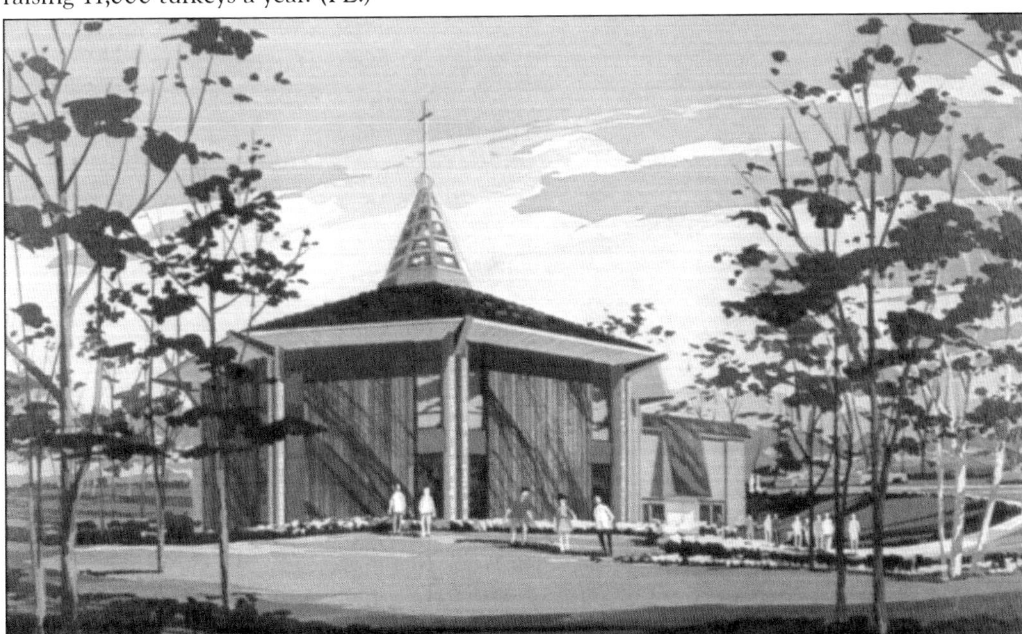

Twin Falls United Methodist Church, located in Munroe Falls, was formed in 1958 from the union of two congregations, the Munroe Falls Methodist Episcopal Church and the Zion Evangelical United Brethren Church. The Methodist Episcopal Church in Munroe Falls dates to 1844. The first service in the new Twin Falls church was on May 24, 1970. (MFHS.)

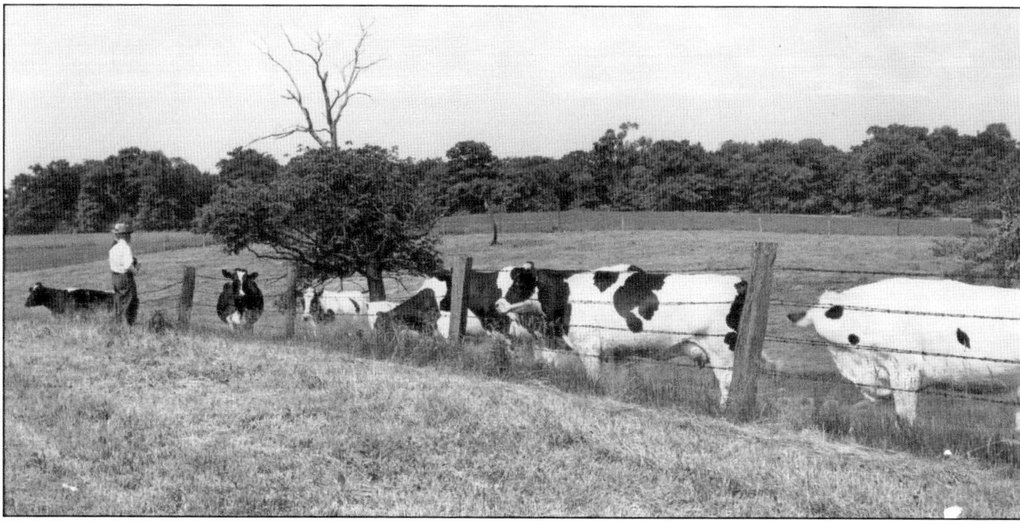

Howard M. Call established a dairy operation on his family's farm when he took over the farm from his father in 1927. Under the direction of his son Charles E. Call, the herd of Holsteins was expanded and by 1966 had 80 milk cows. The farm at that time also had 600 chickens whose eggs were sold to regular customers on a pickup basis. (CJC.)

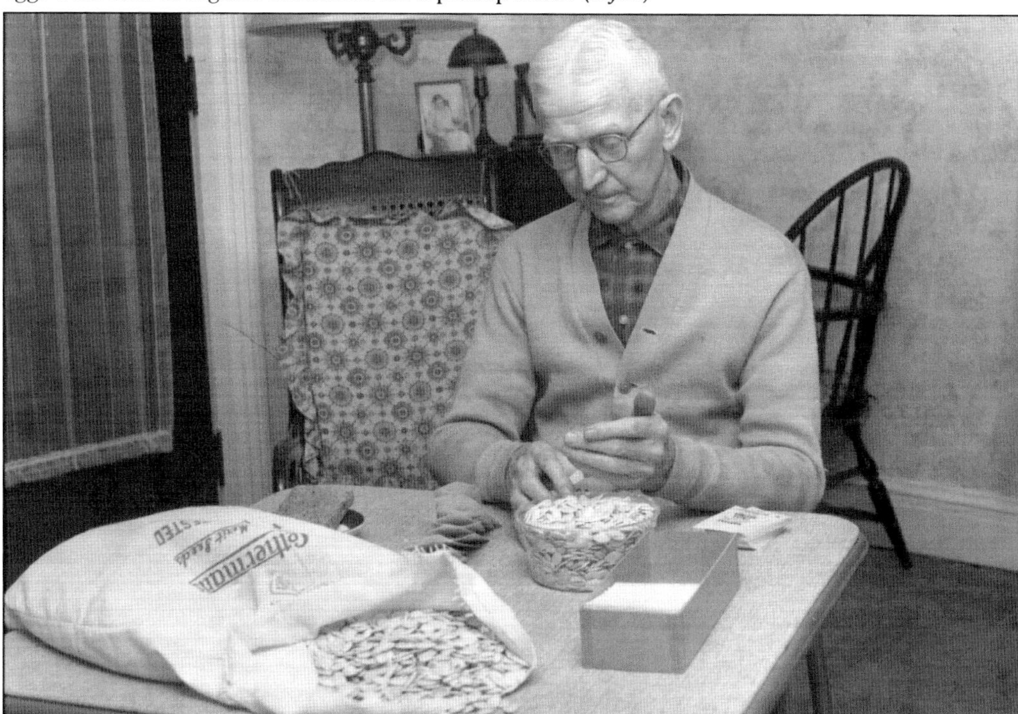

Howard Moses Call is seen here in 1969 packing pumpkin seeds to be used for a contest sponsored by Falls Savings and Loan. Call, a successful farmer, was involved in several organizations, including the Stow Board of Education, the Darrow Street Grange, the Summit County Farm Bureau, the Central Ohio Breeders Association, and the Soil and Water Conservation Movement. His reputation as a businessman earned him a seat on the board of directors of the Falls Savings and Loan Association. (CJC.)

The logo for Osman's Pies was created for Lena Osman upon her retirement. The lady in the old-fashioned dress represents Lena, and the pies—two on the stove and one in her hand—represent the three pies she made on her first day in business. The logo has been used ever since Osman retired in 1967. Osman's Pies continued in operation until 2007, baking 200 pies during a typical day. (CC.)

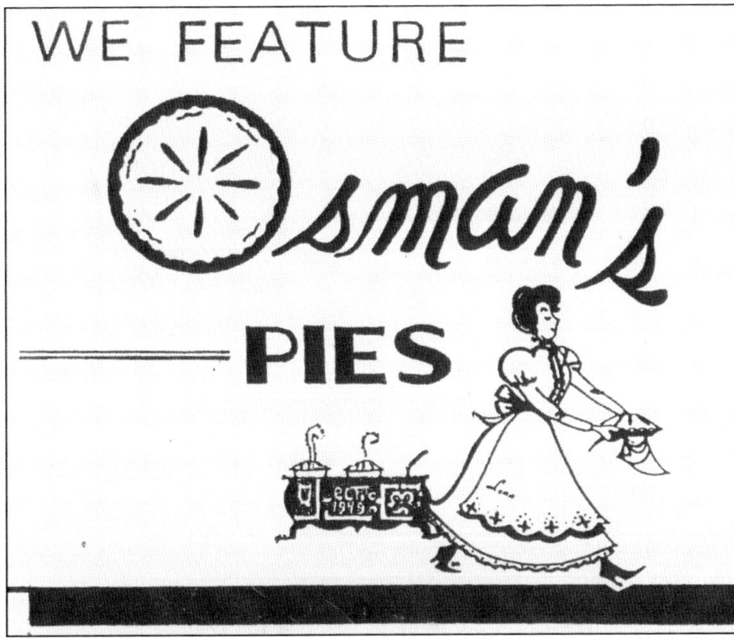

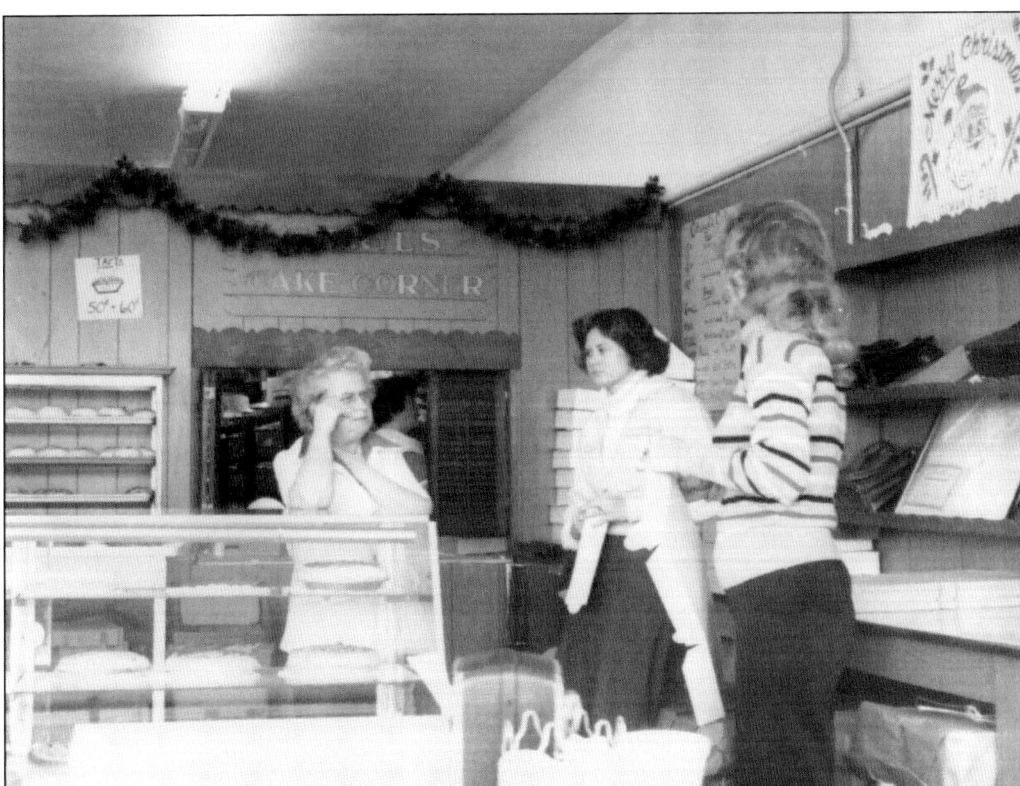

Ethel Osman, owner of Osman's Pies, stands at the pie counter with two employees in the 1970s. Osman took over the Pie Shop from her mother-in-law, Lena. Osman sold cakes as well as pies. Cheryl's Cake Corner was operated by Cheryl Crowe, the daughter of Ethel. (CC.)

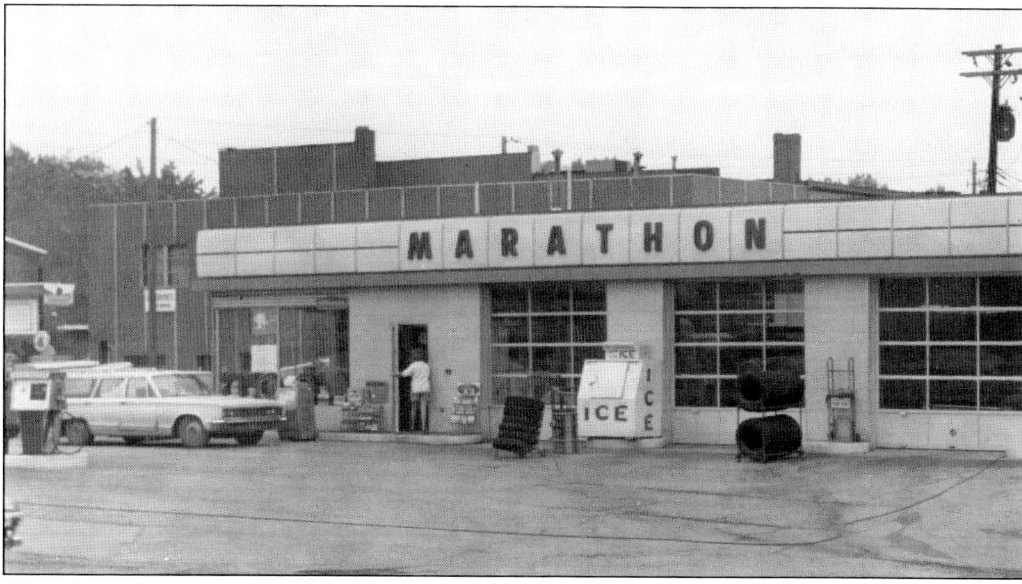

This Marathon station on the southeast corner of the Darrow and Kent Roads intersection was owned by Eddie Parsons until the 1970s. Before this was a Marathon station, it was an Amoco station. Parsons was a longtime business owner in Stow who also had a gas station on Yukon Road before this section of Darrow Road (U.S. Route 91) was opened in 1933. (FL.)

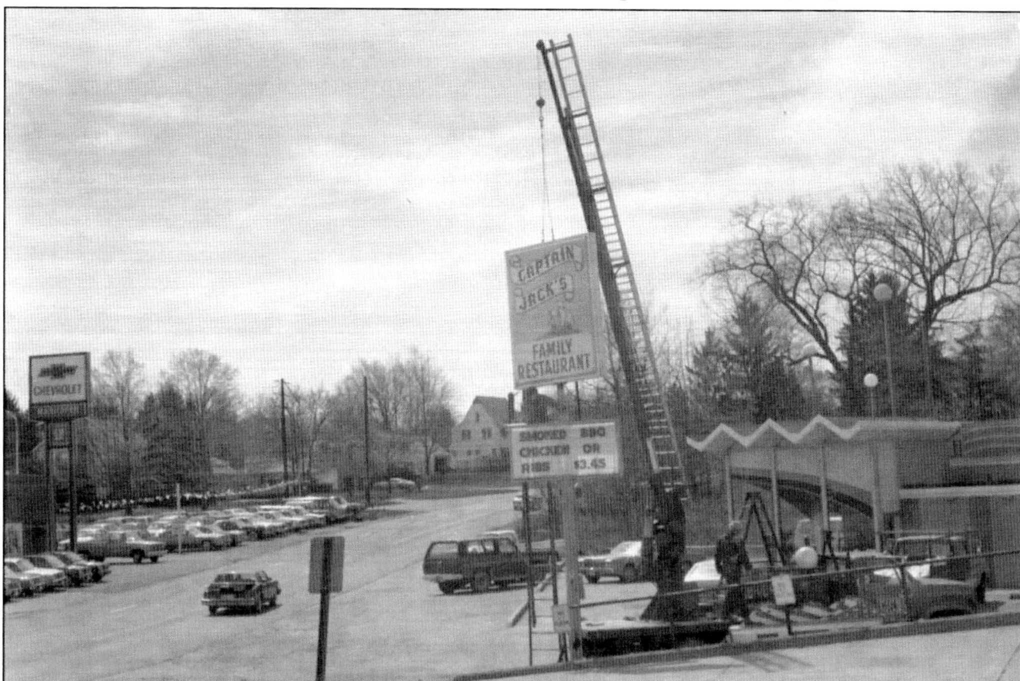

This restaurant at 3428 Darrow Road is situated south of the intersection of Darrow and Kent Roads, across from Marhofer Chevrolet. Behind (south) of the building is a beautiful wooded ravine. The restaurant has had several names over the years, including the original Tip Top Drive-In, the Flagpole, Captain Jack's, Charlie's, and currently Dave's Tip Top. The sign in this photograph features smoked barbecue chicken or ribs for $3.45. (FL.)

Six

Two Communities Looking toward the Future

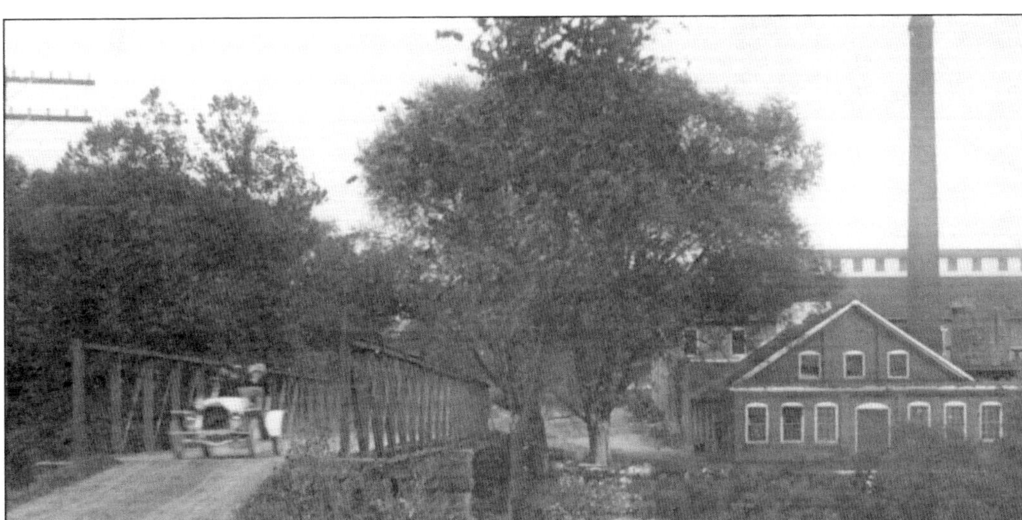

This undated postcard shows an automobile traveling north over the bridge in Munroe Falls. The U.S. Route 91 bridge crossed the Cuyahoga River. Munroe Falls Paper Mill is on the right. Railroad tracks are to the south of the river. (FL.)

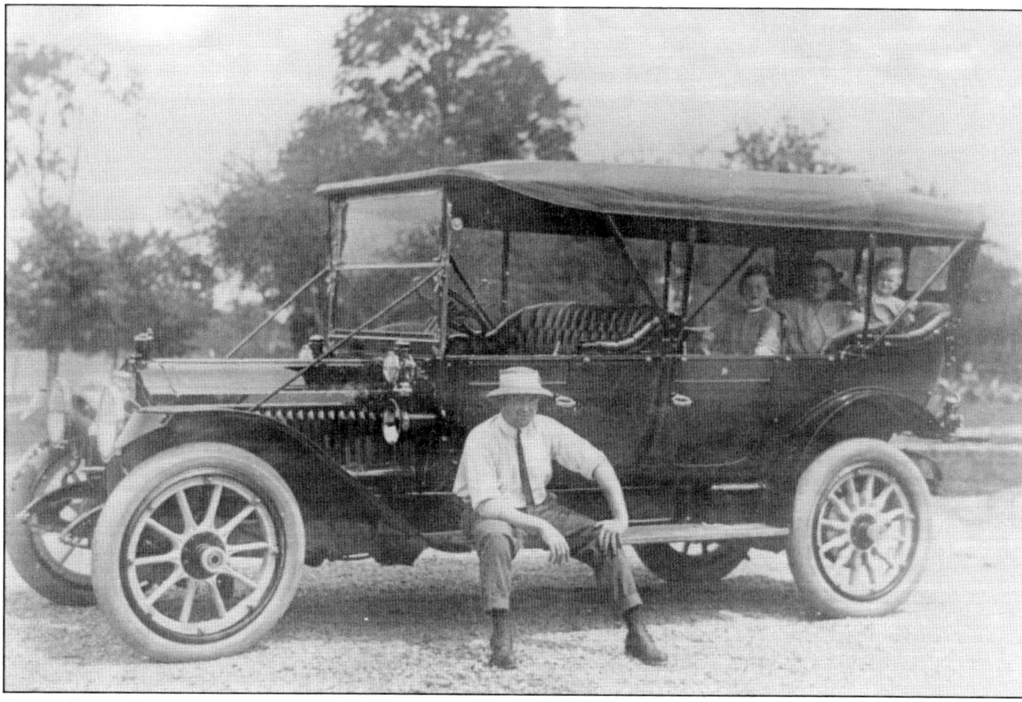

One of the first Packards in Summit County was owned by David Galehouse, owner of Galehouse Farm on Seasons Road in Stow. The property had been owned by William Calkins in the 1800s and by Warren Arnold in the 1920s. Arnold was the developer of Arnold's Acres, where Arndale Road is today. A portion of the original Galehouse 200-acre parcel is now occupied by the Seasons Nursing Home, previously known as Twin Pines Nursing Home. (FL.)

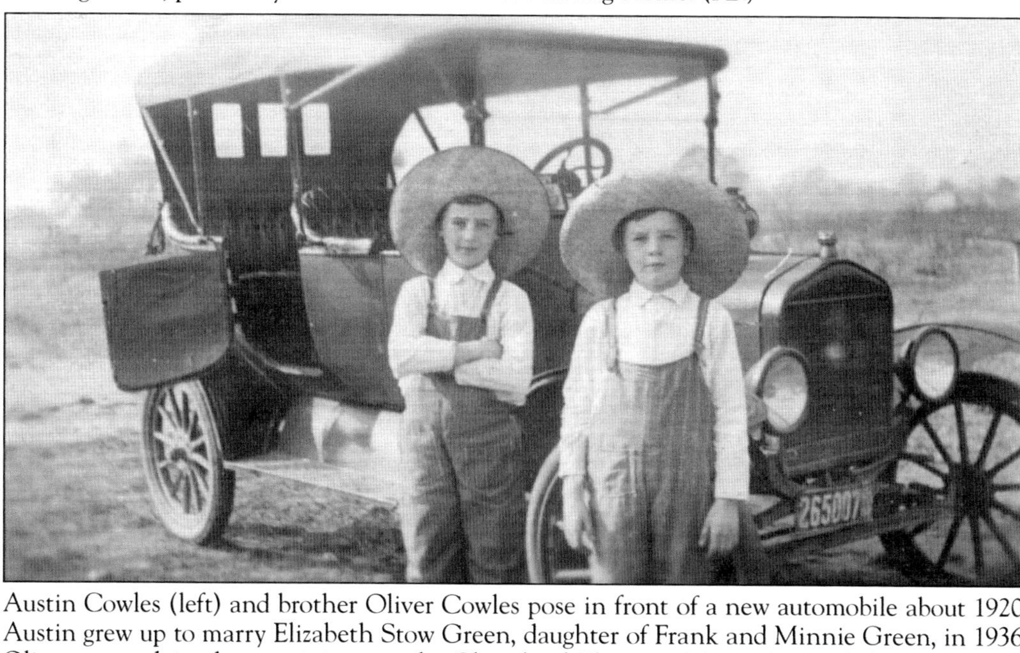

Austin Cowles (left) and brother Oliver Cowles pose in front of a new automobile about 1920. Austin grew up to marry Elizabeth Stow Green, daughter of Frank and Minnie Green, in 1936. Oliver was ordained as a minister in the Church of Christ in May 1931. Both boys graduated from Hiram College. (FL.)

This aerial photograph of Stow Corners was taken around 1939. Note the Church of Christ building in the northeast section. The Stow Town Hall/Stow Public Library building had not yet been moved to become the Children's Chapel. The building on the northeast corner held Acme Store No. 14 and Braunlich's Drug Store. The Sohio station was on the northwest corner and Stow Hardware was on the southwest corner. (FL.)

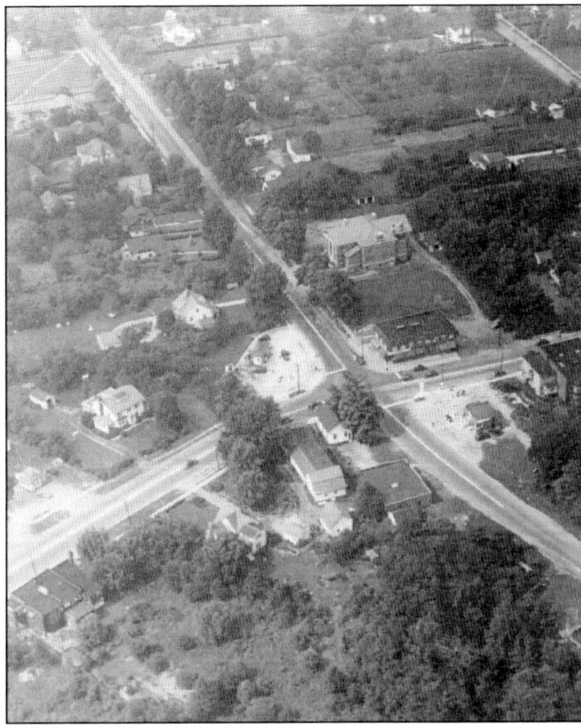

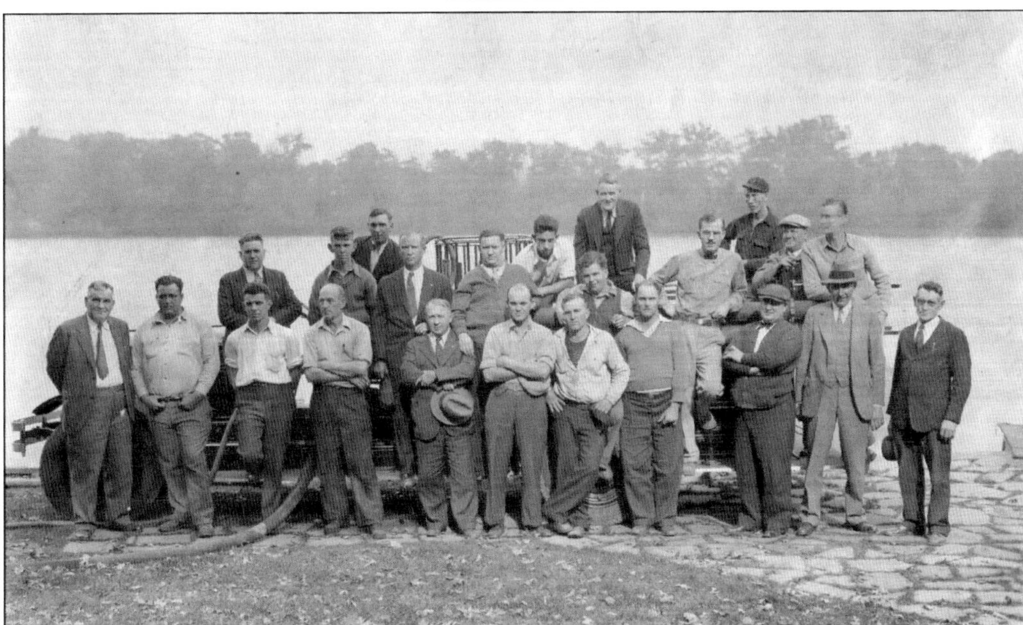

Starting in 1933, Stow was serviced by a volunteer fire department. Volunteers listed on the back of this photograph include, from left to right, (first row) P. R. Kent, K. Deacon, M. A. Patterson, H. E. Osman, W. F. Carlisle, C. W. Marhofer, C. Flitcraft, ? Gilliam, ? Siler, O. Spaght, and ? Herwick; (second row) L. B. Wheeler, K. Putt, J. H. Chipps, A. F. Stein, M. Bee, J. F. Porter, A. Neville, and O. Walters; (third row) H. Spaight, J. Green, J. P. McGrail, and C. Lantz. Silver Lake is seen in the background. (FL.)

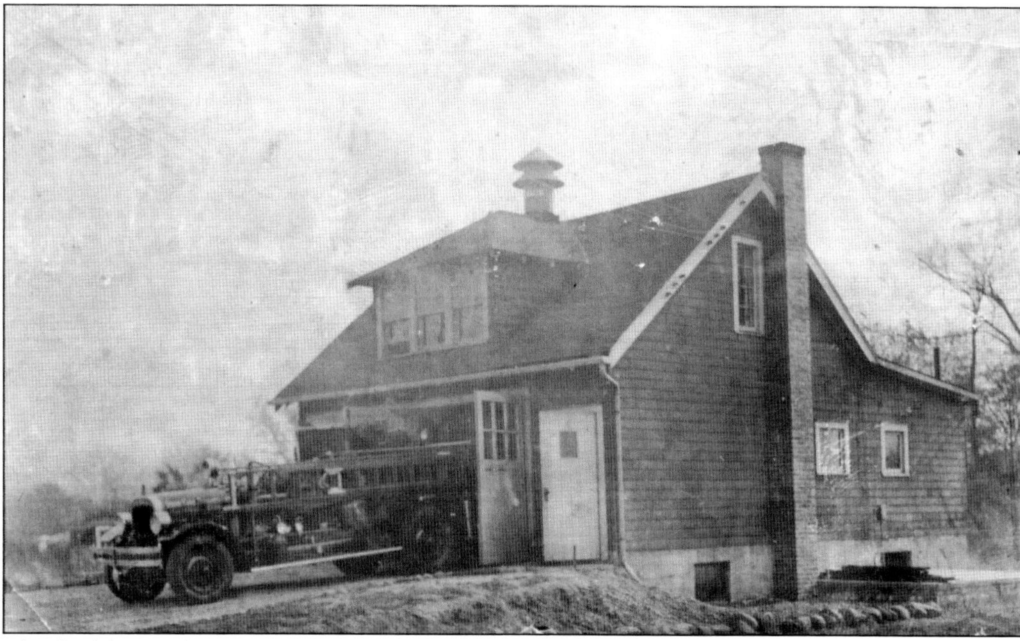

This building, a former garage, was donated in 1941 to be used as a fire station on Kent Road in Stow. In 1940, the Stow Volunteer Fire Department had a roster of 25 members providing fire protection to Stow and the surrounding communities. Twenty-four-hour service was maintained with one man on duty at all times. The equipment included a 1926 Seagraves fire truck with 500 gallons per-minute capacity and one chemical truck. (FL.)

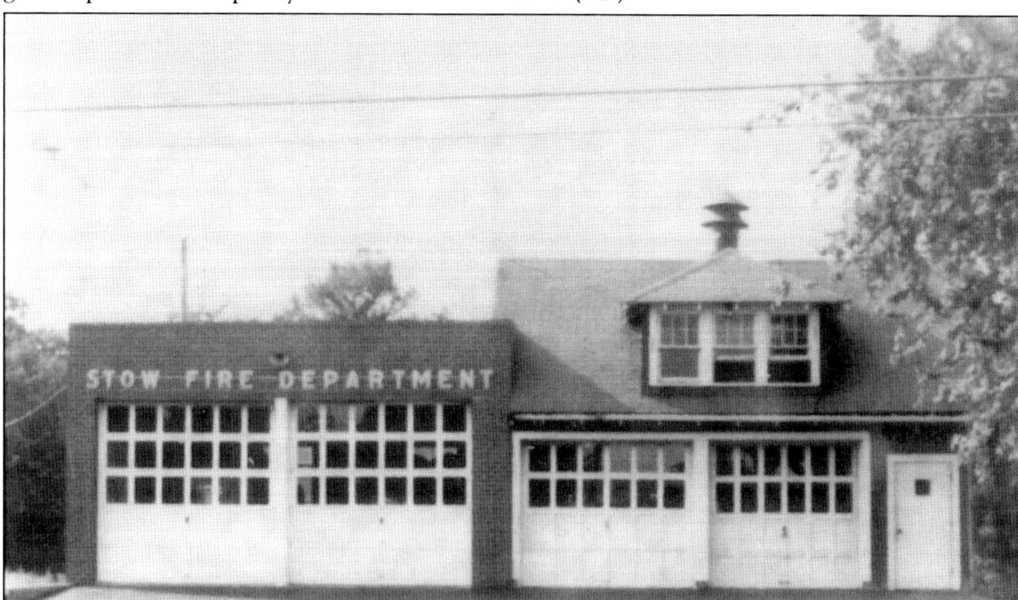

By 1946, the Stow Fire Department had expanded the garage on the first permanent firehouse, which was located on Kent Road. Stow was responsible for the fire protection of Tallmadge until 1943 and of Munroe Falls until 1949. In 1963, a second fire station was built on Commerce Drive. Four years later, a building on the southwest corner of Darrow and Kent Roads was remodeled to replace the first permanent firehouse. (FL.)

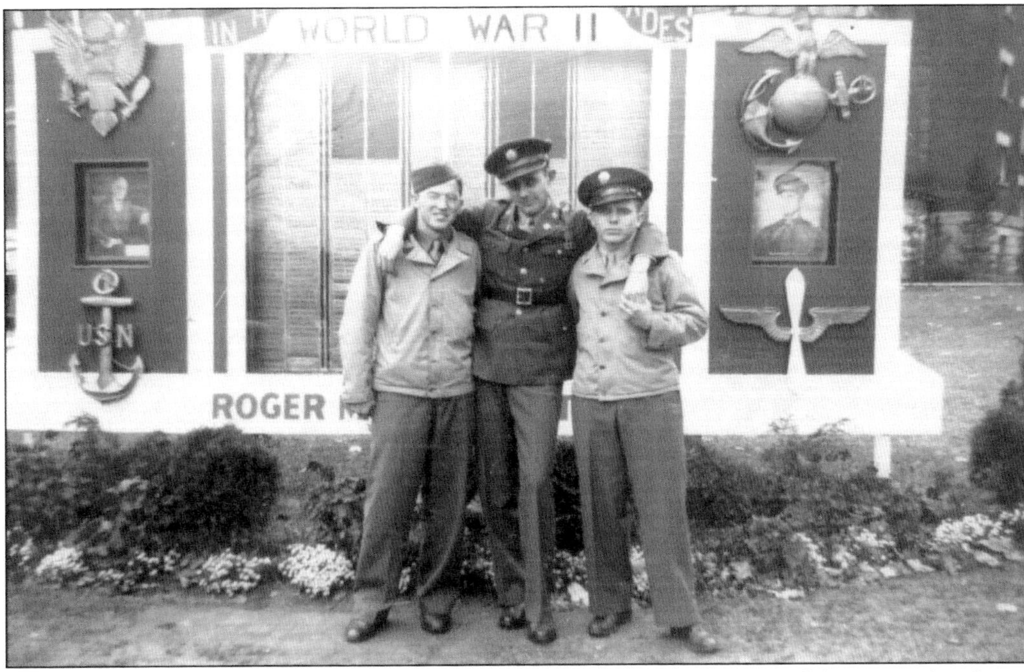

During World War II, a sign was erected in front of Stow Township Hall honoring local men and women serving in the war. Returning servicemen, such as the ones pictured here, visited the memorial as soon as they returned home in order to check on their classmates and friends. Each corner of the billboard held a hand-carved insignia representing one of the four branches of the U.S. Armed Forces. (FL.)

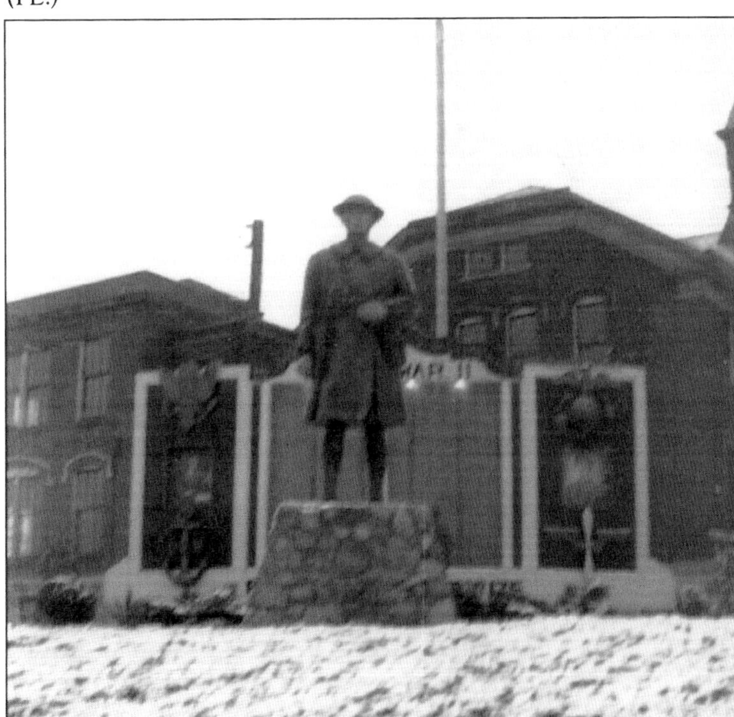

The original World War I Doughboy statue stood in front of Stow Township City Hall for over 30 years. The statue was donated to the American Legion and the City of Stow by Jerry Ricketts of Stow. The doughboy kept watch over Stow until 1979, when it was damaged during the widening of U.S. Route 91. Through the efforts of the citizens of Stow, money for a new statue was raised, and the current doughboy was dedicated on November 9, 1996. (SMFPL.)

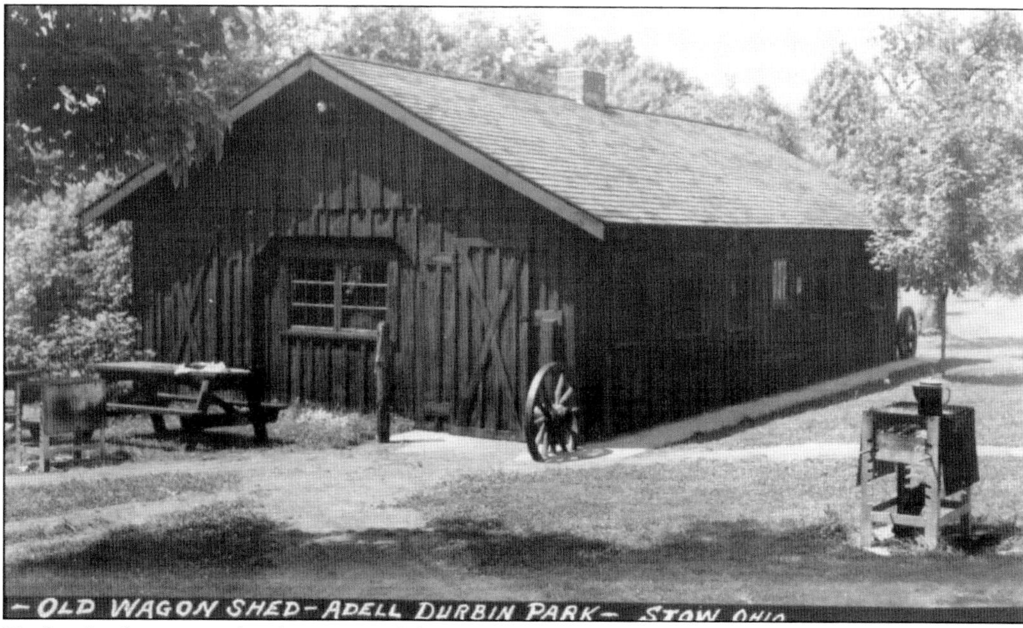

Under the direction of park manager John Denning, several buildings, including Chestnut Lodge (later renamed Denning Lodge), the Sugar House, and the Wagon Shed, were constructed in Adell Durbin Park. Construction on the Wagon Shed was completed in 1950. The building was used for a time by the Stow Historical Society for a meeting place and to store historical artifacts. Denning was park manager from 1946 to 1956. (FL.)

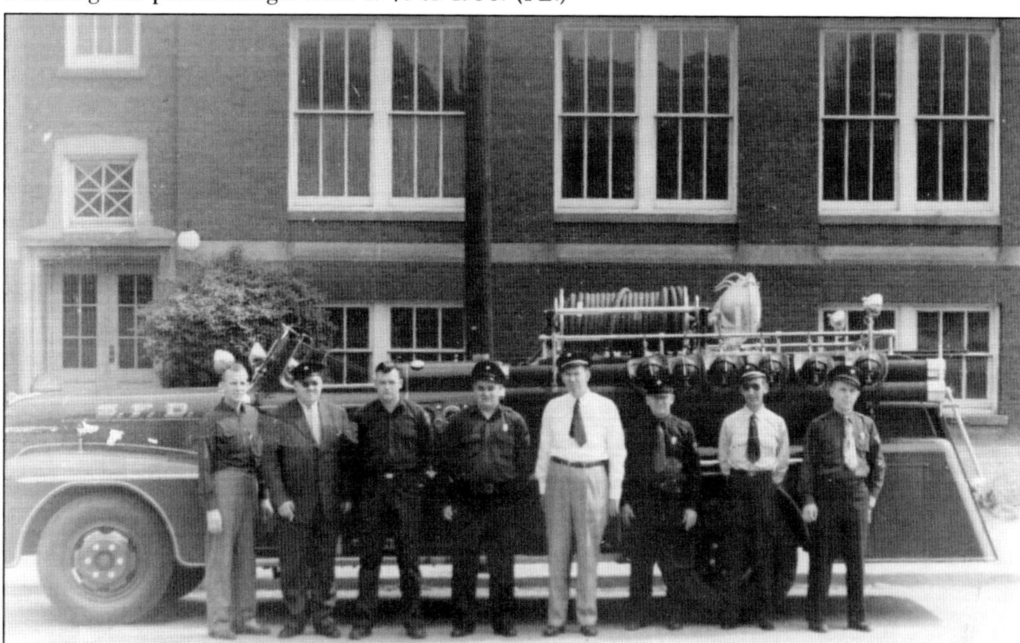

Members of the Stow Volunteer Fire Department pose in front of their Ahrens-Fox fire truck in this photograph taken on Decoration Day in 1950. Pictured from left to right are Paul Montieth, Bob MacAdams, Howard Osman, Jim Worcester, Chief Charles Perrine, Howard Poole, Carl Lantz, and Ralph Saxe. (FL.)

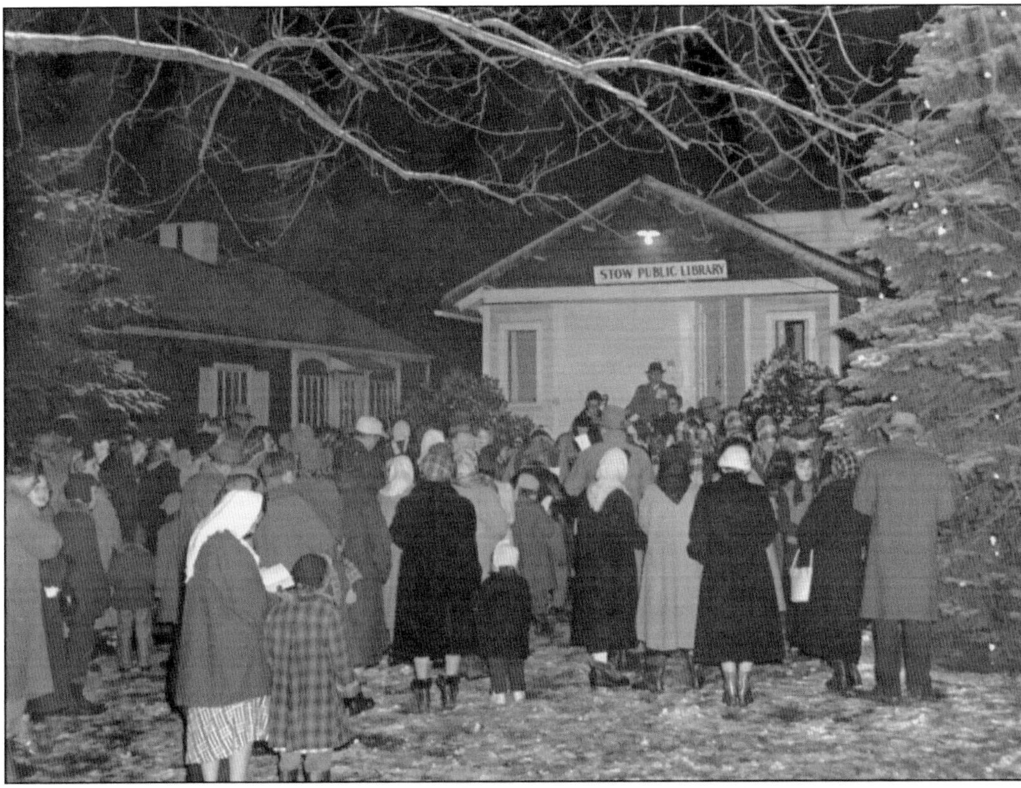

Christmas carolers surround the front porch of the Stow Public Library in this *c.* 1954 photograph. During the tenure of Librarian Marion King, from 1932 to 1937, a spruce tree on the front lawn of the library was decorated by firemen from the Stow Fire Department and a community sing was held. The tree was originally donated by the Stow Culture Club. (SMFPL.)

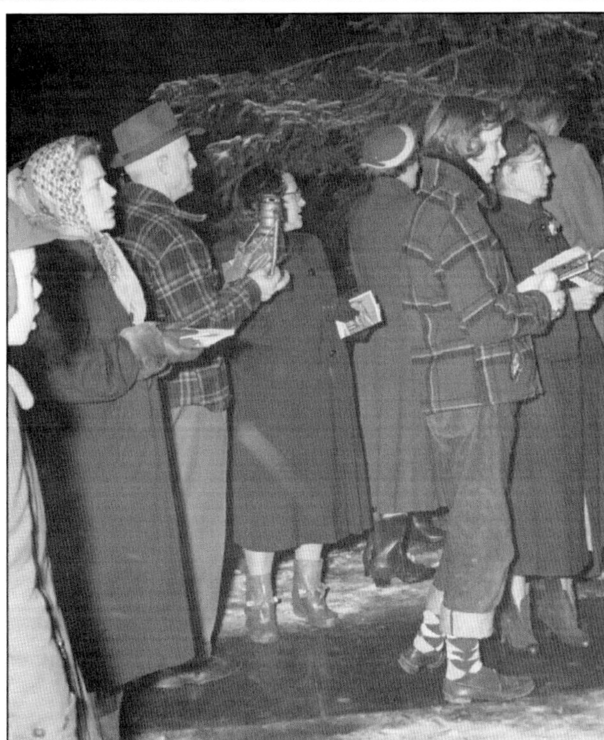

Christmas carolers at the Stow Public Library in 1954 included, from left to right, Steven Lamb, Pauline Bagat, Jack Whalen, Grace Whalen, Kathy Cowles, and Mary Palmer. Dorothy A. Stair (Saviers) was head librarian during the 1950s. (SMFPL.)

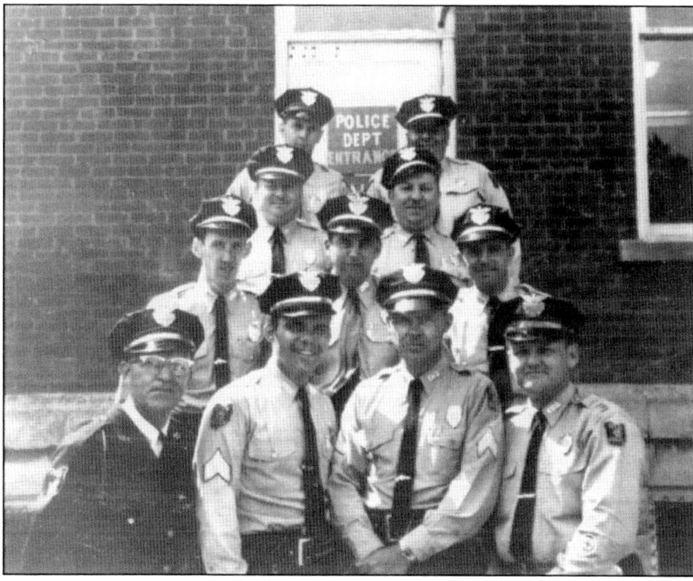

Stow Police Department had seven officers and four volunteers in 1960. Pictured from left to right (first row) are Chief Robert Woodard, Sgt. Richard Robison, Sgt. Robert Flavel, and Capt. Ronald Harper; (second row) patrolmen Dick Saxe, Fred Long, and Phillip Large; (third row) Robert Hill and Frank Polinger; (fourth row) LaVern Speck and Floyd Hill. The police department started with one room in the basement of Stow City Hall. (FL.)

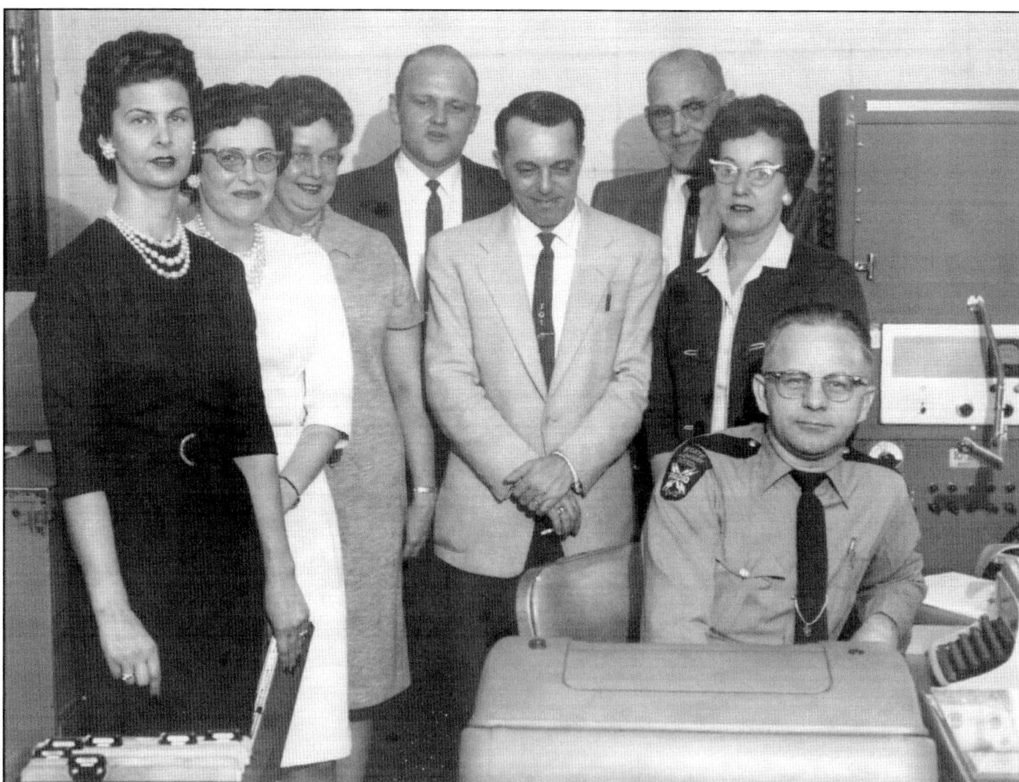

This *c.* 1962 photograph features the Stow Police Department dispatchers and other personnel. Pictured from left to right are dispatchers Macel Chicoine, Charlene (Wickiser) Jenney, and Luella Miller, Stow chief of police Ronald Harper, patrolman Phil Large, dispatcher Harley Hale, secretary Meryle (Cavanan) Large, and (seated) an Ohio State Patrol instructor. (FL.)

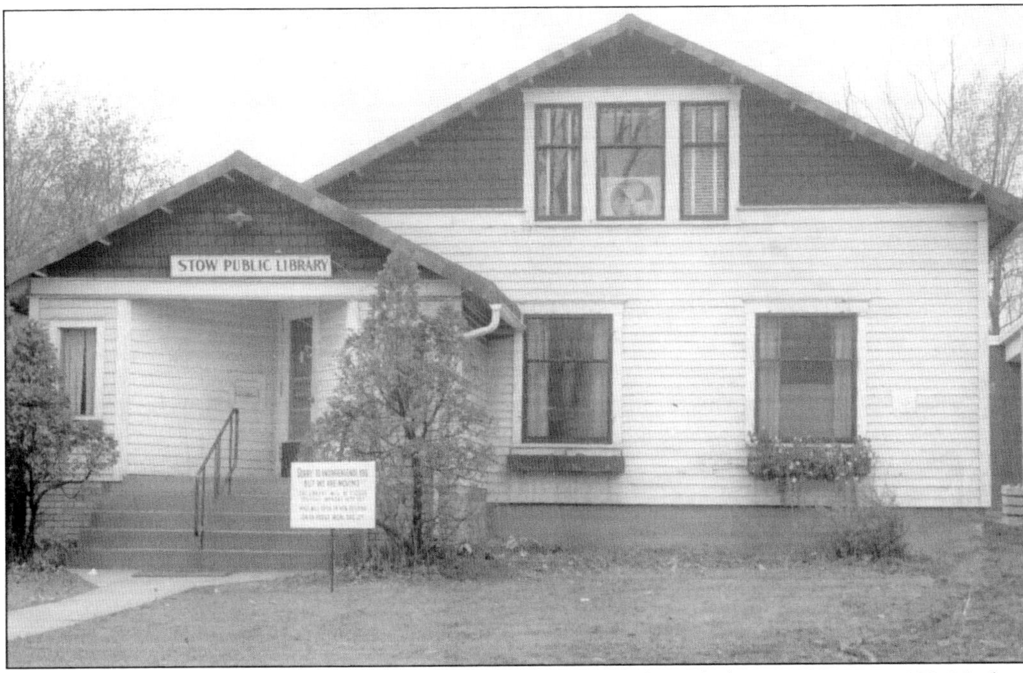

In 1930, the Stow Public Library Board of Trustees purchased this property at 122 Hudson Road (now Darrow Road) for $8,500. The library was then moved from the small township hall building into this house where it remained until 1963. During that time, many changes were instituted at the library, including full cataloging of the collection and detailed circulation records. During the 1940s, the house was enlarged and the side porch was enclosed to accommodate more patrons. (SMFPL.)

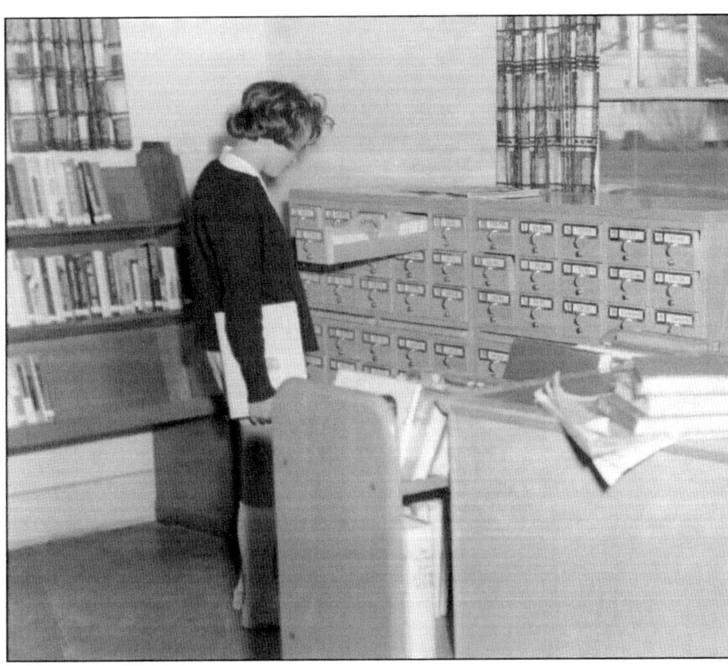

This photograph of a patron using the card catalog was taken before the closing of the old Stow Public Library in 1963. In the 1950s, under the direction of librarian Dorothy A. Stair (Saviers), the library installed its first telephone, purchased a mimeograph machine, hired the first shelvers, and hired the first library assistant. By 1963, the staff had grown to six, and the yearly circulation was over 100,000. (SMFPL.)

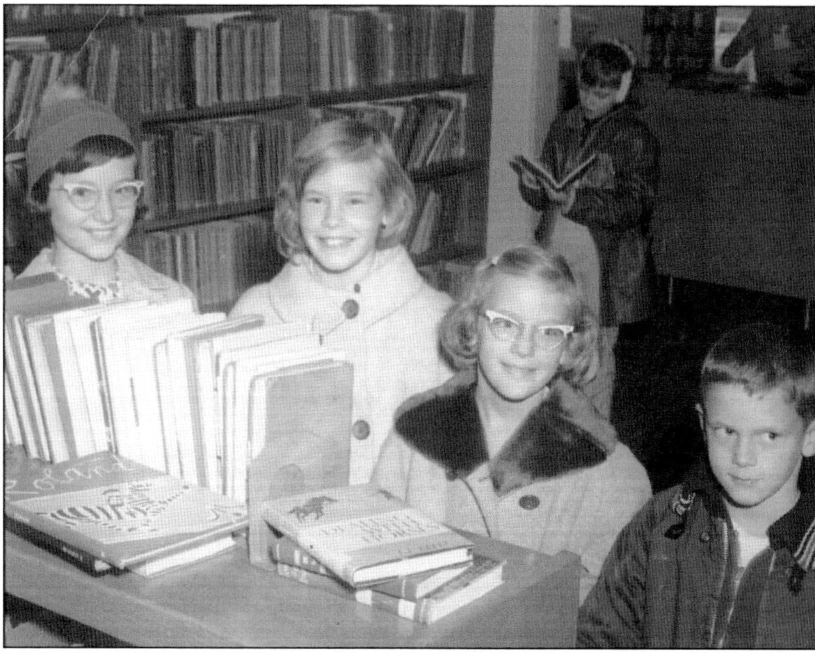

Four young students pose inside the Stow Public Library in 1963. Soon after this photograph was taken, the old Stow Public Library building was closed, and materials were moved into a brand new building next to the old one. (SMFPL.)

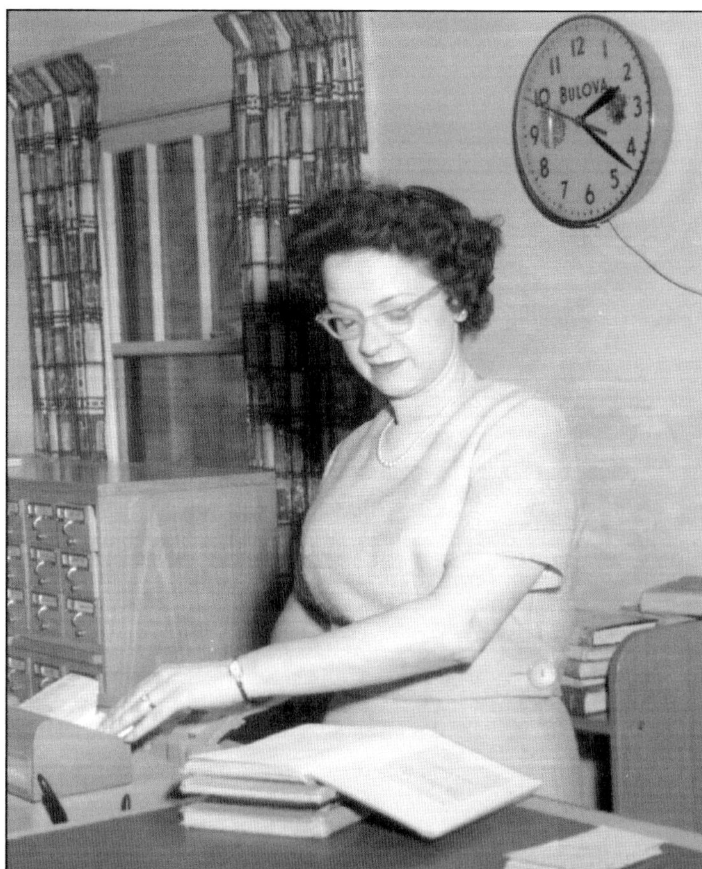

Dorothy A. Stair (Saviers) was head librarian at Stow Public Library from June 1949 to November 1963. Saviers, a graduate of Kent State University, oversaw many changes at the library, including the planning of a new building. In 1963, there were nearly 5,000 registered library borrowers. (SMFPL.)

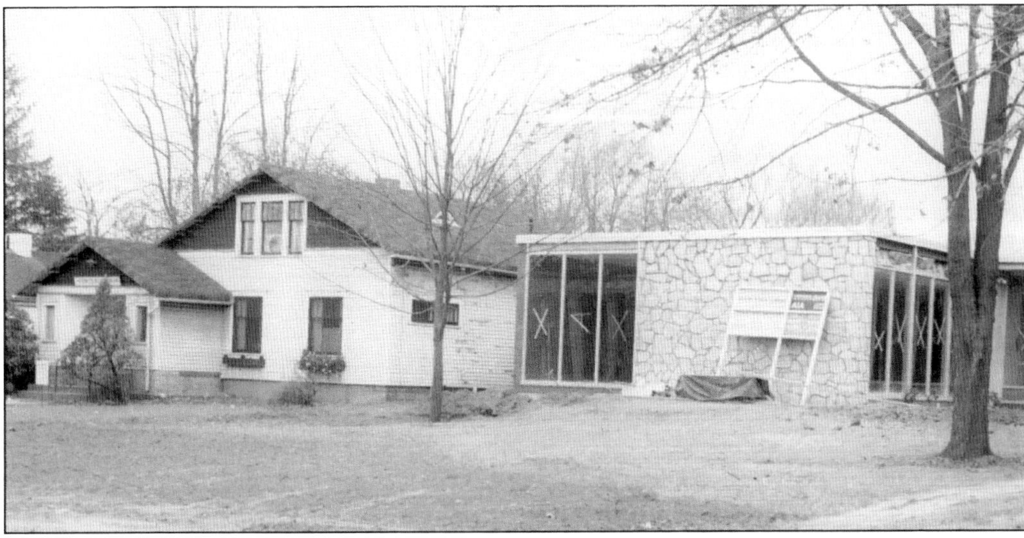

In 1960, the board of trustees of the Stow Public Library purchased property for the building of a new library. In 1963, construction began on the property adjacent to the old library building. The two buildings were so close together that boxes of books were moved via ramps straight from the old building into the new. The grand opening of the new library was held in February 1964. (SMFPL.)

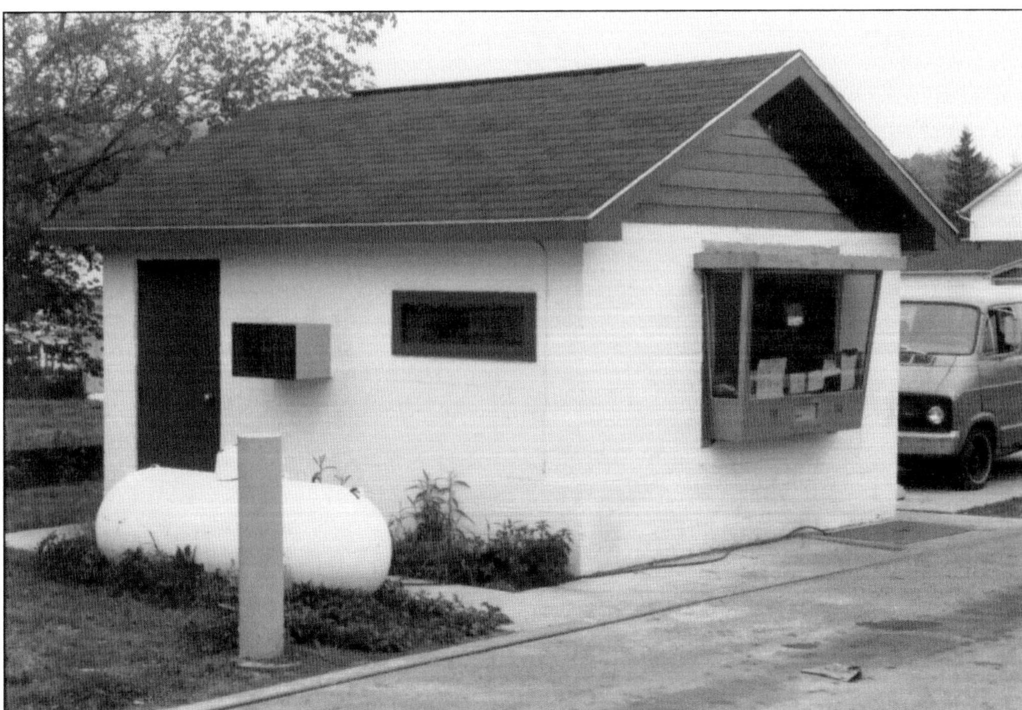

This weigh station in Munroe Falls, built about 1960, was used by residents to recycle paper. Sonoco paid for scrap newspapers to recycle and make cardboard tubes for wax paper, orange juice cans, and other products. An official at the weigh station examined a car before and after the paper was unloaded to determine how many pounds of paper were being delivered. (MFHS.)

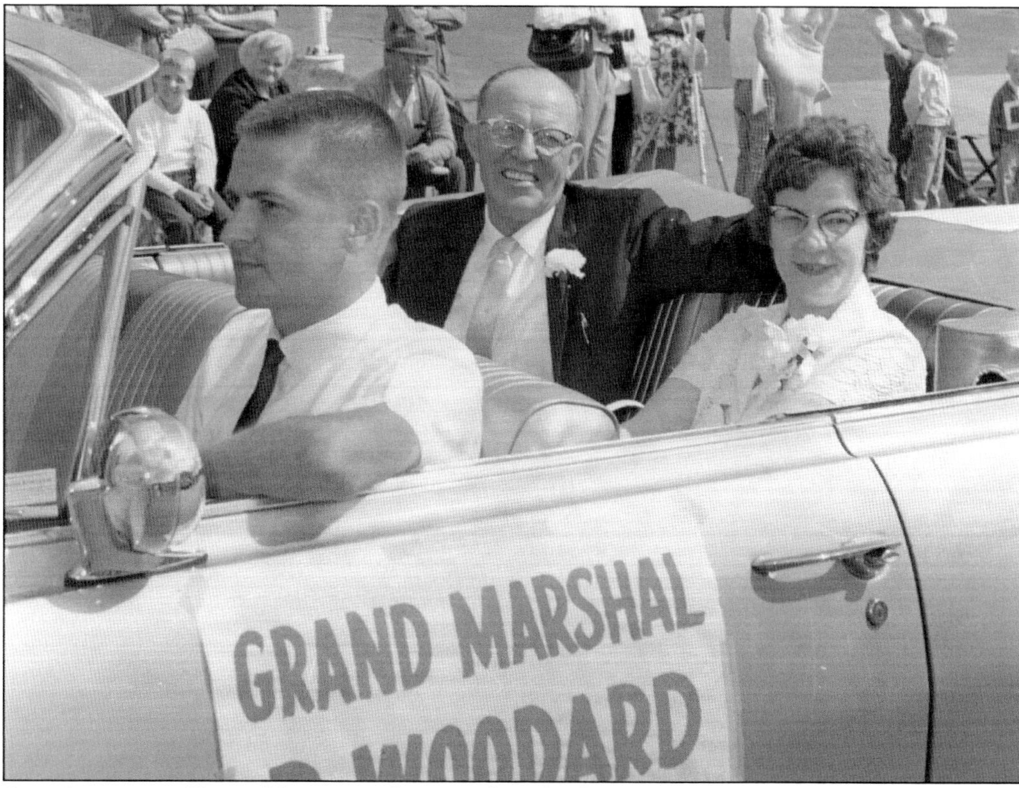

Stow fire captain Howard Osman and Stow police chief Robert Woodard were the grand marshals of the 1964 Stow Independence Day Parade. Osman and Woodard founded it in 1959 and managed to put together a parade of 40 units in less than three weeks. The parade followed the same route it does today, going west on U.S. Route 59 from the Stow-Kent Plaza area to Holy Family Church. The first parade had floats, bands, antique cars, horses, and dignitaries. (Both SMFPL.)

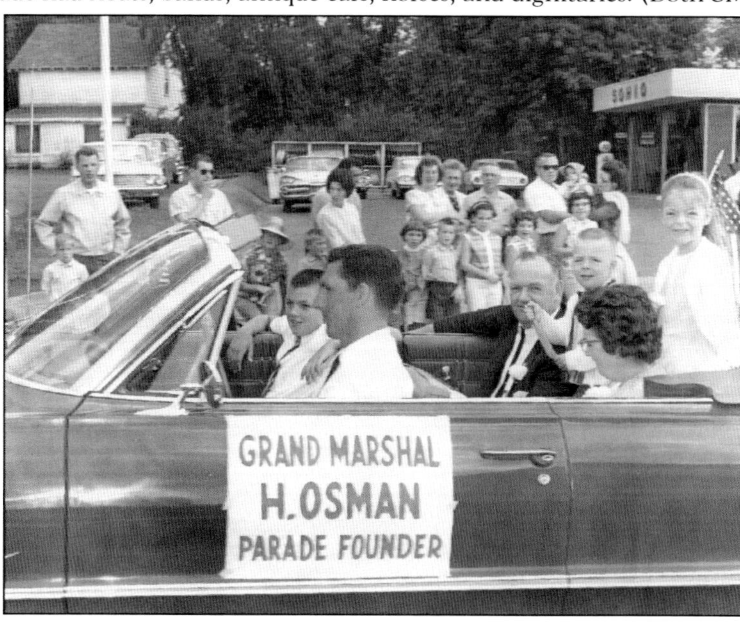

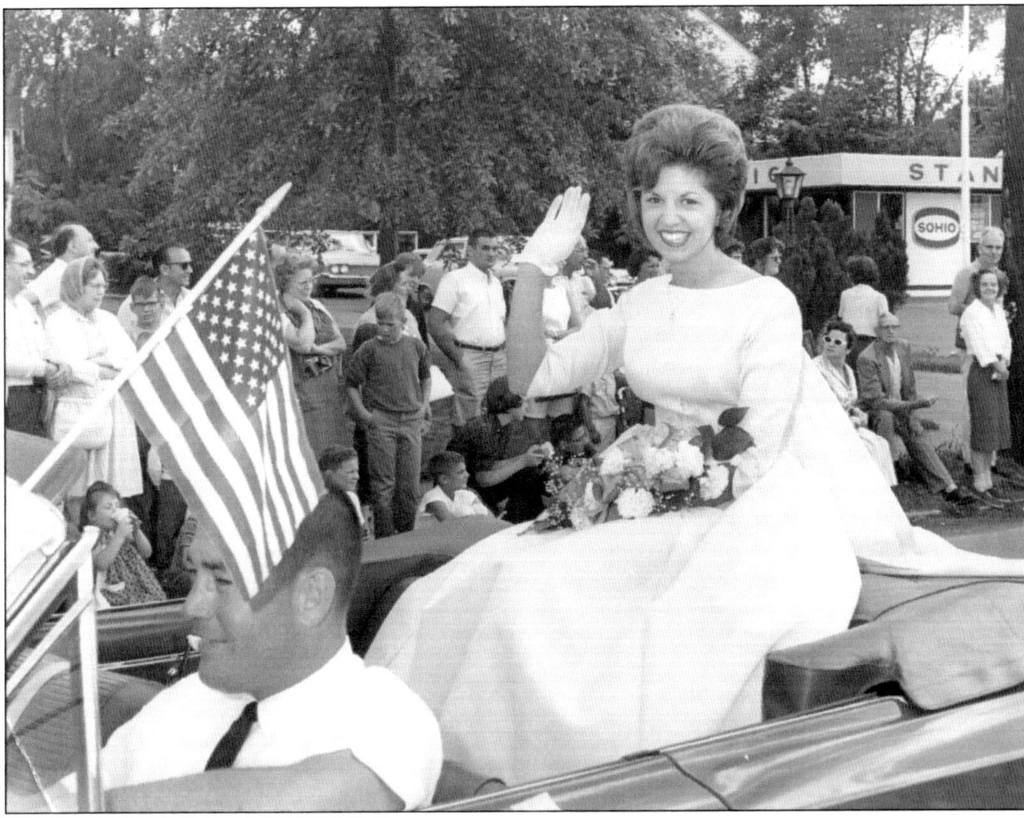

Stow parade queen Karen Breed rides in an open convertible in the fifth-annual Stow Independence Day Parade in 1964. Founded in 1959, the annual parade is one of the largest in the state of Ohio. The 1964 parade had 191 units and included 2,382 participants. (SMFPL.)

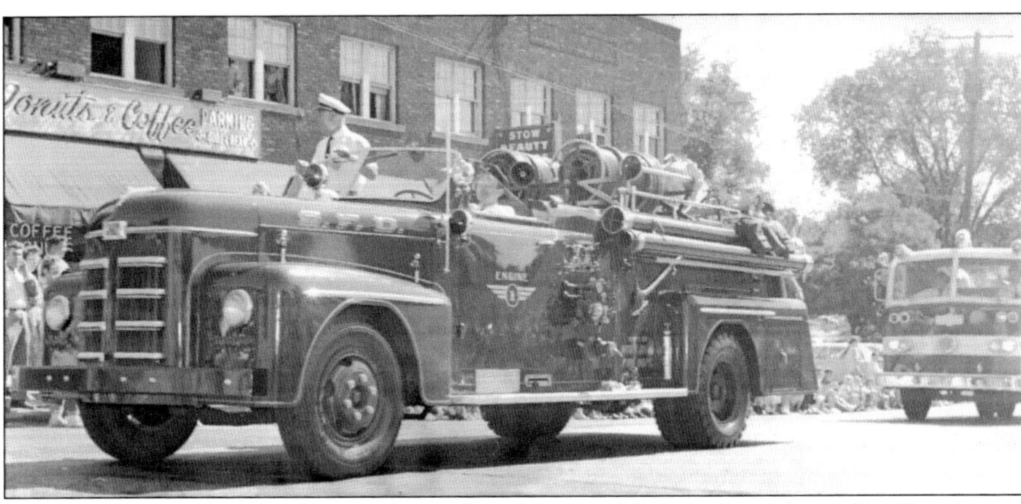

The Stow Fire Department has participated in the annual Stow Independence Day Parade every year since the parade started in 1959. This undated photograph shows Floyd Gaylord driving and fire chief Ralph Saxe standing looking at the crowd. The Ahrens-Fox fire truck is from around 1940. (FL.)

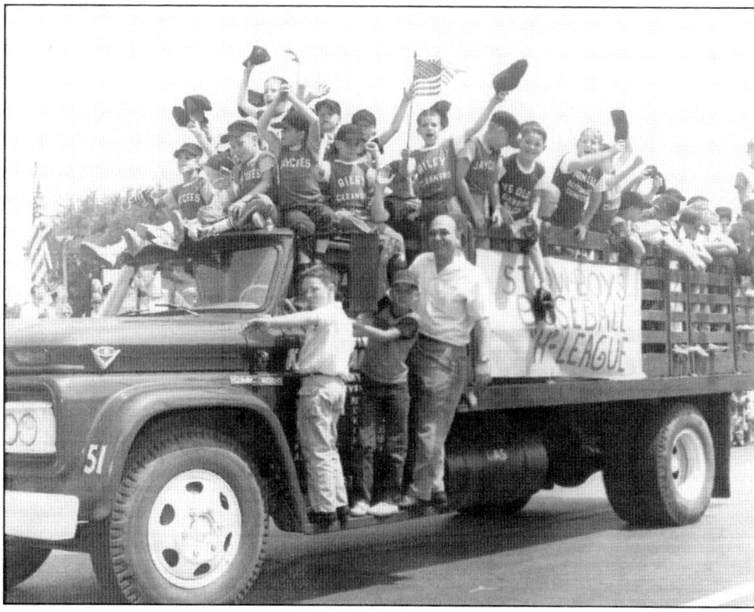

The Stow Boys Baseball League was one of 245 units participating in the 1965 Stow Independence Day Parade. The theme for the parade that year was "The Stars and Stripes Forever." Every participating unit was encouraged to carry a flag in the parade. Some of the league sponsors written on the boys' shirts were Jaycees, Riley Cleaners, and Ye Old Barber Shop. (SMFPL.)

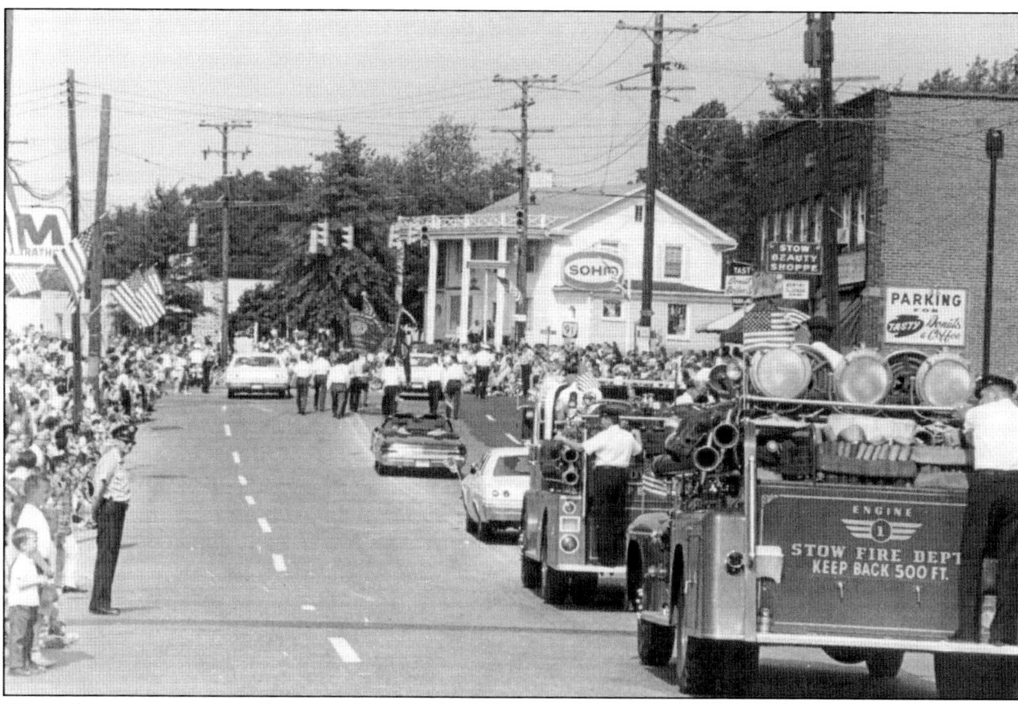

This photograph was taken on July 4, 1965, during the Stow Independence Day Parade. The parade is heading west on Kent Road toward Holy Family Church. The brick building on the right, housing Stow Beauty Shoppe and Tasty Donuts, is no longer standing. The large white building on the right was constructed by Titus Wetmore. Formerly the Gregory Funeral Home, it has been the site of the Dunn-Quigley Funeral Home since 1965. (SMFPL.)

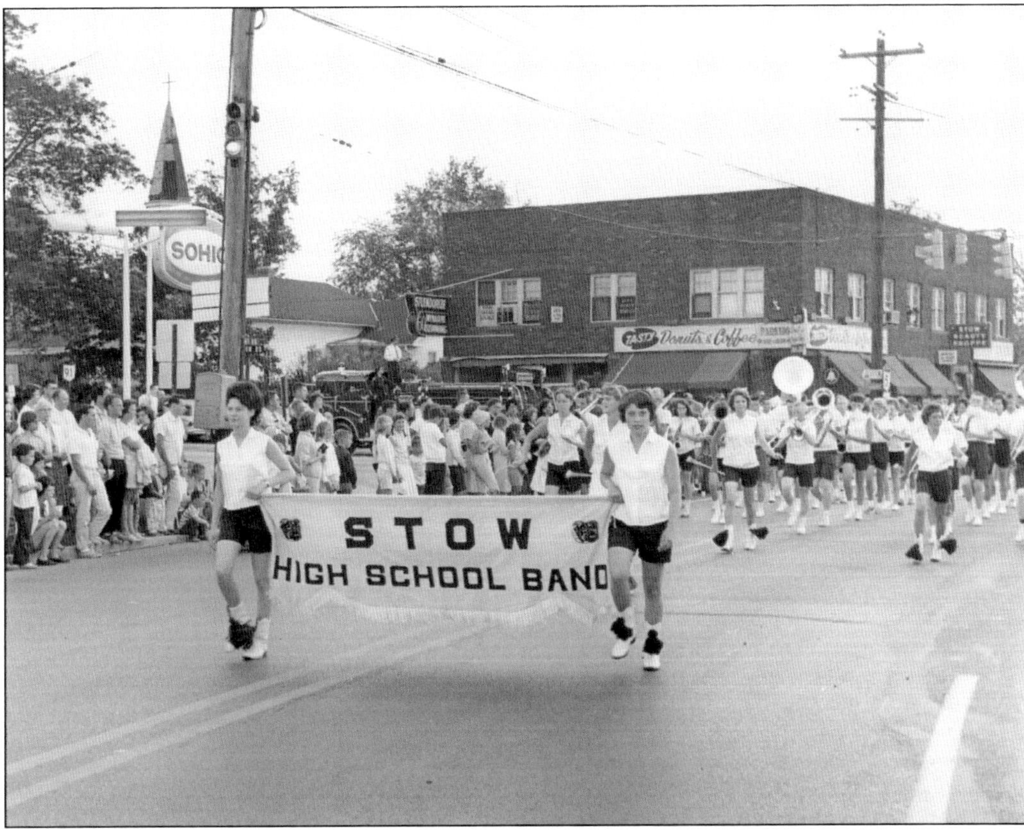

The Stow High School Band marches past Stow Corners in this 1966 photograph of the Stow Independence Day Parade. William Newenheisen was band director. According to the 1966 *Stoanno*, Stow had twin marching bands to liven up the halftime show at football games. (SMFPL.)

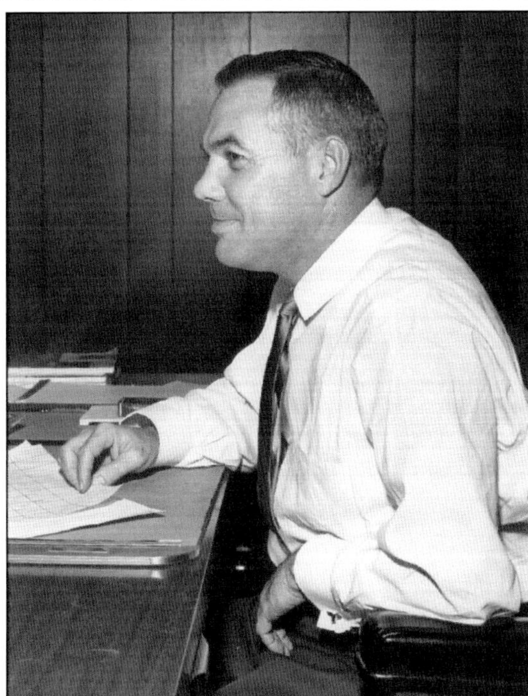

Stow mayor Roger Howard is seated at his desk in this November 1964 photograph. Howard was Stow's second mayor, defeating incumbent Charles H. Montieth. Howard served from 1963 until 1975, when he accepted a position with the State of Ohio. City council president Donald A. Powell then became acting mayor until Paul Hutchison was elected in 1976. Howard is remembered as being very active in bringing Stow from a sleepy, rural community to an up-to-date, modern city. (SMFPL.)

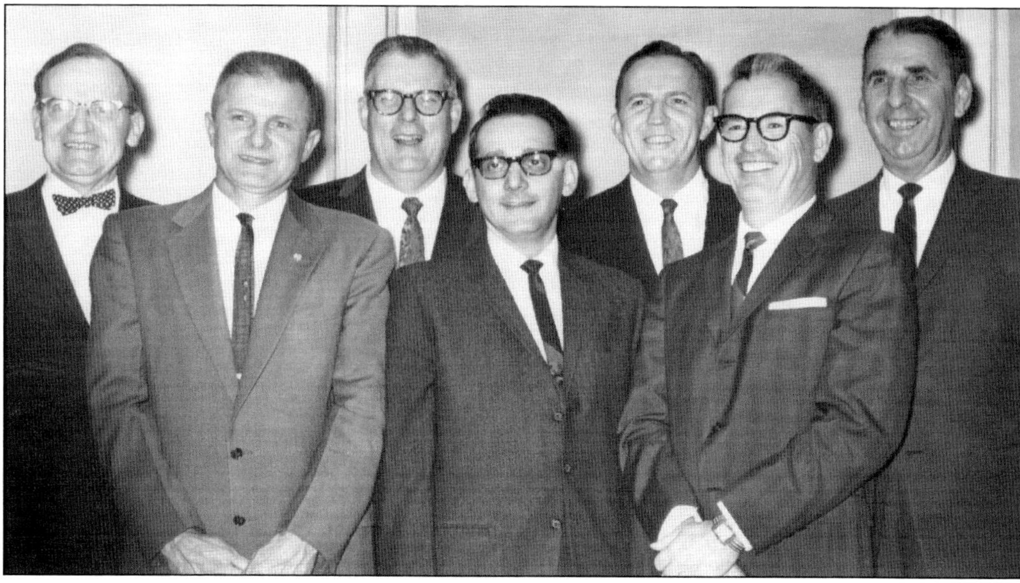

Pictured are members of Stow City Council around 1964. They are, from left to right, Robert Pickton, Melvin Fritz, Harold Patterson, Howard Swiedel, Wesley Clark, Thomas Clarke, and Lawrence Saltis. Members served under Stow mayor Roger Howard. (SMFPL.)

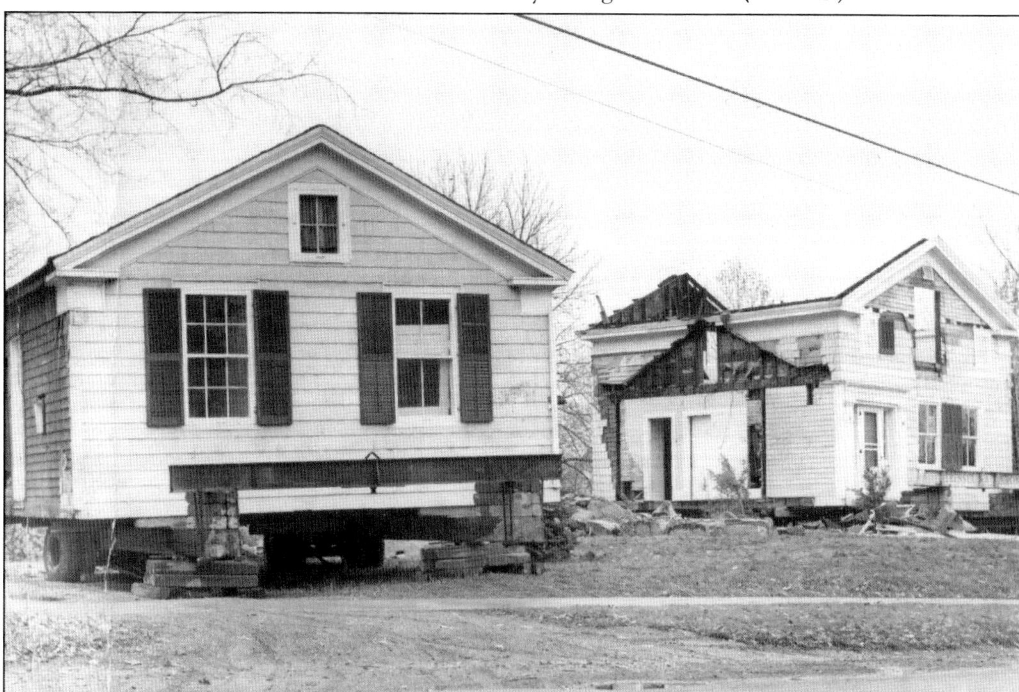

This house, built in 1832, and subsequently owned by the Erastus Southmayd and Edwin S. Wetmore families, was sold in 1966 to the Portage National Bank of Kent as a site for a branch office. The bank generously donated the house to the Western Reserve Historical Society to be placed on the Hale Farm site in Bath Township, where it serves as a testament to the history of the pioneers of the Western Reserve of Connecticut. (FL.)

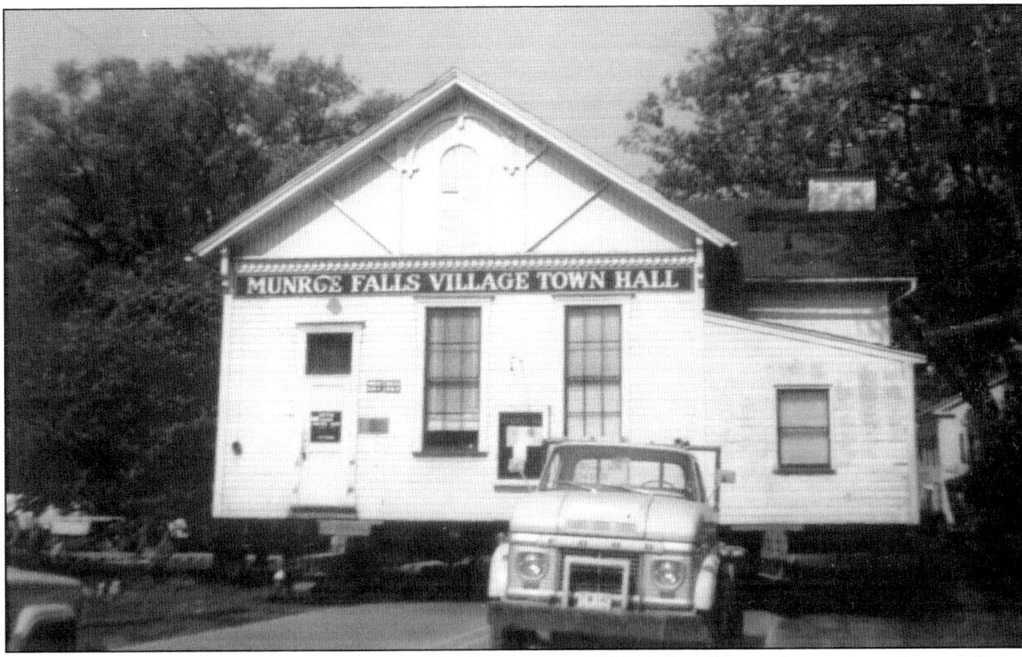

The Munroe Falls Town Hall was originally the Munroe Falls Schoolhouse located on the southwest corner of Munroe Falls Avenue and U.S. Route 91. It was built in 1885 and used for students until 1916 when Munroe Falls merged with the Stow Township School District. The building was moved to its present location at 43 Munroe Falls Avenue sometime in the 1960s. (MFHS.)

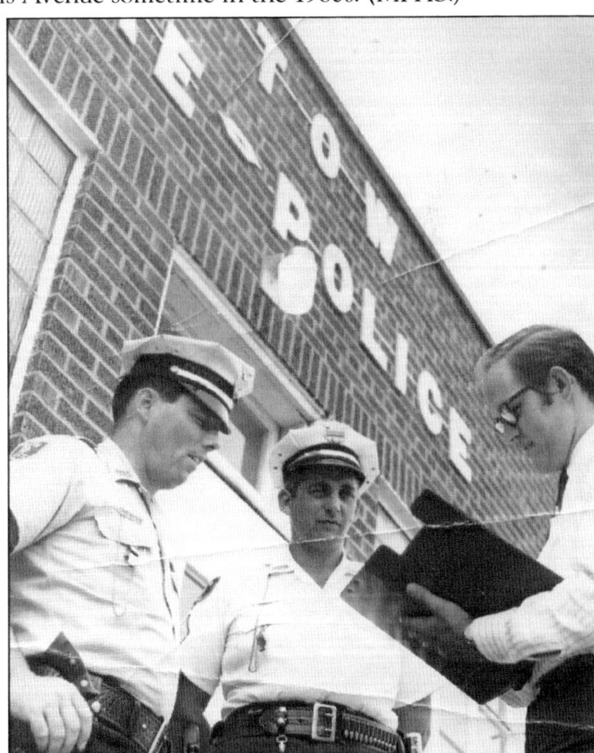

Patrolman Robert Bisbin (left) and Sgt. Fred Long are seen here being interviewed by reporter Jim Strang of the *Record Courier* during the grand opening of the new police station and fire department facility on July 17, 1967. The City of Stow purchased the vacant Becker Wholesale Foods building at the intersection of Kent and Darrow Roads when both departments outgrew their previous facilities. The building was used for another 27 years. (FL.)

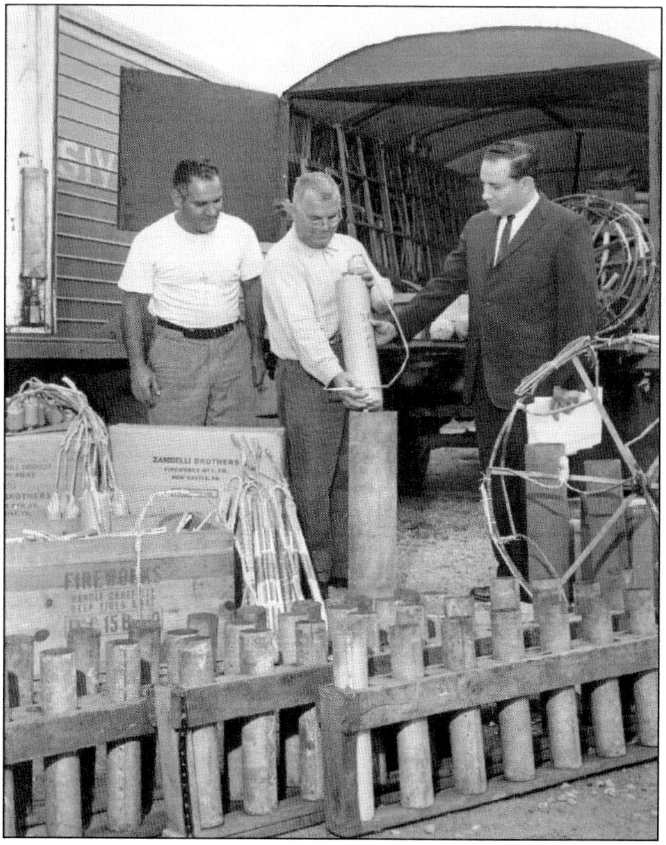

This 1968 photograph is of three men inspecting fireworks for the Stow Fourth of July celebration. The fireworks display, held at the Andrew W. Paton (Kent State University) Airport on U.S. Route 59 in Stow, was sponsored by the Stow Independence Day Commemoration Committee. Fireworks were by the Zambelli Brothers Company. The donation to attend was $1 per car and 25¢ for walk-ins. (SMFPL.)

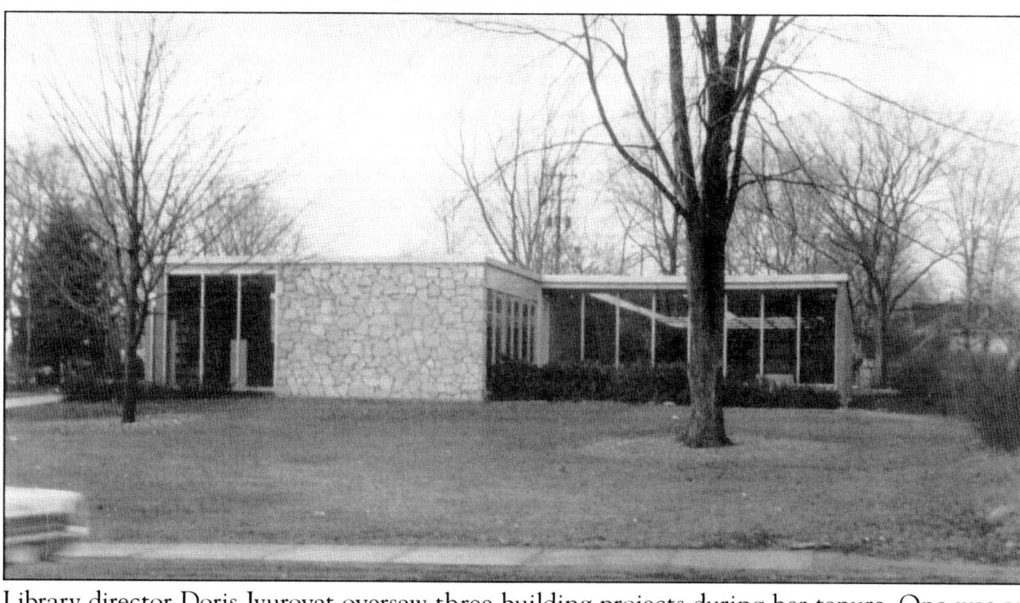

Library director Doris Jyurovat oversaw three building projects during her tenure. One was an additional 1,220 square feet added to Stow Public Library in 1973. By 1974, circulation had grown to over 220,000, and the staff was increased from 11 in 1963 to 22 in 1974. Jyurovat also began evening hours in the 1970s. (SMFPL.)

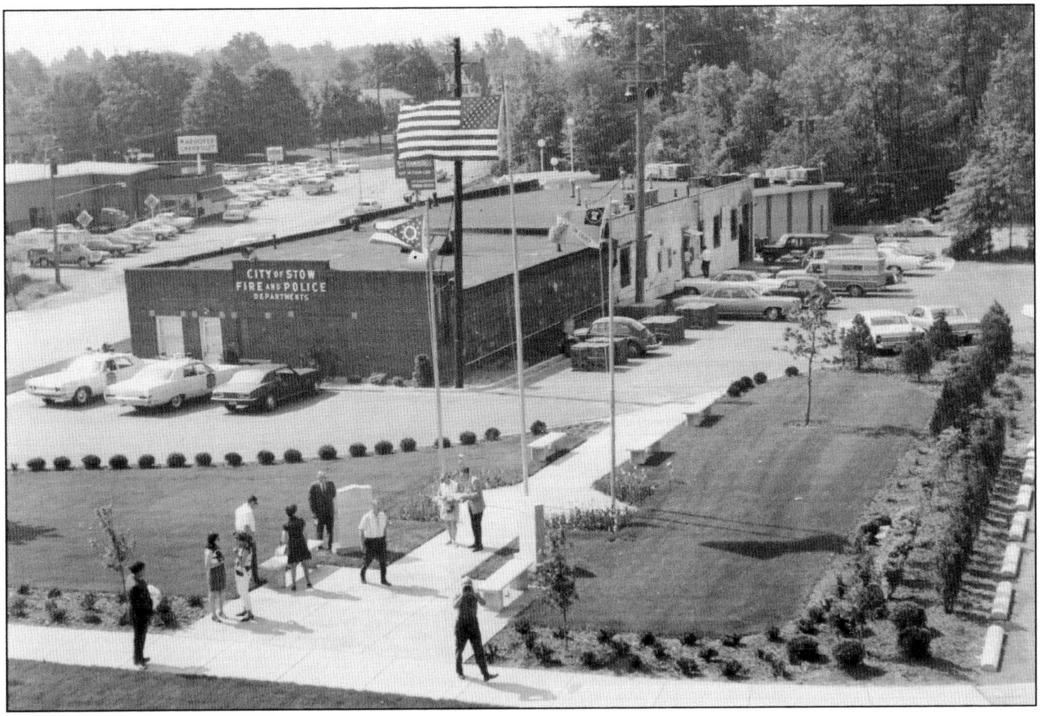

This photograph of the dedication of the Vietnam Veterans Memorial Park was taken on May 30, 1970. The dedication was presided over by Mayor Roger Howard. The park was at the corner of Darrow Road (U.S. Route 91) and Kent Road (U.S. Route 59), which was the southwest corner of Stow Corners. Pictured in the background is the Stow Police and Fire Station, the former site of Becker Wholesale Foods. (FL.)

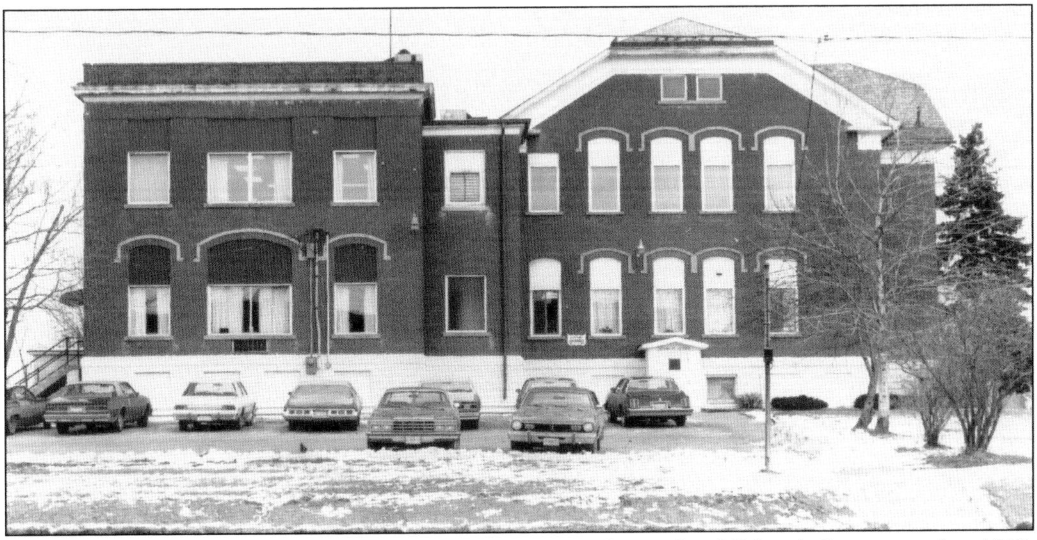

Stow City Hall, shown here around 1970, was once Stow Centralized School. Constructed in 1907, it served Stow elementary and high school students until 1924. At that time, a new high school was built. In 1939, Stow Grade School (Highland Elementary) was built, and the children were moved out of the centralized school. The building on the northwest corner of Graham and Darrow Roads served as Stow Township City Hall from 1940 to 1986. It was razed in 1986. (FL.)

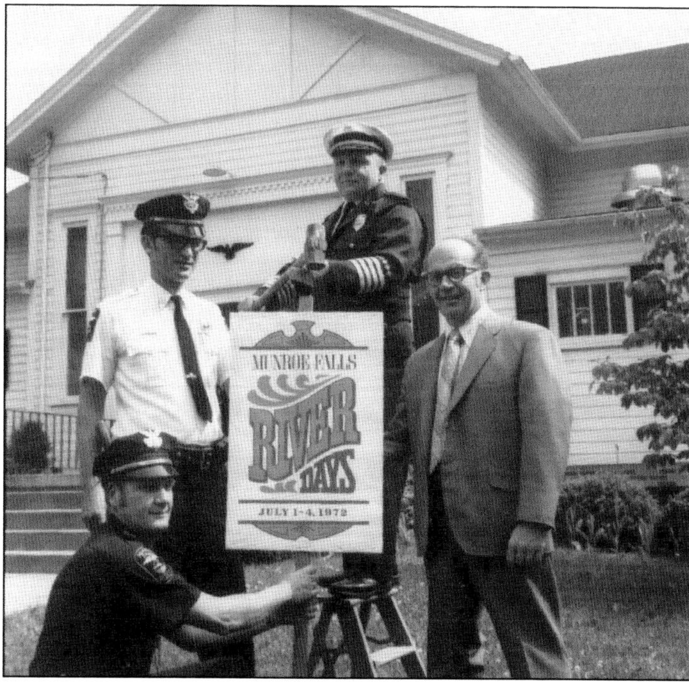

Mayor Gerald L. Hupp (far right) promotes the 1972 River Days festival in Munroe Falls with four members of the Munroe Falls safety forces. Hupp served as mayor of Munroe Falls for 26 years, retiring in 1999. He was a strong leader with a love of history and community. One of his favorite sayings was, "We have a lot to be proud of in Munroe Falls." (MFHS.)

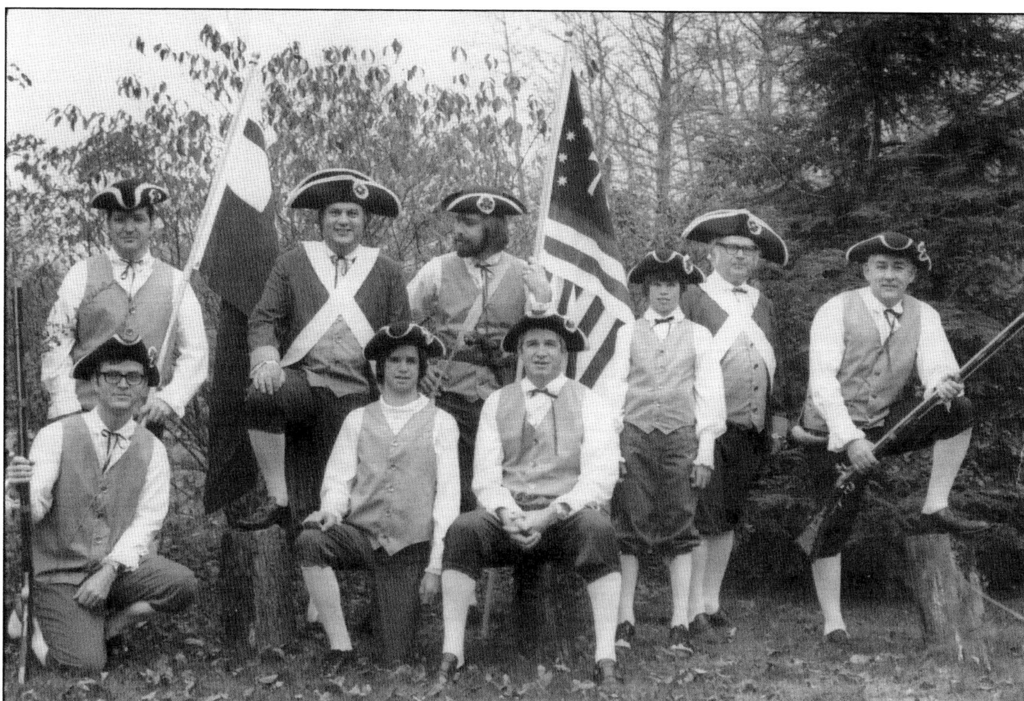

The "Minute Men" of Munroe Falls Lions Club celebrated the nation's bicentennial in 1976 by marching in several local Independence Day parades, including Stow, Brimfield, and Rootstown. Pictured from left to right are (first row) Keith Nixon, Mike Mills, and Marvin Mills; (second row) Roger Benefield, Fred Meine, Doug Scott, Steve Miller, Joe Bishop, and Don Lundquist. The uniforms, not including the hats, were made by Dawn Bishop, wife of Joe Bishop. (MFHS.)

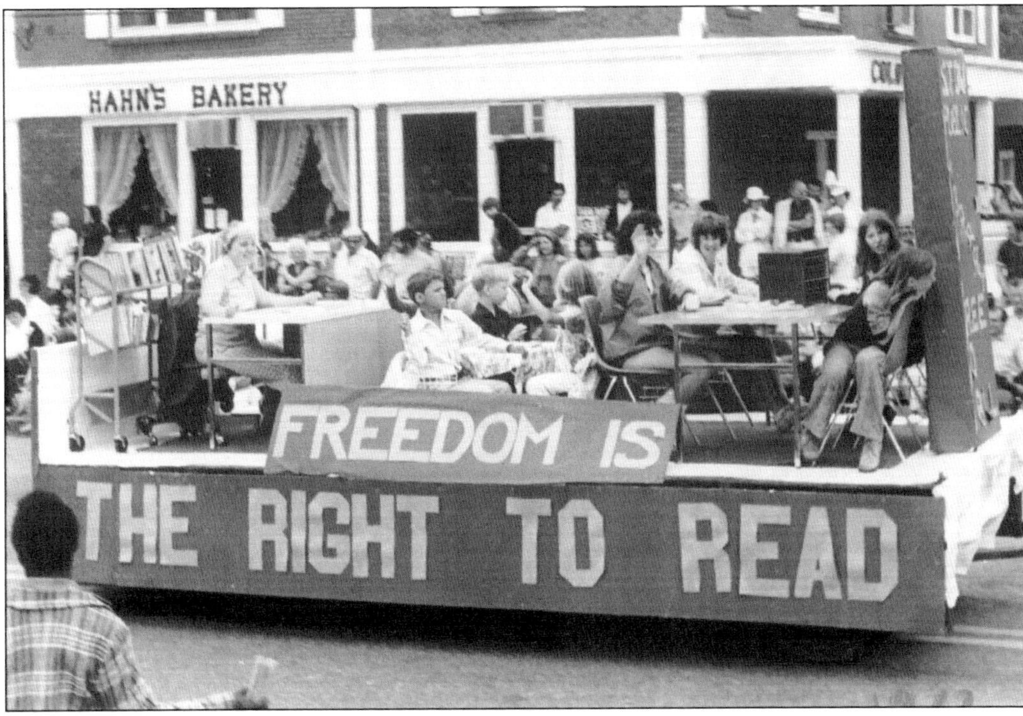

The theme for the 18th annual Stow Independence Day Parade was, "Freedom Is . . . " Stow Public Library director Doris Jyurovat and library staff members rode on the "Freedom is the Right to Read" float, seen here passing in front of the Colonnade Building. Businesses in the building at 3310 Kent Road included Stow Barber Shop, Myers Appliance Service and Sales, and Hahn's Bakery. (SMFPL.)

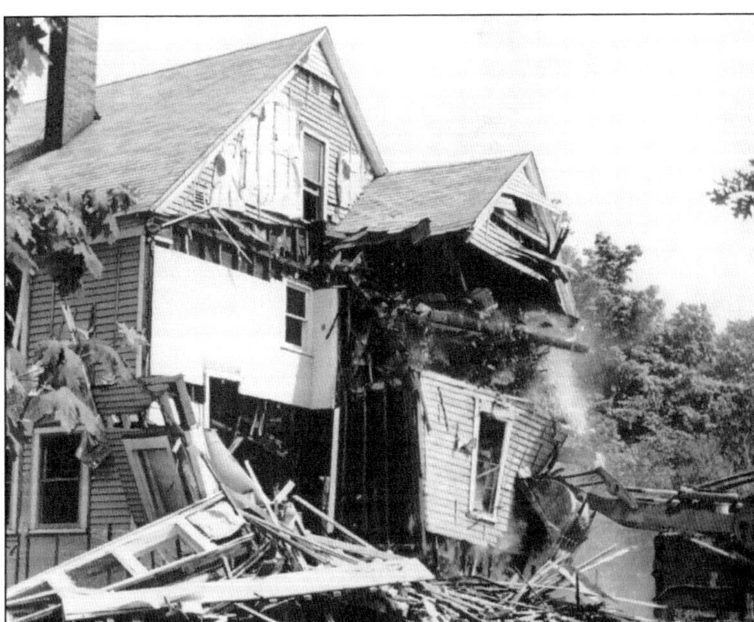

By 1977, the Stow Public Library once again found it necessary to expand. The book collection had filled the library to capacity, patrons were finding it difficult to find a seat on busy nights, and parking was at a premium. Property north of the library was purchased, and this house was razed in June 1978. Construction began on the addition with an expected completion date of December 1978. (SMFPL.)

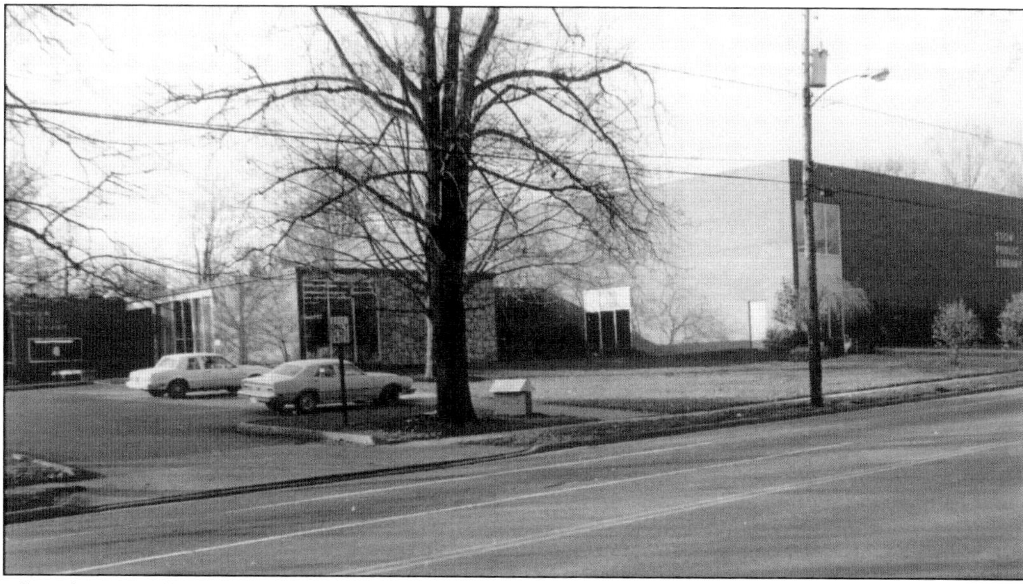

This photograph shows the 10,000-square-foot space that was added on to the Stow Public Library in 1979. Although the original completion date was for December 1978, steel strikes, trucking strikes, and adverse weather conditions moved the date from December to July. The moving of books and materials began on July 23 and was completed in four days by the staff, volunteers, and the Boy Scouts. The open house for the new addition, hosted by the Friends of the Library, was held on September 16, 1979. (SMFPL.)

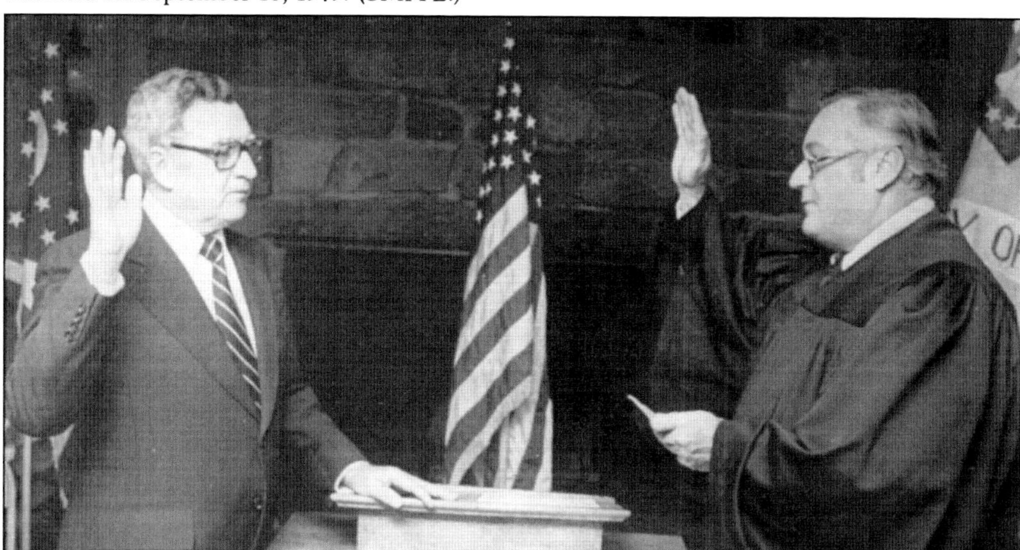

C. Paul Hutchison is seen here being sworn in for his second term of office by Judge William Pike on January 2, 1980. Hutchison was Stow's mayor from 1976 to 1988, serving for three four-year terms. During Hutchison's tenure, roads were improved and sewer and water lines were upgraded. A new city hall was built and completed in 1986. (SHS.)

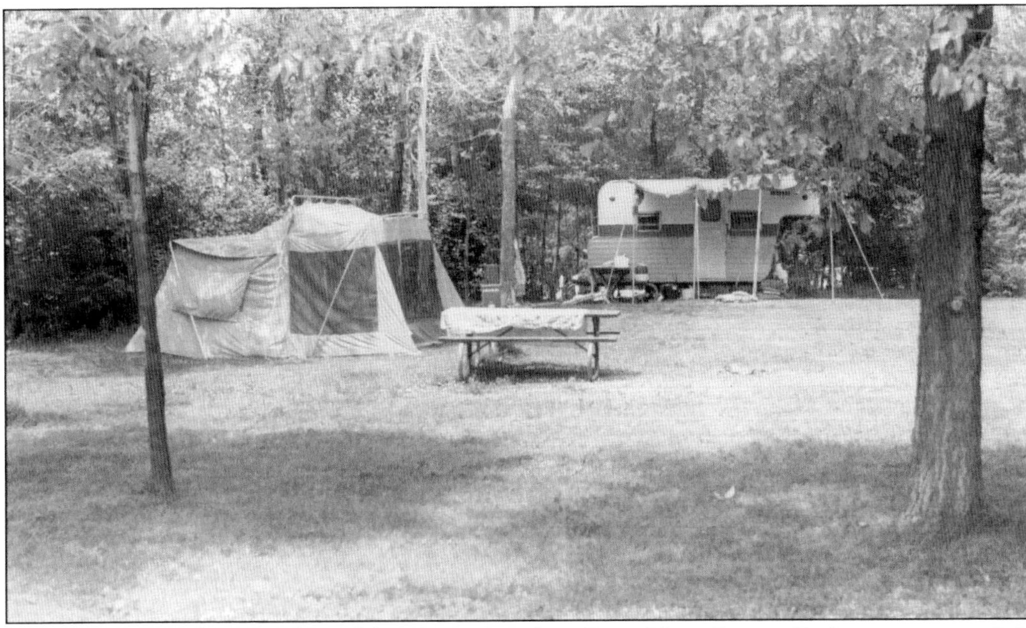

This early 1980s photograph is of the campgrounds at Stow Silver Springs Park, a city-run park in the northern part of Stow. The City of Stow purchased the land for Silver Springs Park in 1967. It is the largest of Stow's parks and contains trails, baseball fields, soccer fields, picnic areas, two lodges, and the campgrounds. (FL.)

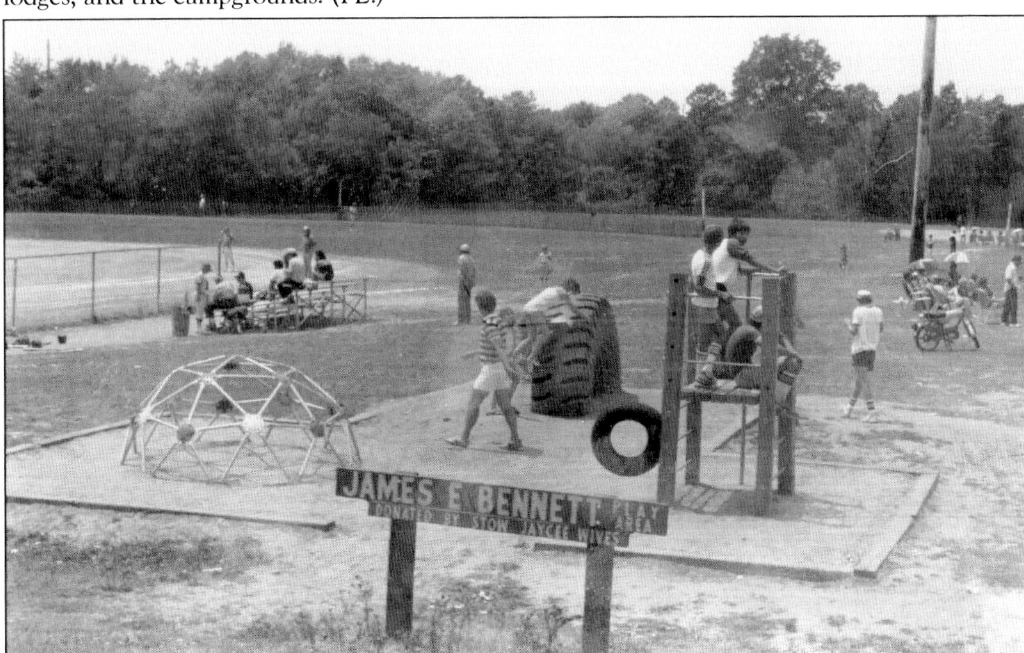

The James E. Bennett play area in Silver Springs Park was dedicated by the Stow Jaycees' wives in memory of Sergeant Bennett of the Stow Police Department, who died in 1981. Bennett served as "Officer Friendly" for the Stow Safety Town program, which he developed for the local schools. The play area was dedicated shortly after his death. (FL.)

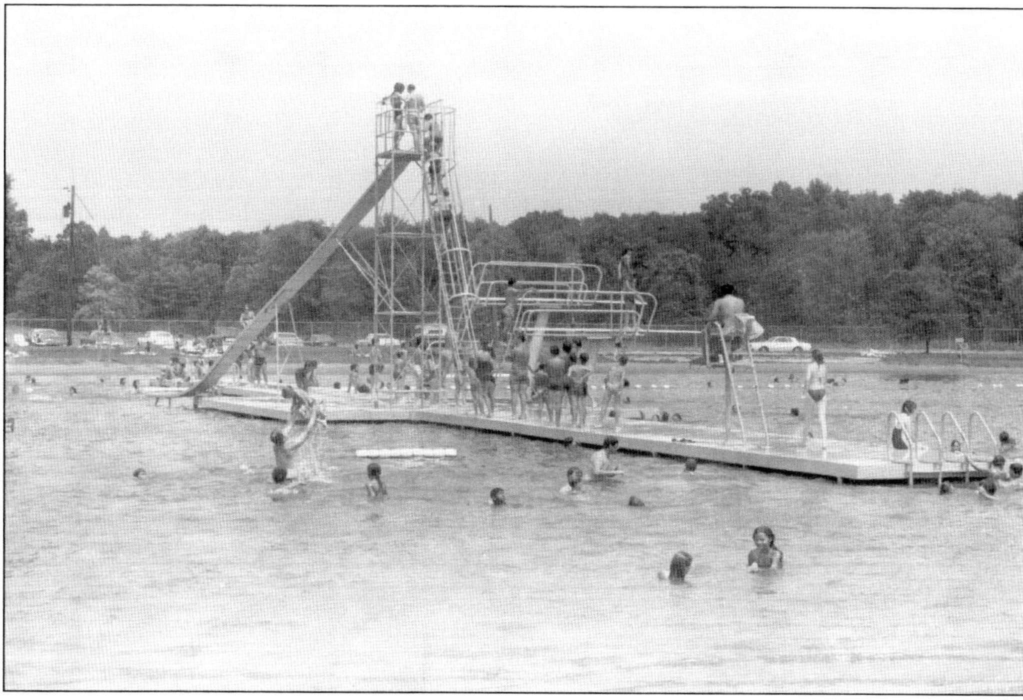

Children and adults alike enjoyed the swimming and water activities at the lake at Silver Springs Park for many years. Bow Wow Beach Dog Park, opened in June 2007 and operated by the City of Stow Parks and Recreation Department, is now in this location. (FL.)

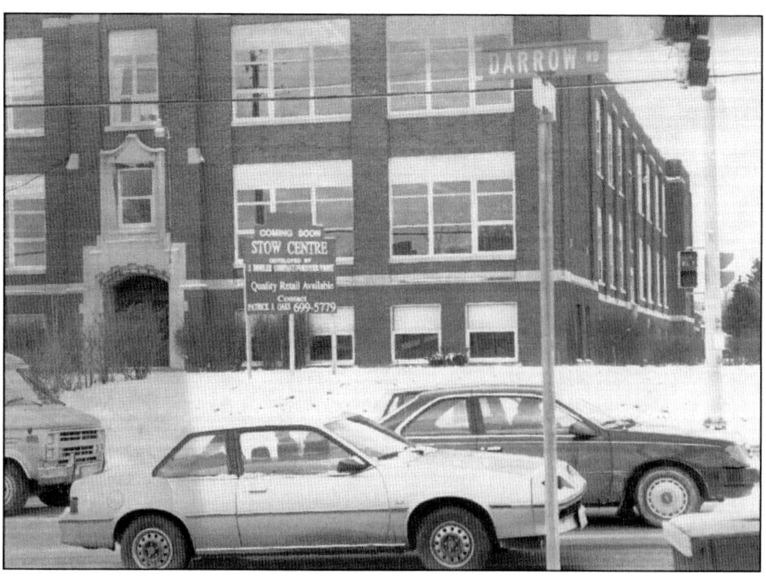

In 1989, Workman High School was purchased by a developer and razed to make room for a new shopping center at the corner of Darrow and Graham Roads. The Workman Building, completed in 1924, served as the high school until a new high school opened on East Graham Road in 1987. Workman was named in 1968 for Stow teacher Velma Workman. (SMFPL.)

BIBLIOGRAPHY

Bronson, Charles Cook. *The Bronson Book; Accounts of the Establishment and Early Settlement of the Connecticut Western Reserve, as Written and Collected from the Writings of Early Pioneers.* Stow, OH, 1954.

Doyle, William B., ed. *Centennial History of Summit County, Ohio and Representative Citizens.* Chicago: Biographical Publishing Company, 1908.

Green, Frank A. *Biographical and Historical Data of Stow, as Copied from the Record Book of Frank A. Green, Sexton of Stow Cemetery from November 1, 1924.* 1924.

———. *Frank A. Green.* Stow, OH, 1996.

Henning Jr., Robert Taylor. *History of the First Christian Church of Stow, Summit County, Ohio.* Lexington, KY: Lexington Theological Seminary, 1982.

James, Peggie Seitz. *Stow, Ohio—Shadows of its Past.* Ann Arbor, MI: Edwards Brothers, Inc., 1972.

———. *Portage and Summit County Pioneer Association, Organized 1874.* 1972.

Lane, Samuel A. *Fifty Years and Over of Akron and Summit County.* Akron, OH: Beacon Job Department, 1887.

Long, Fred. *Recollections of Living and Working in Stow, Ohio 1936 to . . .* Stow, OH: Stow Historical Society, 1997.

———. *Stories From a Stow Native.* Stow, OH: Stow Historical Society, 2001.

Morar, Virgil C. *Education of Stow City Schools.* Kent, OH: Kent State University, 1967.

Myers, Katheryn. *History of the Village of Munroe Falls, Ohio.* Munroe Falls, OH: Munroe Falls Historical Society, 1980.

Perrin, William Henry. *History of Summit County, Ohio.* Chicago: Baskin and Barrey, 1881.

Stockman, H. J., ed. *Community Church News.* Stow, OH: 1934–1948.

Stuckey, Helen Potter. *Summer Memories of Ohio 1895–1909.* South Strafford, VT: Kemp and Cary Press, 1985.

Woodward, Phyllis. *History of the Stow Public Library 1924–1974.* Master's research paper, December 1975.